THE CLIENT DECIDES

A LITIGATOR'S LIFE:
Jackie Onassis,
Vice President Spiro Agnew,
Donald Trump,
Roy Cohn, and more

MARTIN LONDON

Eastlake Press

1285 Avenue of the Americas, Suite 3140

New York, NY 10019

Hardcover ISBN: 978-06928158-7-8

Softcover ISBN: 978-06928158-8-5

Library of Congress Control Number: 2016921606

Design by Deborah Perdue, Illumination Graphics

www.illuminationgraphics.com

Table of Contents

Dedication

Mom and Dad:

All the "higher education" was just trim

on the structure you guys built for us.

Epigraph:

"We do not decide what kinds of cases we try;

the client decides that for us."

Simon H. Rifkind

Preface

How did the kid from Carroll Street between Schenectady and Utica Avenues in Crown Heights, Brooklyn end up doing a tour of duty as the Chairman of Paul, Weiss, Rifkind, Wharton & Garrison, one of the nation's, indeed the world's, leading law firms? In 45 years at the firm, I represented President Kennedy's widow, Jacqueline Kennedy Onassis and their son, John, as well as Vice Presidents Agnew and Humphrey, and a long list of distinguished banks, businessmen, doctors, lawyers, and some just plain Joes. I beat Donald Trump in court and in my *pro bono* work I rid the bar of unethical lawyers (including Roy Cohn), rid the bench of unprincipled and incompetent judges, and I struck an important blow for women's reproduction rights by helping to represent a group of brave physicians who refused to knuckle under to anti-choice fanatics who threatened their lives.

Most of the cases that came my way had one thing in common: hard work, intellectually and physically. No fact could be ignored, every document wrung out to reveal any hint, connection, or suggestion that might help the cause, every legal principle challenged, tested, and applied or rejected with persuasive reasoning. It's a process that demands maximum effort and requires a team of exceptional talent. I was lucky to find that at Paul, Weiss.

Under the guidance of our leader, former federal judge Simon H. Rifkind, the Paul, Weiss litigation group took on a great variety of matters. Rifkind was right: it was the client who decided what kinds of cases I tried. For reasons I cannot ascertain, many of my significant cases involved the First Amendment. It just happened that way. Again and again, I found myself confronting those historic words, "make no law . . . abridging the freedom of speech, or of the press." Lawyers know the words neither mean what they say, nor say what they mean. There is, in fact, much speech that is "abridged" by the law (e.g., threats, libel, etc.) and lots of "non-speech" conduct that is nevertheless considered protected speech (e.g., silence, contributing money to political or other causes, etc.) More than that, the meaning of The Amendment changes with time and politics. It became my job sometimes to try to limit the reach of that clause, and other times to expand its impact. My clients' interests dictated the direction of my argument.

Cumulatively, I have spent thousands of days in courtrooms all over the world, representing clients in a great spectrum of commercial and *pro bono* cases.

Of the hundreds of diverse cases I have handled in my career, I reflect on these 20 matters, which I have divided into five groups: i) cases implicating the First Amendment; ii) cases involved in my *pro bono* practice, at least one of which also involved the First Amendment; iii) cases involving politics or political figures; iv) "hard work" cases involving disparate subjects some of which required me to spend months in the courtroom and all of which compelled me to learn stuff they never taught in law school; and v) a potpourri of smaller cases that were fun and interesting.

What a ride!

Part I:

"MAKE NO LAW… ABRIDGING THE FREEDOM OF SPEECH"

Jacqueline Kennedy Onassis, The Secret Service, and Me

*T*he tribulations of Jacqueline Onassis tested the reach
of the First Amendment. Was her tormentor immunized
from judicial sanction because he labeled himself a
"journalist"? Did the President's widow lose all her privacy
rights because the paparazzi anointed her a "public figure"?

*In the face of the substantial deference our courts pay
to the freedoms guaranteed by The Amendment, it fell to us
to challenge its application to the conduct of the self-pro-
claimed paparazzo Ronald Galella, whose photographs of
Mrs. Onassis frequently appeared in the popular media. Her
determined resistance to his assault on her privacy led me
to a fruitful friendship with a good woman, brought some
tranquility to her life and that of her children, and led to a
novel and important legal precedent.*

◆

When President John F. Kennedy was killed on November
22, 1963, his widow and two young children were entitled to

3

Secret Service protection. Jacqueline lost that when she married Aristotle Onassis in 1968, but John and Caroline retained their coverage until they reached age 16.

On September 24, 1969, when John was nine, he and his mother were riding bikes in Central Park – John in front, followed by his mother, followed by a Secret Service agent. As the boy approached the end of the path that emptied onto the sidewalk on the west side of Fifth Avenue, Ronald Galella, a photographer whose obsession with Jackie had tortured the family for years, jumped out from behind a bush onto the path to snap pictures. His sudden appearance frightened John, who swerved, almost lost control of his bike, and risked either falling or careening into traffic. The incident was witnessed not only by his mother and the agent following behind her, but also by the two agents stationed in front of the family's Fifth Avenue residence directly across the street. The agents immediately accosted the photographer and took him to a police station. There he got into a contretemps with one of the agents, and that resulted in Galella receiving a summons for criminal harassment.

The New York City Criminal Court judge dismissed the charge with the casual comment, "I don't know who was harassing who." In July, 1970, Galella sued Jacqueline Onassis and the Secret Service agents for $1.3 million dollars for false arrest and "interference with his right to take pictures of the family." (He claimed he had not been on the path of John's bike, and, furthermore, had heard Jackie tell the agents to smash his camera. Both assertions were later proved false by eyewitness testimony and other evidence.)

The case was removed to the Federal District Court. In a conversation with an Assistant U.S. Attorney representing the Secret Service agents, Galella's lawyer admitted that he sued because he was "sure that [Mrs. Onassis] will settle out of court to avoid any court appearances and adverse publicity."

Galella seriously miscalculated. He had no idea of the extent of Jackie's steely determination to protect her family. She adamantly refused to settle. In her answer to Galella's complaint, she not only denied his meritless claims, but sought injunctive relief from his alarming and dangerous harassment of her and her children.

In Galella's suit, Jackie had been represented by another firm, but in November of 1971, her husband Aristotle Onassis retained my senior partner, former federal Judge Simon H. Rifkind, to represent Jackie. I had been a partner at Paul, Weiss for less than three years, and was hard at work at my desk late on a Saturday afternoon when Rifkind, with whom I had already tried several cases, knocked on the doorpost, and we had the following conversation:

> Rifkind: Good Afternoon, Martin, I am sorry to disturb you. Got a minute to chat? (Really, that's the way he spoke – all the time).

> London: Sure, Judge, good to see you. Have a seat. What's going on?

> Rifkind: You busy? I wanted to know if you can take something on. Aristotle Onassis has just retained us to take over his wife's case. Can you help?

Busy? Was he kidding? I was drowning in work. That's why I was there late on a Saturday afternoon, and planning to work the next day too. I responded as any reasonable young lawyer would do in those circumstances. I lied:

> London: Busy? Not really. Sure, Judge, be happy to help. Send me the file and I'll get right on it!

We chatted some more, and he departed. Thirty seconds later, I boogied down the corridor into the office of Lewis Kaplan, a brilliant first year associate who had so little work to do that he, too, was in the office on Saturday afternoon. Though Kaplan was a new kid on the block, I knew he was not only smart, but an agreeable teammate. The London/Kaplan conversation was basically a repetition of the Rifkind/London one. I asked the same questions and he told the same lies. Five minutes into my representation of Jacqueline Onassis, I had already increased our likelihood of success: I had recruited Kaplan as another of her champions.

And so began an extraordinary experience: The team of Rifkind, London, and Kaplan (one immigrant, two children of immigrants) representing the former First Lady of the United States, and, indirectly, the deceased president's children as well.

Two weeks into my involvement in the case, on November 30th, 1971, Galella violated an outstanding court order, and on December 2nd, we moved to hold him in contempt of court and for further injunctive relief.

To support our application to the court, we needed to offer up proof of the pertinent facts. This normally requires, at the start, a written sworn statement reciting the facts upon which the claim for relief is based. I spoke to our client on the phone, drafted the document, and now needed her to sign it and swear to the truth of its contents before a Notary Public. (When I was a new lawyer, I applied for and received a commission as a New York State Notary Public. It's not difficult to be appointed. But I soon encountered a hazard; the law required the signatory of a sworn statement to physically appear before the Notary, and swear to its truth. But colleagues were inclined to ask me, as a convenience, to notarize the signature of an absent affiant. I always refused to comply with those requests, and that sometimes engendered ill will, so I let my notarial commission expire. Kaplan was a Notary, but still too young to recognize the inconvenience of that office). The two of us traveled to the client's apartment at 1040 Fifth Avenue to get Jackie's affidavit signed and notarized.

This was a major event. Up to this point, I had not met Jacqueline Onassis. Now I was going to meet American royalty, and she was my client yet. Was I intimidated? You bet.

We were admitted by a housekeeper and identified ourselves. She said she knew who we were and asked us to give her the papers; she would take them to Mrs. Onassis, get her to sign them, and then she'd bring them right back to us. There was no way I was going to let that happen, and even had I acquiesced, Kaplan would have withstood the rack before notarizing an unwitnessed signature.

I explained to her why that wasn't possible, and we cooled our heels in the elegantly furnished living room, taking in the outstanding views of Central Park, while she delivered our message to the client. I was not calm. I had already met my share of prima donnas and I assumed the former First Lady and international fashion icon would rank high on that list. Yikes, was I going to screw up this representation on the first meeting? I spent an anxious ten minutes mentally crafting the explanation I would offer up to Judge Rifkind for losing his celebrated client. Then Jackie came out wearing a peach dressing gown, hair brushed, no perceived makeup, and with a warm smile, apologized profusely for keeping us waiting. She had been out late the night before, had gotten the kids off to school, then had gone back for a snooze. Jackie could not have been more gracious. We sat on a couch, she read the document, put it on the coffee table, signed it, Lew notarized it, she thanked us again, and we were off and running. We filed the motion and got an additional temporary restraint from the judge. *The New York Times* made fun of me the next day because the document I drafted for the client said she lived in "dread fear" of Galella, which was substantively accurate but redundant. There was a real human interest story there of a family being abused while trapped in a gilded cage, but the *Times'* writers, not for the first time, revealed an instinct for the capillaries.

We never did get to argue our December 2nd motion. Galella had put in sworn answering papers denying any involvement in the November 30th event, and the judge decided to skip all the preliminary motion practice and just try the entire case – ten weeks hence! Remarkably enough, in the 18 months before we had been retained, neither side's lawyers had done much of anything in the way of actually getting ready to try the case. No depositions, no document demands, no exhibit or witness lists, no outlines, nada. What pressure! We were now in a round-the-clock crash course of trial preparation. We had to prepare our client for her deposition and trial testimony, depose Galella after examining his thousands of photographs, prepare for his trial testimony, look for, interview, and prepare scores of other witnesses, compile witness and exhibit lists, etc., all in 2-1/2 months. (Twenty-five witnesses testified at the five-week trial. The transcript ran to 4,714 pages).

Jackie understood immediately that this was our game, our trade, and she made herself totally available to us. She spent days with Lew and me in the Paul, Weiss 29th floor conference room going over each one of more than 40 incidents of harassment, intrusion, bumping, touching, surveillance, insulting remarks, and conduct dangerous to her and the children – who were by now frightened of Galella. We examined thousands of Galella's photographs and talked about the events surrounding each one of them. We worked five days a week with our client, and on Saturdays and Sundays without her. Lunch consisted of sandwiches from Star's Delicatessen across the street. (After the trial, I think the firm had to paint the conference room to get rid of the smell of pastrami and pickles). And when the former First Lady went off to dinner, Lew and I went down the block to our favorite Japanese restaurant where we had scotch and steak before returning to work. (I'm proud that, to this day, Kaplan gives me credit for teaching him to drink Scotch whiskey.)

As the trial date approached, Galella retained new counsel, Al Julien, a renowned plaintiff's (i.e., negligence, medical malpractice, etc.) lawyer with a sterling success record. He took Jackie's deposition at the federal courthouse, the session lasted six hours, and my witness was superb. She followed our instructions to a "T": listen to the question, answer it directly, no exaggeration, just tell it like it is. I was proud of how she handled what was for her, a totally foreign experience. As we left the courthouse, several photographers were waiting. A nice shot of both of us sitting in the back of the car with shit-eating grins made the front page of the *New York Daily News*.

★★★
FINAL

DAILY NEWS

NEW YORK'S PICTURE NEWSPAPER ®

10¢

Vol. 53. No. 172   Copr. 1972 New York News Inc.   New York, N.Y. 10017, Wednesday, January 12, 1972★   WEATHER: Sunny and mild.

CHURCH SCHOOL
AID BARRED

Court Voids $33M State Plan

Stories on Page 3

Jackie Keeps Her Powder Dry. Rain flecks window of her car, but Jackie Onassis seems to be in sunny disposition as she leaves Federal Courthouse with attorney Martin London. She survived barrage of questions during four-hour pretrial hearing of her legal battle with cameraman Ronald Galella. —*Story p. 4*

NEWS photo by Paul DeMaria

That photo prompts the following recollection. When I graduated from law school, my father owned a coin-operated self-service laundromat on Utica Avenue in Brooklyn, just four blocks from where I grew up. He wanted me to hang a shingle in the front window of his store, and said he had room for a desk in the back, behind the dryers. I could work from there, rent-free. When I told him I planned to work as an associate in a Manhattan law firm, he was troubled. He had always been in business for himself since he was a teenager, and he could not understand why, with all my education, I would go to work for somebody else and be an *employee!* But years later, when that picture of Jackie and me appeared on the front page of the *New York Daily News*, he paraded up and down the aisle of a crowded airplane bound for Florida, holding out the front page photo and proclaiming to all, "My son, the lawyer. Partners with Rifkind."

The Trial

The trial began on February 16, 1972 before U.S. District Judge Irving Ben Cooper, at the Manhattan federal courthouse. There was no jury, and the court made the jury room available to us as our base during the trial, while Galella's team was awarded other space. Jackie was in court every day, on time, and diligently followed the proceedings. While the rest of us were drained by the crushing tension of trial duties, she was calm and focused on practical issues: "Marty, can I have a piece of paper to park my gum? I don't want to be seen chewing when we walk up the courthouse steps," and "What do you all want for lunch, so I can have it delivered to our jury room?" I had (and still have) chronic back issues and she gave me the name and telephone number of Dr. Janet Travell, in Washington D.C., and told me,

"She helped Jack tremendously. Marty, you should call her immediately." I never got around to that. Maybe that's why I still suffer. (I came across that note, in Jackie's near perfect handwriting, just recently).

On the day we called Bernadette Carrozza, the editor of *Photoplay Magazine*, to the stand, her "reward" was to join us at lunch. She couldn't believe her good fortune – chicken salad on rye with Jackie. Bernadette was bubbling over.

We were on trial four and a half days a week. Judge Cooper had a motion calendar on Friday afternoons, and our trial team usually went uptown for lunch at the Brussels Restaurant, a block from our office. One Friday, Jackie said Caroline, then 15, was going to join us, and ten minutes after we arrived at our table, in breezed Caroline in jeans and a sweater. The other diners were already chewing on their silverware gawking at Jackie, but when Caroline came in, all eating stopped. We laughed when she told us that she had been running late, had come down on the Fifth Avenue bus while her Secret Service detail was delayed getting their car out of the garage, and she lost them. I am told they forgave her.

At trial, as we expected, Julien called Jackie as his first witness, and hit all the points we anticipated: How could she be frightened while so many pictures showed her smiling? The answer was that she plastered a smile on her face because she knew that his pictures would have been more valuable (and, therefore, even more frequent) if she looked frightened or angry. Sad but true. One magazine editor who purchased Galella's pictures testified that Galella had told him that "he hides, he jumps out from wherever he is hiding to get emotion and expression in the pictures."

Then there was what I call a "Julien special" section of his cross-examination. He was a master of cross via indirection and confusion. Very effective before juries, not so much before a judge. A big chunk of his cross involved Jackie's testimony about an incident at the P.J. Clarke's restaurant. A lot of stuff about pulling down a window shade or not, changing tables or not, she didn't recall, etc. It went on for days, and was neither relevant nor material to the case, but I was impressed by how effectively Julien used it to divert a listener's attention from the key issues at the heart of the litigation. One could almost forget what the case was about. But *we* didn't forget, neither did Judge Cooper, nor later, the Second Circuit Court of Appeals.

There was even a section of the cross when Julien sought to embarrass the witness (and us) by raising a question of whether Kaplan actually was present when she swore to her December 2nd affidavit. He was stunned when she told the story of that morning.

After Julien's examination of Jackie, Rifkind handled her direct. It was a pleasure watching that team, a master litigator and a well-prepared witness. But after the first week, with some 20 witnesses to go, Rifkind, good soul that he was, said to me, "You know, Martin, I've got a lot of stuff back at the office, and I don't think you two really need me around here, so is it okay if I go back to the office and take care of other things?" And he left!

The team of London and Kaplan carried on. At some point, a classmate of Lew's who had been in the gallery watching for days, cornered him during a recess, and said, "Holy shit, you and I just got out of school a year back, and here you are examining witnesses and arguing objections like a real trial lawyer. How'd you do that?" Lew shrugged and said, "Y'know, I just watched Rifkind and London and did what they did." (Kaplan is now a federal judge in the same court).

As one might expect, the trial drew capacity crowds. The gallery was always full, and those waiting for an empty seat stood in a roped off line in the corridor. One day a reporter approached me in a recess and quietly inquired, "Marty, I am embarrassed to ask you this question, but my editor insists. Are the buttons on Mrs. Onassis's jacket brass or real gold?" What made him think I would know the answer to that question?

You're Right, Counselor, I Lied

While Jackie was the public celebrity, when it came to the merits of the dispute, Galella was clearly the most important witness in the trial. His testimony was the center ring of a Liar's Circus.

In my first year in law school, Perry Mason was my relief valve from the pressure of exams. Yup, those novels were my escape from Torts 101 and Introduction to Administrative Law. Fast forward 16 years, Galella is on the witness stand, and the_New York Daily News_ ran a piece that began:

> Perry Mason couldn't have done it better. The scene in federal court yesterday was one with which TV fans are familiar, but one which real trial lawyers seldom experience.
>
> The setting was the trial of Jackie Onassis being sued for $1.3 million by freelance photographer Ronald Galella....
>
> Galella is in the witness box under the intense cross-examination by Martin London, co-counsel for Mrs. Onassis. London, tall, gaunt-faced, intent, has been hammering away at one point for what seems like an hour ...

The denouement of my "hammering away" was one of several instances where Galella uttered the equivalent of the witness's statement at the end of every Perry Mason cross-examination: "You're right, Mr. Mason, I lied."

Some background for that bit of cross:

Galella's conduct at the *Metropolitan Museum of Art* on November 30th, 1971, was in clear violation of an earlier injunction, and he knew it. Our December 2nd motion was directed at that incident, and when we moved to hold Galella in contempt for the November 30th offense, he challenged Jackie's version of the facts and swore in a responsive affidavit, "I had nothing to do with that incident." It was that denial that precipitated the court's decision to try the case promptly.

Galella's affidavit was but the first in a long string of his lies relating to that event. The second lie came when Galella, at his pre-trial deposition, swore he had fully complied with our deposition subpoena requiring him to produce to us all of his photographs of Mrs. Onassis. In an effort to protect the first lie, he omitted from his production the pictures he took on November 30th.

At trial, Galella repeated the lie about having produced all his pictures, but qualified it by swearing he had produced all the photographs "under my control." We knew that, too, was a lie; we had learned from our pre-trial investigation that he not only had taken pictures of the November 30th event, but had tried to sell them to *Photoplay Magazine* and had asked Photoplay editor Bernadette Carrozza to hide her copy of the pictures he submitted. When my cross of him revealed that we likely knew the truth, he telephoned Carrozza at the end of that court day and asked her whether she had produced the pictures to us even though he had asked her to hide them.

When she said "yes," Galella told her:

> On the QT, the injunction was against me . . . I could
> get in trouble if they know that I had taken these
> pictures. I wasn't supposed to be photographing her
> then . . . I could go to jail.

The stream of perjury surrounding this incident soon
overflowed its banks. The next day, in an apparent attempt
to expunge his perjury, Galella brought to court two copies
of his photo contact sheet showing the pictures he had taken
of Mrs. Onassis on November 30th. He still tried to justify
his earlier failure to produce the contact sheets by testifying
that when he received our pre-trial subpoena he didn't have
the pictures because he had earlier given them to *Photoplay
Magazine*, as was evidenced by the large red initials "PP"
on one sheet. Those initials, he swore, were placed there by
the editor of Photoplay, Ms. Bernadette Carrozza.

His testimony on this subject can be described only
as "tortured." He was still trying (and failing misera-
bly) to avoid responsibility for his earlier contumacious
failure to produce the pictures in an effort to hide his
November 30th conduct. At first, he testified he gave
Carrozza a single copy of the contact sheet that *she* had
scribed with the "PP" initials. When I pointed out that
his retained second copy bore the exact same initials,
he changed his testimony and said he had given her
two copies and she initialed both of them. But when I
questioned him further about the need for the magazine
to have identical copies of the same contact sheet, and
reminded him that he had already testified he had given
her only one copy, he changed his testimony again and
swore he gave her only one, and he kept the second one
for himself. But that left him to explain the "PP" initials

on the second copy and he then testified that Carrozza initialed the first copy, and he initialed the second copy. But when it was pointed out to him that the initials on both copies were virtually identical, he swore to yet another version of the facts. He said while Carrozza had initialed her copy, he had attempted to forge her "PP" on his own copy in the hopes he "possibly" could deceive the court on the issue of where his contact sheet was when it was subpoenaed!

Given Galella's multiple contradictions in this single series of cross-examination questions, the judge had had enough. Cooper interrupted my cross, called a recess, and urged the witness to have a private chat with his lawyer about the criminal penalties for perjury. When court resumed, we heard yet another version of the facts about this exhibit. This one had the ring of truth; Galella admitted that *none* of the initials were placed there by Ms. Carrozza, *all* the initials on both contact sheets were inscribed by him in an effort to deceive us and the court. To nail this down, his prior inconsistent testimony was read back to him. While listening to his own testimony, Galella confessed, "That's false!"

In the course of the trial, we pointed out to the court more than 30 instances where Galella's trial testimony was flatly contradicted by Galella's own testimony at or before trial. That may be an all-time record, I dunno. What I do know is the trial court found:

> Certain testimony was so utterly corrupt that its value is to demonstrate [Galella's] willingness to lie. The record is studded with instance after instance where [Galella's] testimony was clearly perjurious. Often his own testimony exposed the perjury and at other times his very testimony compelled its

rejection; on occasion, he was forced to acknowl-
edge the falsity of his testimony.

Upon reviewing the trial transcript, the Circuit Court of
Appeals, later wrote:

> [Judge Cooper's] findings on credibility are indeed
> broad, but they are supported in the record. Galella
> demonstrated a galling lack of respect for the truth
> and gave no indication of any consciousness of the
> meaning of the oath he had taken. Not only did he
> admit blatantly lying in his testimony, he admitted
> attempting to have other witnesses lie for him.

Galella's Conduct

By the end of the trial, we had submitted evidence of
more than 40 instances, here and abroad, of Galella's outrageous behavior. He barged into theatres, hid behind coat
racks in restaurants, bumped, pushed, and chased Jackie,
bribed doormen, attempted to bribe Caroline's tennis
instructor, romanced maids, tracked Jackie's purchases,
interrogated clerks and waiters about what she bought and
ate, intruded into the children's schools, endangered them
when they were at horse shows, water skiing, swimming,
sledding, bicycle riding, etc.

He knew no bounds, and admitted as much. In an interview that appeared in *Esquire Magazine*, Galella told Bruce
Jay Friedman (who testified at the trial) that he had no mari-
tal plans because "I would have to find a girl willing to vault
out of bed in the middle of the night to catch Jackie coming
out of the Carlyle. How many girls like that are there?"

Galella told Friedman of his "ultimate coup" when he stated
he had learned from a source at a boutique that Jackie had a
pair of "hot pants," and he wanted to catch her wearing them.

Galella knew he was causing pain to Jackie and the children. On one occasion, Galella found himself in a sidewalk conversation with Aristotle Onassis, in which Mr. Onassis remarked that his wife has had a great deal of trouble in her life, and he asked Galella why he was harassing her. Galella did not deny he was inflicting pain. Instead, he appointed himself her apparent therapist even stating "I am not a sadist . . . this will help her forget her troubles!"

But this so-called "photojournalist" was after more than pictures. Galella asked Aristotle Onassis for a job at Olympic airlines. In the event that signal was not clear enough, Galella created and mailed a "Christmas Card" to the Onassis family.

The Christmas Card

Galella's two-sided Christmas card, sent to the Onassis family in December 1970, bore the banner "Peace on Earth, Good Will Toward Men." The front of the card had images of Galella and a Santa Claus wearing dark glasses (Aristotle Onassis always wore dark glasses.) The characters were standing side by side and Santa was holding a fistful of cash. In the background is a picture of Jacqueline and nine-year old John wheeling their bikes across Fifth Avenue after the frightening incident when John almost fell. There is also an Olympic Airlines poster (Mr. Onassis's company) with pictures of Jackie and Caroline on the poster. And the key, an easel with a poster reading, "Meet Santa, Starring Aristotle Onassis as Santa and Ron Galella as the Paparazzo in THE 'PAYOFF.' " The reverse side of the card is the same except for one major difference: *Galella is sitting in Santa's lap receiving cash from him.*

A paragraph from our post-trial brief, quoted in the opinion of the District Court, urged:

> Whatever else may be said about this case – about
> harassment, about freedom of the press, . . . one
> thing is clear; no one has the right, constitutional or
> otherwise, to conduct a coldly calculated and mali-
> cious campaign to drive another into paying him
> off. And that is just what Galella has done here.

While much of Galella's offensive conduct was not
denied, throughout the trial, in court and out, his lawyers
urged that Galella was a "photojournalist", his pictures
were the equivalent of "speech," his news gathering activities were protected by the First Amendment, and the court
had no right to abridge them. Moreover, he claimed that as
a "public figure," Jacqueline Onassis had no privacy rights,
and the First Amendment barred the imposition of *any*
restriction on his right to photograph her.

Galella's purported Constitutional justification for
his outrageous conduct was bogus. The First Amendment
does not immunize tortious conduct. Even a real journalist is bound by the same civil and criminal laws as
everybody else when it comes to conduct employed to
gather the news. Journalists have no more immunity to
violate laws against harassment, than they do to commit
burglary or assault. This case was not about "speech" or
"freedom of the press," it was about conduct – outrageous
behavior that breached the social contract. A reporter or
photographer who assaults his subjects, harasses them
beyond reason, endangers them and their children, gets
no pass from James Madison.

The trial court agreed. The judge's opinion listed the differences between a real journalist and Galella:

1. Assaults and Batteries. Galella's physical move-
   ments . . . jumping, lunging, leaping, rushing out,

bumping, scuffling, blocking, thrusting. . . . Threat of physical harm; it appeared that the propeller of [Galella's] boat might cut John's legs, or capsize his boat, or that John would fall from his bicycle or his horse.

2. Offensive mouthings. Unlike other members of the press, Galella grunts, yells, makes strange sounds, laughs and calls to defendant, "How do you like me?" "The marines have landed," "Snuggle up to Santa" [he had hired a Santa he used on several such occasions], and "Glad to see me back, aren't you, Jackie?" And [in my mind, anyway, the worst] to Caroline when he intruded on her tennis court in Central Park, "I am not making you nervous, am I, honey?" and "How do you like the great paparazzo back again?"

3. Bogus events. Galella forces his subjects into ersatz happenings. He hired a costumed Santa to try to force himself close to the defendant so as to create an unusual situation. This false, forced, attempted pose echoes the startled expression which Galella seeks to arouse by his assault and taunts. News is real; Galella promotes the phony.

4. Self-Aggrandizement. . . . [Galella] persistently arranged to have himself photographed with Mrs. Onassis. He has posed for photographs to be published in nationwide and worldwide magazines disclosing the "disguises" he dons to photograph Mrs. Onassis.

5.   Seeking a "PAYOFF." No self-respecting reporter will suppress his story for a price. Not so Galella, who offered to cease his activities for money or a job. The Christmas card was intended by plaintiff to communicate an offer to cease his harassment of defendant and her children in exchange for money to be paid to him or a job to be given to him by Mr. Onassis.

6.   Incessant surveillance. . . . The result of Galella's surveillance is that Mrs. Onassis may not enter or leave her home without Galella's knowledge and is faced with the constant fear that he will follow her hour after hour wherever she goes.

7.   "Secret Agent" tactics. Outside of movieland, reporters do not normally hide behind restaurant coat racks, sneak into beauty parlors, don "disguises," hide in bushes and theatre boxes, intrude into school buildings, and when ejected, enlist the aid of school children [when Galella was caught inside of John's school, he was evicted, but on his way out, he tried to give his camera to another student to take pictures of John!], bribe doormen, romance maids. The chases that figure in the trial record here would not be performed by any news reporter when there is no news afoot.

On appeal, the Circuit Court unanimously affirmed the District Court findings:

Evidence offered by [Mrs. Onassis] showed that Galella had on occasion intentionally physically touched Mrs. Onassis and her daughter, caused fear of physical contact in his frenzied attempts to get their pictures, followed defendant and her children too closely in an automobile, endangered the safety of the children while they were swimming, water skiing and horseback riding. *Galella cannot successfully challenge the court's finding of tortious conduct.*

and,

. . . Galella's constant surveillance, his obtrusive and intruding presence was unwarranted and unreasonable. If there were any doubt in our minds, Galella's inexcusable conduct toward defendant's minor children would resolve it.

Galella does not seriously dispute the court's finding of tortious conduct.

The district judge enjoined Galella from coming within 50 yards of Jackie and 75 yards of her children. The Circuit Court unanimously affirmed the trial judge's conclusions, but inexplicably voted 2-1 to reduce those distances to 25 feet from Jackie and 30 feet from the children. The majority erred. The low-hanging clouds up on the 17th floor of the courthouse must have obscured their vision of what was so clear in the District Court below. The appellate judges had misjudged the culprit. Galella later thumbed his nose at them and violated their order too.

Some twenty-plus years after the trial, Galella continued to manifest a distant relationship to how awful his conduct had been. One night, when my wife Pinks and I were walking east on 45th Street after seeing a Broadway show, we encountered him and several other photographers standing in front of another theatre, cameras in hand, waiting for a celebrity or a cast member to exit. He spied me, and as if we were the best of old friends, called out with gusto, "Marty,

Marty London, come over and meet the guys!" With a big smile, he turned to his colleagues and said, "Hey guys, this is Marty London. He set out to make me out to be a liar, and boy, did he ever succeed!" He laughed, I said hello, and we went on our way.

Immediately following the trial, Jackie and I developed an easy social relationship, but instead of pastrami sandwiches in the 29th floor conference room, it was real food on real plates in the Four Seasons Grill Room in the Seagram Building. We discussed real-life issues. John was the same age as my son Jesse. They even looked alike. We talked about our concerns for their futures, what'll they do when they grow up, etc. This was New York City, and safety was something we both worried about. We talked about how difficult it was to teach our kids how to deal with situations that are universally troublesome; if your 15-year-old son is accosted on his bike by three or four kids who demand he give it up, what's the answer? There's a time for fight, a time for flight, and a time for ignominious surrender. How do you teach judgment? There are no right answers of course, but it was helpful, for me at least, to discuss this kind of stuff with an intelligent and concerned parent. We also gossiped. There were lots of Kennedys, and like everybody else in the world, Jackie had differing views about the members of her large clan of in-laws. I confess I loved to listen to her talk about that stuff. And she had gone into the publishing world, and urged me to write a book. She sent me a copy of one written by famed litigator Edward Bennett Williams. "See," she said, "look how easy this is, Marty. Do it!" I laughed. Ed Williams was a lion of the trial bar and I was a young striver. My head was 110% in my law practice. I couldn't imagine adding a book to my work load.

In the late 70's, when I was single, Jackie invited me to a Saturday night Christmas dinner party at her apartment. But though I no longer lived on Carroll Street, I had not outgrown my roots, and foolishly wore my favorite yellow cashmere turtleneck and a brown hound's-tooth sport jacket. When I arrived, the women were wearing haute couture gowns and jewels, and the men wore dark blue suits, white shirts and impeccable ties. I felt like a circus clown, and worse, in a short time I was sweating as if I were in a sauna.

But it got worse. I recall this incident as if it happened yesterday. Across the room, standing alone by the piano, was Diane Keaton. Gorgeous. Dazzling. I screwed up my courage, went over to her, started a conversation, and I actually thought we were getting along fine. She was charming, I was charming, and I was so intently focused on her it took me a while before I became aware that a third person had joined us. I put out my hand to shake his, and said, "Hi, I'm Marty London." He took my hand and said, "Glad to meet you, Marty, I'm Warren Beatty." He then released my hand, put a proprietary arm around Diane's waist, said, "Nice to have met you, Marty" and took her away. Duh, was I the only person in the room who didn't know that Warren Beatty and Diane Keaton were a storied Hollywood couple? I guess so. Not my field.

Jackie and I lost touch for a while, and a number of years later, ran into each other at the gas dock in Menemsha Harbor on Martha's Vineyard. Jackie was on a 24-foot center console with Maurice Tempelsman at the helm, and Pinks and I were on my 28-foot Grady White fishing boat, fueling up for our four-hour trip back to the Hamptons. Jackie invited us and the kids to come back to the island at the end of the summer for her Labor Day beach picnic. We accepted, and the kids got to hang with Teddy, John, and the Kennedy clan. (Years later, my daughter Stephanie worked for John at *George Magazine*). Given the circumstances of how my relationship with Jackie began, I had brought no camera to the picnic. I thought that would be highly inappropriate. Duh, I was the only one who thought so, and everybody took pictures except me!

My relationships with the family continued. Though I had nothing to do with recruiting her, Caroline spent a summer at Paul, Weiss after her second year at law school, and I became a legal advisor to John when he started *George Magazine*. At his request, I wrote an article on abusive "photojournalism" for the magazine. He edited the piece himself and published it.

But some of his mother's troubles with "journalists" got passed along to John. He was the victim of some bizarre instances of articles reporting on totally fabricated interviews with him, and a raft of bullshit stories, most of which I was able to knock down if we learned of them before publication.

By and large, he bore the assaults on his privacy with equanimity. But after he married Carolyn Bessette, he attracted an increasingly larger swarm of paparazzi ass-holes, and the strain was magnified.

On Friday afternoon, July 16, 1999, five years after Jackie died, John called me at the office. I had left early for the week-end, and my secretary Ellin Ossandon, who treated both John and me as if we were her children, gave John my number at the beach and assured him I would not mind taking his call. He declined, said he did not want to bother me on the weekend and would call me on Monday. Later that day, John piloted his small plane, with his wife and sister-in-law aboard, headed for Martha's Vineyard. Their departure had been delayed, and in the haze and gloom of the receding daylight, John became visu-ally confused and flew his plane into the sea.

We did not speak that day, but I know what he was calling about.

In the National Interest: The Resignation of Vice President Spiro T. Agnew

Prior to the second term of Richard Nixon, no President of the United States had ever resigned, and only one Vice President had done so; in 1832, John C. Calhoun, a lame duck Veep, quit his office with less than three months left in his term, to take a seat in the Senate where he could speak more vigorously to advance his political views. One hundred forty-one years later, Vice President Spiro T. Agnew resigned under vastly different circumstances. While he vigorously denied accusations that he took bribes as Governor of Maryland, the government was intent on bringing felony charges. But the prosecution was short-circuited when we, on the Vice President's behalf, made an application to the court that raised serious First Amendment issues. At least the national media and the government thought it did. The hysterical press reaction to an order made by the judge assigned to the case imposed significant pressure on the government to find a way to resolve the case without confronting messy and distracting Constitutional conflicts. At bottom, we did

*our job, the press did its job, and the resulting clash provided
a unique result that served the national interest.*

✦

On the evening of August 5, 1973, as the Watergate scandal intensified, my partner Jay Topkis called me at home and told me he had just received this call:

> Caller: Mr. Topkis, this is ...., from the Colson law firm in Washington, D.C. Are you free to come to D.C. tomorrow to meet a new client? This is a sensitive criminal investigation.
>
> Topkis: Does the client have a name?
>
> Caller: He is a high government official and the matter is so sensitive I have been instructed not to mention his name on the phone.
>
> Topkis: A high government official? A Congressman?
>
> Caller: No, higher.
>
> Topkis: A Senator?
>
> Caller: No, higher.
>
> Topkis: A cabinet member?
>
> Caller: No. higher.
>
> Topkis: Holy shit, the President?
>
> Caller: Ahhh, . . . not *quite* so high!

Jay asked me if there was any reason we should not take

the case. I asked, "Are we getting paid?" Jay said, "Yes." I said, "Then I can't think of any reason not to take the case."

A chance to represent the Vice President of the United States in a criminal case? For that opportunity, I was more than willing to put my personal political preferences aside. (I was not only a Democrat, but had been a candidate for local office on the Democratic ticket, and soon thereafter became Chairman of the Ossining Town Democratic Committee). I said, "Jay, for you, anything!" He laughed and we made arrangements to meet at 10 a.m. at Charles Colson's law firm the next morning.

Jay Topkis was a brilliant partner with whom I had worked during my years as an associate. He helped me learn how to write, and that means how to think. He was wickedly irreverent and his cutting sense of humor was capable of inflicting serious injury, but I almost always managed to duck. I recall one instance, though, when he did draw a few drops of blood.

Soon after I had arrived at the firm, Jay asked me to try a case with him in New York Supreme Court. Young associates do not often get speaking roles in trials, but Jay gave me one of the several witnesses. After the trial, as we walked down the courthouse steps, he offered up an appraisal I cherish to this day: "Hey, London, nice. You could really be a trial lawyer someday." From Topkis, this was as good as it gets. But he soon punctured my balloon. This was not a jury case, and we had to submit a post-trial brief summing up our proof, applying what we considered to be the applicable law, and arguing our cause. It was my job to write the brief. I knew Topkis's reputation as the hardest of markers, and I slaved for weeks over a 30-page typed draft before I sent it to him. After a week of radio silence, I received in the interoffice mail twelve legal size yellow pages of tight handwriting in green ink, topped by a buck slip: "Marty, this is our brief. Yours stunk. Jay."

Oh, yeah, we lost that case.

The morning after Jay's call from the Colson firm, I boarded the Eastern Airlines Shuttle to Washington, D.C. At LaGuardia Airport, the Shuttle "terminal" in 1973 was an oversized Quonset hut in which prospective passengers were corralled in a switchback line and were boarded on a first-come, first-served basis. When the plane was full, those left behind had to wait for the next flight, usually an hour later. When the plane reached cruising altitude, a stewardess would come down the aisle collecting fares like a train conductor.

When I got out of my car at the Shuttle parking lot and removed my suit jacket from the hook above the rear side window, I noticed a problem; a six-inch-long, inch-wide strip of lining on one flap of the center vent was hanging down. My Bar Mitzvah suit had grown a tail.

As I boarded the plane, I asked the stewardess if she had a needle and thread. She laughed and said, "Are you kidding? It's all I can do to get the fares and offer coffee on this run. I can't help you." But when she collected my fare, she said, "Sorry I snapped at you. This is a stressful flight for us because it is so short and we have so much to do. Anyway, I found something that might help," and she handed me a big diaper pin with a yellow plastic safety cap at the closure end. I was familiar with the device. My kids had been born before God invented disposable diapers. Piece of cake. I shrugged out of my jacket and pinned my satin tail back up out of sight.

For an hour, Jay and I were briefed at the Colson law firm and then the two of us, accompanied by young Colson partner Judd Best, walked over to see our new client. The Vice President's office was across a small blocked-off street adjacent to the White House, in what was formerly known as the Treasury Building, later called the Executive Office Building. The Secret Service security procedures were thorough. The contents of our bags were examined, and we were required to pass through metal detectors before we were ushered to Agnew's second floor office.

I have never been to the Oval Office, but I have seen pictures of it. The Vice President's office looked every bit as commodious, albeit rectangular. Big desk, upholstered couches and chairs, nice rugs, all very impressive. After introductions, the Vice President thanked us for coming to see him, retained us, and we started to discuss the problem. But before we got too deep into the facts, I had to break off – coffee at home, coffee on the plane, coffee at the lawyer's office, my back teeth were floating. I got directions to the men's room. There was a private bathroom attached to the Veep's office, but on this occasion, I used the one in the hall. As I walked down the corridor, I was keenly aware how closely I was being observed by the guy in the dark suit wearing a button in his ear, who was stationed just outside the Vice President's office. Upon my return, the door-watcher spoke his first words. "Sir, would you mind telling me what that thing is hanging down from the back of your jacket?" Ugh, I knew before I looked. Sure enough, my safety pin had become undone, and I had been visiting the Vice President of the United States while sporting a satin tail with a bright piece of metal and yellow plastic at the bottom end of it. Talk about humiliation! What must the client be thinking of his new lawyer? While I pinned the tail back up to the jacket, I told my story to the Secret Service agent. He laughed, and said they were wondering what it was when I passed through security. Some thought it might be some sort of antenna, but no suspicious device showed up when I went through the scanner and they had been reluctant to question the Vice President's invitee. Nice guy. He wished me well. I was sure that story would be told over beers at a cop bar that night. Hey, I have told it myself dozens of times.

The Spiro Agnew we faced that morning was nothing like the person I had expected to meet. The "nattering nabobs of negativism" candidate turned out to be a warm and likable guy. I could see how he got elected Governor, and then Vice President. We reviewed the state of play, which is no secret now. The U.S. Attorney for the District of Maryland was investigating allegations that Agnew, while serving as the Governor of Maryland, had accepted "pay-for-play" bribes from architects and engineers. Given the status of the target, the matter had the attention of the highest level of the U.S. Department of Justice.

Our meeting with the client lasted for hours. At one point, he spoke to the President on the phone. I could hear the unmistakable timbre of Nixon's voice, but could not decipher what he was saying.

We moved from the chairs opposite the Vice President's desk to the couches and club chairs at the other end of the office when we were joined by Attorney General Elliot Richardson, who'd come over, he said, because the President had suggested it. Richardson was an imposing patrician figure. *The New York Times* once described him as "the archetype of the cultivated New England Brahmin." Especially following my "clothing malfunction," I was immediately taken by his attire. It was an extremely hot and humid day, but Elliot was dressed so immaculately I would not have been surprised to learn that an assistant had steamed out the wrinkles in his Savile Row suit just before he walked into the room.

Richardson appeared to be an intelligent, thoughtful guy, despite his inability to speak concise declarative sentences.

All speech was in the form of lengthy, contemplative paragraphs. He had held four previous cabinet positions, had been a U.S. Attorney, and was already overwhelmed with the burgeoning Watergate mess when the Agnew problem fell into his lap. He struck me as a straight shooter, whose focus was on the best interests of the Department of Justice and the country, and when he assured us the Agnew investigation was "not political," I believed him.

(Richardson's integrity was on national display one week after the Agnew matter was concluded, when Elliot refused to obey President Nixon's order to fire Archibald Cox, the Watergate Special Prosecutor. When Nixon pressed, Richardson resigned. When the President then issued the same order to Elliot's next in command, William Ruckelshaus, he too refused to obey and resigned. The next Department of Justice official down the line was none other than Solicitor General Robert Bork, who survived the "Saturday Night Massacre" by doing the President's bidding. Nixon promised him the nomination for the next open seat on the Supreme Court, but was not President long enough to keep the promise. Nine years later, President Reagan made good on Nixon's commitment, but Bork was rejected by the Senate. His compliance with Nixon's directive was cited as one of the several reasons for the Senate's decision).

At our August 6th meeting, Richardson supplied a minimalist description of Maryland U.S. Attorney George Beall's investigation into the alleged bribery payments to Agnew. No evidence had yet been submitted to a grand jury, but Beall already had some guilty pleas from the alleged bribe-givers. The Attorney General's account of the matter was a view of the case from 30,000 feet, and he suggested we meet with Henry Petersen, the head of the Department of Justice Criminal Division, for more details.

We said "sure," and in the ensuing days we did meet with Petersen, who was accompanied by Beall and his assistants. They gave us a few more details, but, as we were soon to learn, the information they offered up was not nearly as detailed as one or more people in the DOJ were giving to the press.

We immersed ourselves in developing a strategy. Preparing for trial was not our first option. As in any criminal inquiry, the first goal is to find a way to avoid indictment, and this case had unique opportunities for that. For openers, we had a strong argument that a sitting Vice President was immune from criminal prosecution unless and until he'd been impeached by the House and tried and convicted by the Senate. Why? We argued that the Constitution said so.

Article II, section 4, reads:

> "The President, Vice President and all civil Officers of the United States, shall be removed from Office on Impeachment for, and Conviction of, Treason, Bribery, or other high Crimes and Misdemeanors."

And Article I, section 3, provides:
> "Judgment in Cases of Impeachment shall not extend further than to removal from Office, . . . but the Party convicted shall nevertheless be liable and subject to Indictment, Trial, Judgment and Punishment, according to law."

Those paragraphs certainly suggest that the "Party convicted" by the Senate after impeachment by the House could *then* be "subject to Indictment. . . ." That's a pretty powerful argument that criminal indictment comes only after impeachment, but it's hardly conclusive. The word "then" is nowhere found in that clause of the Constitution, though we thought it was implied.

Second, while nothing in the Constitution explicitly says so, constitutional scholars unanimously held the view that a *President* is absolutely immune from criminal prosecution while in office. Could it not be argued that the *Vice President*, who is also an Article II officer, benefitted from this criminal-immunity-while-in-office umbrella as well? No surprise, there was no judicial authority either way.

If either argument prevailed, any criminal proceeding against the Vice President would be barred unless and until he was removed from office by impeachment or until his term expired. And if he were not removed by impeachment, then he couldn't be prosecuted for another three and a half years and even that is assuming his stint as an Article II Executive Officer ended at that time. After all, as a result of Watergate or other misadventure, the Vice President might become President in advance of that date, or he might be elected President (or Vice President) in 1976. In all, Mr. Agnew could possibly be in office for another eleven or more years!

Whether or not the Vice President had pre-impeachment immunity from criminal prosecution, it was certainly clear Congress had the power to impeach. But the remaining questions were complex. Would the DOJ present evidence to Congress? If so, what happens to grand jury secrecy? Could we confront adverse witnesses in Congress prior to a court trial, something not available to defense lawyers in an ordinary case? Would the DOJ simultaneously prosecute?

Consider this realistic scenario: i) a court rejects our constitutional arguments, and rules the government can prosecute a sitting Vice President; ii) the House takes up the matter and does not impeach, or it does impeach, but the Senate does not convict (it takes only 37 votes to block a conviction and there were 45 Republicans in the Senate at the time), and iii) the DOJ wins a criminal conviction and the judge sentences Agnew to prison. The result? Spiro Agnew would still be the Vice President of the United States, but would be in a federal prison cell. Does he keep his Secret Service protection there? If the President is disabled, or dies (or resigns!), does the imprisoned Vice President then become an imprisoned President? Could he then play his get-out-jail-free card and pardon himself?

And what happens to the country in the meantime, especially with the President hanging on to his job by his fingernails as the Watergate scandal grows exponentially? To add to the stew, this was not exactly an otherwise quiet period outside the United States. The Yom Kippur War started while we were discussing our legal issues with Richardson & Company, and the President had to make a crucial decision whether to re-supply the overrun Israeli army.

At the same time, the press learned of the "secret" criminal investigation and were publishing daily reports of leaked information. Article after article began with "We have learned from high Justice Department officials," or "A reliable Justice Department source," or "Prosecutors said," etc. And the DOJ knew those attributions were accurate – on September 5th, the *Washington Post* reported:

> Attorney General Elliot L. Richardson said yesterday he has been told by news media representatives that the Justice Department has been a source of leaks about the investigation of Vice President Spiro T. Agnew.

The Vice President publicly denied the alleged bribery and extortion charges, but those denials were drowned out by the media frenzy fueled by the prosecutorial leaks.

On September 10th, exactly one month before the end of the matter, Jay Topkis and I called Elliot Richardson and asked if we could meet. Elliot said that was a good idea and asked if Petersen and Beall could join. We said "Certainly." When Richardson asked what was on the agenda, we said no more than, "We think we are at the stage where it is useful to get together." Richardson agreed, and we made a date for a few days hence, in his office.

The physical office of the Attorney General of the United States is only a bit smaller than a regulation basketball court. The wall opposite the windows was plastered with photos, diplomas, awards with red ribbons and gold seals, and a poster in Latin, the translation of which is, "Grab them by the balls, and their hearts and minds will follow." Richardson, in a genuine effort to set a relaxed tone, referred to the big room as the "Martha Mitchell Memorial Dining Room," and then led us to a smaller room at the far end, which he used as his working office. It was not much larger than my office at Paul, Weiss. He told us he never used the big room, though Bobby Kennedy had.

Richardson said he was pleased we were talking and wanted to have a general discussion of the options for all of us to consider. The ever-shy Jay Topkis opened with, "No midnight indictments while we are talking, right?" Richardson agreed. Then Topkis said, "Well, for openers, we think the Vice President is immune from criminal prosecution as long as he is in office." Richardson calmly said he did not agree, they had done work on this question, and he believed they could indict the Vice President and try him.

In that meeting, and a number of meetings thereafter in the Attorney General's office, we did what negotiators do, at least the good ones; we isolated the several points of agreement and worked on the others. We made our priorities plain. Our client would resign, but only if the criminal case ended with his retaining his freedom and dignity. The government's priority was to be sure the result served the national interest and preserved the integrity of its prosecutorial function.

Throughout, Richardson was tortured by the question of what was in the "national interest," a point on which the Department was divided. Elliot conceded that the Vice President could try to instigate impeachment proceedings, and seek a "political" verdict, but he maintained if that happened, the DOJ could nevertheless go forward simultaneously with a criminal indictment and trial. He thought that ugly show would likely last at least two years, and *that* certainly was not in the national interest. And while it was unnecessary to say it, we all knew the President was severely wounded and might not last that long. Put the problems together and you had the makings of a major national crisis that, as one political observer noted, "could threaten the viability of the nation." Again and again, Richardson said he needed a result that showed the DOJ was acting responsibly, this was a serious criminal case, and not a political putsch.

At one of our meetings, Richardson mentioned a *personal* concern that took us aback. As the Attorney General, he was in the line of succession in case of a Presidential vacancy. We were surprised because he was number seven – the Vice President, Speaker of the House, President Pro Tem of the Senate, and Secretaries of State, Treasury, and Defense came before him. But he was now talking about a deal moving him up the line to number six, and with a weak President, he might well advance to number five, with a national election still three and a half years away. Furthermore, if the Vice President resigned, the President would appoint a successor. Who knows who that would be? Elliot said he feared people would accuse him of forcing

Agnew to resign to benefit his own standing. We thought the likelihood of anyone attributing that motive to the Attorney General to be remote, but we were not sitting in *his* chair. Richardson's concern gave rise to one of my favorite anecdotes.

At that point in the meeting, Jay suggested a break. Our team left Elliot's small office, repaired to the far end of the basketball court, and Jay said to me, "Marty, Elliot is genuinely concerned about this, and feeling poorly because of it. We need to buck him up." Using the Yiddish word for "flatter," Jay said, "Marty, can you think of a way to *schmeichel* the Attorney General?"

I could, and did. Richardson was a compulsive doodler. He doodled while speaking and listening. But he was no ordinary black-pencil doodler. He had an array of colored felt tip pens in a cup on his desk, and applied a multicolored array of swirls, circles, and loops to the top page of his lawyer's notepad. They were quite attractive. Soon after we returned to the meeting room, I told him I admired his work. He beamed. He said others had also complimented him, and his doodles hung on walls throughout Washington. I asked if I could have one too, and he brightened even more, tore off the completed work on the top page, and endorsed it "To Marty, with great respect, Elliot Richardson" and reached across his desk and handed it to me. (I had it framed and hung on a sunlit wall in my office. Little did I know that Elliot used cheap materials, and after one summer, the doodle faded to nothing and I was left with a blank sheet of white paper in a black frame! A metaphor for something? What?)

Resignation was always part of the package, but the remaining issues were:

1. What would Agnew plead to?

We offered to plead *nolo contendere* ("I admit nothing, but do not contest the charge") to a misdemeanor. They wanted Agnew to plead guilty to a felony. We wanted a tax count, they wanted bribery and extortion. When we got close to a deal we could live with, Richardson raised a problem for them that plagued the negotiations throughout: they had cooperators in Maryland who had signed guilty pleas to felony bribery counts and were facing jail sentences. How could the government agree to jail the cooperating bribers but let the alleged bribee go free? It seemed Elliot, under pressure from Beall and Petersen, was retreating from his earlier acquiescence to a tax count and was now back to talking about a plea of guilty to bribery. I scribbled a note on my yellow pad and showed it to Jay. "What is this shit – we are back to GO!" I do believe that Richardson and Petersen were honestly worried about these issues and were not raising them as part of a negotiating strategy, but we always made it clear this was a deal-breaker. Richardson finally acquiesced on the tax count issue, but said he needed to get the IRS on board. Topkis was Topkis, and remarked, "Well, Elliot, that goes one inch toward solving a mile-long problem." Eventually, the government agreed to a *nolo* plea to a felony tax count, and did not retreat from that.

2. Government Statement

Richardson insisted that the Government needed to publish a lengthy statement listing all the evidence of guilt of bribery, so that the public could see this was a serious criminal matter and not a political maneuver. When it looked like the deal was foundering on the language of that document, the White House got involved in the issue. Jay and I accepted an invitation to walk across the street to the White House and meet with Nixon's Chief of Staff, General Alexander ("I am in charge!") Haig and the White House Special Watergate counsel, Fred Buzhardt. Haig (a/k/a "The Nurse") was just as advertised: aloof, efficient, and a man who behaved in every respect as if he had a stick up his ass. He didn't speak English so much as what became known in D.C. as "Haigspeak," which has been defined as "a particularly verbose, obscure and semantically strained" speaking style. I thought of it as a cross between military jargon and Yogi Berra malapropisms. The General also tended to see all problems through what I would call "Haiglenses." I thought his role in the Agnew matter was helpful but hardly in the center ring, but Haig told Petersen that he saw himself "in the spotlight of history."

Fred Buzhardt, on the other hand, was succinct, realistic, an honest broker, and an excellent mediator. In short, he got the job done. His presence on the scene says a lot about the pressure Agnew's legal problems were putting on the administration. After all, Buzhardt was up to his chin in alligators dealing with Watergate, and was nevertheless now weighted down by being drafted to help with the Agnew crisis. I had little doubt the President wanted Agnew gone, and his White House staff worked to accomplish that, despite the view of some that as long as Agnew was Vice President, Nixon was "impeachment proof."

3. The Sentence

This was the toughest nut to crack. For us, it was fundamental to any plea deal that the Vice President's offer to resign was contingent upon a "no-jail" sentence. This turned out to be more complicated than anticipated, and was not resolved until the day before the Vice President resigned.

Throughout September, Richardson was adamant that the government could not make a sentence recommendation.

He said it was imperative the DOJ stick to its standard posture: sentencing was exclusively the province of the Court. We said, "fuhgeddaboudit," we needed an iron-clad no-jail assurance from the judge, and we surely could not get that without a firm recommendation from the government. At one point, at the end of one of his Hamlet-like soliloquies, the Attorney General conceded, "Well, I will do it if I have to, but not up front. I will bite the bullet later."

Petersen's attitude was negative. He reiterated that it was not the U.S. Attorney's practice to make agreements as to sentence. Moreover, the matter had been assigned for all purposes to District Judge Walter E. Hoffman of Virginia (all nine Maryland federal judges had recused themselves), and Petersen said he knew that it was Judge Hoffman's practice to give no advance notice of his sentencing intentions. Petersen repeatedly raised the problem of the other defendants in the case who faced prison sentences on their pleas of guilty to felony bribery.

Jay suggested that perhaps we could make progress on the open issues by sounding out the judge on what he needs to render a no-jail sentence, and Richardson agreed. Moreover, he said he would refrain from submitting evidence to the Grand Jury until we met with Hoffman. Topkis chided him by adding that until the government found a way to stop the flow of leaks coming from its people, submitting evidence to the Grand Jury was a major risk for them. No response.

We thought it was clear from the meetings with Richardson, Petersen, and Beall that the government was divided on virtually all the issues, even the ones we thought had been locked up. While Elliot was concerned about the damage to the nation that would be associated with a years-long criminal proceeding against a sitting Vice President, with possibly a contemporaneous impeachment proceeding against one (if not both!) of the country's Executive Officers, Henry Petersen and George Beall were stuck on DOJ procedural issues involving sentence recommendations and deals already made with the alleged bribers. I thought Beall and his team might also be dreaming of a sensational career-making historic trial. While all this was cooking, there was the rapidly approaching cyclonic cloud of the leak issue. While the government lawyers vigorously denied responsibility, I did not for a moment believe all those journalists were fabricating their reports.

The division within the DOJ led to a breakdown in the talks. On September 25th, Richardson called Jay and me and told us that after consulting with his colleagues, he had decided to release a statement saying negotiations had failed and the criminal case would go forward with the submission of evidence to the grand jury. The press reported his statement and the fat was in the fire.

We were prepared for that contingency, and two days later, the Vice President sent a letter to the House of Representatives asking that body to commence impeachment proceedings in the interests of "preserving the Constitutional stature of my Office and accomplishing my personal vindication." Our letter argued that the House was the only body constitutionally authorized to act in these circumstances, and cited as precedent a request by Vice President John C. Calhoun in 1832. (Calhoun had been accused of siphoning off money on military procurement contracts. The House took up the matter and he was vindicated).

The Agnew letter, like the Calhoun letter, pledged full cooperation with the House inquiry. Agnew visited Speaker Carl Albert, who was non-committal, though he had earlier indicated that if the House did go forward, he would appoint a special committee to study the matter and make recommendations to the House. But two days after Albert met with the Vice President, the Democrat said he would not consider the matter because of the "ongoing criminal investigation."

Speaker Albert's decision created a pickle. We argued the DOJ was frozen until the House acted, and now the House said it was frozen until the DOJ acted. We needed to shock the stilled negotiations back to life. How do we incentivize the DOJ to relent? Aggression, that's how. We attacked the government directly. On the day Speaker Albert refused our request for impeachment hearings, we launched a missile that exploded not only in the offices of the DOJ, but in media offices throughout the land. We sued the federal government, and asked for two injunctions.

> We wanted the court to enjoin any submission to the Grand Jury on the ground that criminal prosecution of a sitting Vice President was barred by the Constitution. Our motion was accompanied by a legal brief the Paul, Weiss team had been working on since day two of our representation. (In the summer of 1973, we had a brilliant student intern from the Harvard Law School working at the firm, but I do not recall whether young Charles E. Schumer actually contributed to this effort).

And,

> ii) We sought an injunction against any further illicit press communications coming out of the government. We accused the prosecutors of an "obviously deliberate campaign of leaks."

When the national press read that second request, it went berserk. While journalists were inclined to report on sophisticated Article I and Article II Constitutional issues with a degree of equanimity, the attack on government leaks hit them where they lived. Editorials attacked us for "trying to wage war against the First Amendment," and the story competed with the Arab-Israeli war for front-page space in *The New York Times*. The government called our application "frivolous," and declared that all its people were willing to take lie detector tests.

We asked for a conference with Judge Hoffman, and he convened an October 3rd meeting in the Baltimore federal courthouse. Present were the defense lawyers, U.S. Attorney George Beall, and two of his assistants. There were two items on the agenda.

First, given all the press reports about the Vice President's alleged wrongdoing, the judge said he felt obliged to give a supplemental charge to the Grand Jury about its obligations. He gave us a copy of his draft and asked if we had any comments or suggestions. When I read the text, I sat quietly but I wanted to cheer – I thought his words helped our cause, and indicated that Judge Hoffman was an acute thinker. He knew the First Amendment was not an absolute bar to *any* abridgment of speech; there were other Constitutional rights of equal, and competing, importance. He would tell the grand jurors:

> It would be a tragedy to the cause of the administration of justice if grand jurors returned an indictment merely because they may have heard or seen reports from the news media.
>
> **We are rapidly approaching the day when the perpetual conflict between the news media, operating as they do under freedom of speech and freedom of the press, and the judicial system, charged with protecting the rights of persons under investigation for criminal acts, must be resolved.** [Emphasis mine]

We were satisfied, and the government people sat in uncomfortable silence, but obviously could not and did not object.

Second, we then turned to our accusation of government misconduct via their leaks to the press. We complained bitterly about contamination of the grand jury. The prosecutors said, "It ain't us." We said, "Well, the press says it is," and the sensible Judge Hoffman turned to us and said, "Look, fellas, these reporters are not always truth tellers. This is a hot story. Why should I believe them that the government is leaking when the government tells me it is not?"

We were ready for that question. We said, "Ok, Judge, somebody is not telling the truth. Let's put both sides under oath. Let's take depositions of these reporters and we'll find out if their reports are true, and while we are at it, let's depose the prosecutors and see if they deny the leaks under oath."

I thought the U.S. Attorney from Maryland would ricochet off the ceiling. He and his colleagues became highly agitated at such an outrageous proposal: that had NEVER been done before, there was no provision in any statute or rule that provided for that remedy, blah, blah, blah, etc., etc., etc. These lawyers were dangerously exercised. I loved that scene. Still do.

Judge Hoffman, on the other hand, was a calm, sensible judicial officer whose job was to resolve disputes in accordance with facts and reason. He was unmoved by the government's apoplectic opposition. He calmly told us, "First, if you did that, it would need to be limited in scope. I can't let you take too much time and delay the government's efforts. Second, I would have to consider the details of precisely what kind of order to enter, and that would take some time, so I dunno." Bingo! A softball, right down the center of the plate. "No problem, Your Honor. In preparation for this meeting, we drafted an order for your signature. We'll depose a limited number of reporters and prosecutors, all to be promptly designated by us. For openers, we will depose Elliot Richardson, Henry Peterson and George Beall." I reached into my briefcase, pulled out several copies of a draft order I had prepared for the occasion, distributed them to the judge and the prosecutors, and while the latter sputtered and got red in the face, Judge Hoffman serenely looked over the draft, nodded, took out his pen, signed the document, and gave it back to us for filing. At one point, one of Beall's assistants sputtered, "Are you *really* intending to take depositions of the Attorney General of the United States, the Chief of the Criminal Division of the United States Department of Justice, and the United States Attorney for the District of Maryland?" Topkis smiled, and said, "Yes, for starters," and the AUSA said something to the effect of, "Well, in that event I'm not sure the Justice Department has enough attorneys to cover the depositions!"

The further details were all to our advantage. When the prosecutors complained that the reporters' depositions would be full of objecting lawyers and refusals to answer and would take forever, Hoffman said he would take care of that: the depositions would be in his courthouse and he would preside and make instantaneous rulings compelling answers where appropriate. And the depositions would be sealed.

The New York Times ran the story at the top of the front page. The headline read "Judge Grants Agnew Right to Investigate News Leaks." The paper predicted that Judge Hoffman's order "seemed certain to open a new area of controversy and litigation." That was a material understatement.

We had created another formidable adversary; we had stuck a pointed stick in the eye of the Fifth Estate, and the

First Amendment Bar shifted into warp gear. Media lawyers asserted Judge Hoffman's order created a "Constitutional dispute that was one of the gravest in the history of the free press." This was a desecration of the Holy Temple. From the Fundamentalists point of view, nobody could question a reporter about anything. That simply is the way these people read the Constitution. Ridiculous? I thought so. While the issue of confidential sources is highly contentious (though I cannot find the word "source" in the Constitution, publishers' lawyers and a number of judges can see what I cannot see). We thought the reporters had already given up their "sources" when they reported their information came from "Justice Department officials." That was good enough for us. We believed we needed to go no further than that. We intended to ask each reporter only two questions: "Did you write this article," and then, pointing to the paragraph that said the source was a high government official, "Is this true?" We expected to get answers to those questions, one way or another, and we did not think *any* reading of the First Amendment forbade that. I still don't.

The press mobilized for all-out war. Combative anxiety prevailed. Reporters and media executives, up to and including Arthur Hays Sulzberger, the publisher of *The New York Times*, and Katharine Graham, the publisher of the *Washington Post*, declared they would go to jail before revealing sources. The publishers hired more lawyers, chartered airplanes, and located appellate judges "just in case." A bombardment of motions to quash the reporters' subpoenas rained in on us.

We had served nine reporters with subpoenas. The journalists publicly vowed to go to jail *before answering any questions at all.* They fashioned lapel buttons proclaiming, "*FREE THE AGNEW NINE.*" A subpoena became something of a badge of honor, and there was talk of "subpoena envy" among those who didn't get one. In the midst of this chaos, a reporter called me:

> Reporter: Marty, you have got me in a lot of trouble with my boss. I am in deep shit here.
>
> Me: Why?
>
> Reporter: You did not give me a subpoena and my boss wants to know why everybody else has government sources and I do not.
>
> Me: Look, _____, I apologize, but we sent subpoenas only to reporters who published articles saying they had received confidential information from government sources.
>
> Reporter: I did that! I did that!
>
> Me: No problem. Send me a copy of your article and I promise to send you a subpoena.

He did, and I did, and the "Agnew Nine" became the "Agnew Ten."

Not all inquiries from the press resulted in subpoenas. Some of the reporters covering the Agnew story withstood the hysteria and acted responsibly. Lesley Oelsner, a young legal reporter for *The New York Times* (who had, a year earlier, written an intelligent article about the First Amendment questions associated with the Jacqueline Kennedy Onassis case) called me on August 17th:

> Oelsner: I want to pass on to you the latest "Daily Hot Tip" from Baltimore: "Beall got permission from

Petersen to go forward with enough indictments to fill Oriole stadium." Do you know that to be true?"

London: [Laughing] No.

Oelsner: Well, do you know of any forthcoming indictment of the Vice President?"

London: No.

Oelsner: Thank you for taking my call.

Oelsner did not run the "Hot Tip" in the paper.

The most absurd call came weeks after the matter was resolved when Bill Sherman, the Managing Editor of the *New York Daily News*, called:

Sherman: Marty, there is a rumor floating around that one of the reasons Agnew settled was a story about sex orgies involving the Vice President.

London: Bill, that wins the prize for the most irresponsible story in this case. It is no more credible than one involving little green men from Mars influencing the settlement.

Sherman: Yeah, I agree. We won't run the story, but I had to check it out before throwing the story away.

The government, of course, vigorously denied leaking. Though Petersen said they would all take lie detector tests, it was clear to us they were worried. So worried, the DOJ tasked the FBI with making an investigation. Scores of government personnel signed a leak-denial form affidavit drafted by the FBI. How could any government employee who wanted to keep his or her job refuse to sign that? Again, it all came down to who was lying – the reporters or the government.

The question of whether a District Court should enjoin the criminal proceeding against the Vice President because of the provisions of Articles I and II of the Constitution was troublesome enough for the government. Solicitor General Robert Bork's brief described that issue as "momentous and difficult." Add to that mix the "leak" depositions, and you had extreme pressure on the government. The prospect of the Attorney General and his minions being questioned under oath regarding their relationships with the press must have been thoroughly uncomfortable. We had no doubt that Elliot Richardson and Henry Petersen would never consciously violate the rules, but it was highly likely that some Justice Department people down the line would perjure themselves (or had already done so in signing affidavits during the FBI investigation). Just the precedent of DOJ officials being deposed in a leak investigation had to be extremely troubling for the Department. All this happening during the Watergate scandal created a "perfect storm" that incented the government to find a way out.

Hoffman's order dominated the press and government reactions. To represent the government witnesses at their depositions, the DOJ brought in the U.S. Attorney from Chicago, who, undeterred by his ignorance of the facts and legal issues, got his fifteen minutes of fame by making aggressive comments to the press, which, of course, added fuel to the fire.

Four days after Judge Hoffman ordered the leak depositions, Elliot Richardson blinked; on Sunday, October 7th, he called Judge Hoffman and asked if His Honor would help the parties reach a settlement by attending a conference *the next day*. Richardson suggested they use the empty chambers of a federal judge in Baltimore. Hoffman agreed to a meeting, but rejected the notion of convening at the courthouse. He wanted secrecy and directed his staff to book rooms at the Old Colony Motel in Alexandria, Virginia. We agreed to attend, and were told the judge's instructions were that if we saw press in the vicinity of the motel as we approached, we should retreat and call the judge in his motel room.

Surprise, surprise, as our taxicab approached the motel parking lot that Monday, October 8th, we saw the reporters and cameras. We followed orders, and told the cab driver to take us to the nearest gas station, where we called the judge from a pay phone. Hoffman was pissed. He said the secret was out, Petersen and his team had already been photographed on the way in, and we might as well come ahead. Richardson did not attend.

The meeting lasted for several hours, and was unlike any I have attended. The two teams of lawyers faced one another sitting on the edges of the twin beds in the sparsely furnished motel room. Judge Hoffman sat on a chair at the foot of the beds. The DOJ's team of Petersen, Beall, and the latter's assistants indicated the government's intransigence had melted in the new environment. We made progress.

When the defense lawyers wanted to caucus, we went to the bathroom. But it had no phone! The judge suggested we go to the room next door, which had been left unlocked for that purpose. (The judge had sent his wife to the movies.) We made our calls, came back, and affirmed parts of the deal: resignation, *nolo* plea to one felony tax count, government statement of its view of the case, and Agnew agreed to make a statement that he should have paid some $29,000 in additional income taxes.

But the major issue remained unresolved: would the government recommend a no-jail sentence, and would the judge agree in advance to accept the recommendation?

Petersen insisted that the DOJ would make no recommendation and would leave the sentence to the judge. Topkis said we would not go forward unless we knew the bottom line; we would not plead unless we knew what the court was going to do. The judge had indicated his normal sentence for a tax felony was a "split sentence," i.e., prison and a fine. What's more, he said, in this case his hands were tied by the government's position. "I can't plea bargain with myself. If the government does not make a recommendation, I have nothing more to say." But then Hoffman added, "Even if the government came forward with a recommendation, I could not commit myself to accept that recommendation in advance of the plea hearing. Plea bargaining does not contemplate an agreement by the court."

Petersen then blundered. He told the judge the government was not cowed by the pendency of the leak depositions, and everyone on his team was prepared to take a purity oath. The judge was not impressed. He said:

> Look, Henry, someone on your team has leaked, and you have to face that. Look at the news coverage of this meeting in this obscure motel. Henry, ya gotta clean your house.

We took a break, conferred, made a call to Buzhardt, who said he would call Richardson, and we went back to the meeting and asked the judge if we could meet again tomorrow. Topkis took one more crack at the judge's reluctance to give an advance blessing to a no-jail sentence recommendation in a plea deal. Before we left, Jay said, in substance:

> Your Honor, in an ordinary case, if an accused person had an agreement with the government to plead guilty or *nolo* as part of a no-jail plea agreement,

and you disapproved of the agreement in open court, you would allow that defendant to withdraw his plea and change it to "Not Guilty." But this is not an ordinary case. It sets no precedent for future plea bargains involving other people. You cannot leave the Vice President of the United States in that position. The Vice President of the United States withdrawing a plea in open court is not in anyone's interest, and certainly not in the national interest.

The judge said he would think on it.

We scheduled two meetings for the next day, Tuesday, October 9th: one in the morning with the Attorney General and his team, and a 2 p.m. meeting with the same cast, plus the judge, both meetings in Richardson's basketball court. In the morning meeting, Elliot was still tortured over the sentencing issue. After hours of back and forth, he finally said, "Okay, I said before I would bite the bullet if I had to. If the Judge says he will bless the deal if I do it, I will do it." But he was so troubled, he said he was not sure he would attend the plea in open court. He worried that his presence in court might make it look like the result was a political maneuver. Jay said, "Elliot, this is too important for you to miss the hearing. First, if you need a yard, you should call your own number. Second, you should go because if you don't, the press might suggest you are ashamed to be there." I did not know Brahmins could blush, but Elliot did, and said, "I hadn't thought of that. Thanks, Jay. I'll be there."

At the afternoon meeting, the judge pressed the Attorney General. "Can you commit to a government sentence recommendation?" Richardson delivered a tortured speech, but concluded, in substance,

If there is no deal, Agnew will be the Vice President
for two to three years while the investigation con-
tinues, a charge is brought, and a trial is had.
That is certainly contrary to the national interest.
Therefore, if you require it to bless this deal, you
have my recommendation. *The government agrees
with the Vice President's counsel.*

Topkis then scribbled a message to me on his pad. It
read, "Note for history."

Richardson concluded with a statement that it was in
the public interest that the Vice President resign and a new
Vice President be appointed. He repeated,

For all these reasons, notwithstanding the bad evidence, we nevertheless recommend a sentence
without confinement.

Whew. Halfway there. But now we needed to move the
ball the rest of the way down the field. There was still no
deal if Hoffman would not depart from his normal practice.
We needed his assent before we entered the plea and submitted Agnew's resignation.

Judge Hoffman then made what was for him, an unusu-
ally long speech. He, too, was seriously concerned about
the national interest and now agreed with our position that
this case was not a precedent for plea agreements in other
cases. But his conversion was not specific enough for me and
I wrote a note to Topkis: WE DO NOT YET HAVE A FIRM
COMMITMENT FROM THE JUDGE. Topkis pursued, and
finally we heard the magic words in plainspeak. The judge
said he was concerned about the appearance of a departure
from his normal practice in such cases, i.e., a split sentence
of confinement and a fine, and he realized "we will all be

taken to task by some people for what we do here today," but **he agreed the national interest was paramount, *and as long as these considerations were part of the public record, and there was full disclosure of these conversations*, given the extraordinary circumstances and the recommendation of the Attorney General, he would abide by the government recommendation and approve the agreement.**

What a relief. I think I lost ten pounds in two months. We then cleaned up some details: no fingerprinting, no photographing, etc., and the judge said he would schedule a hearing for the next day at 2 p.m., and would say nothing in the hearing notice as to the purpose of the court session. That was it. Well almost. After the last detail was hammered out regarding tomorrow's proceedings, Judge Hoffman said, "Okay, gentlemen, Thank you. This concludes the matter. The Agnew matter is ended."

But Richardson, his pride wounded, wanted the last word, and made a classic trial lawyer error – he failed to leave court the moment he had the result he wanted. Instead, he repeated the mistake Petersen had made the day before, and complained to the judge that he was upset by our "attack on the prosecution." If he were looking for a reprimand of the defense lawyers, he got the reverse. Judge Hoffman responded, in substance:

> Elliot, as I told you on the phone, someone in the Department of Justice is leaking information. You have to face that. I cannot identify the sources of the leaks in the Department, but you cannot deny you have some.

Now we needed to get back to the client's office, report, and draft some letters. When we convened at the Veep's office, we were surprised by the number of Agnew advisors in attendance, including a lawyer sent by Agnew's friend, Frank Sinatra!

First, the resignation letter. What should it say? Each meeting participant was impressed with his own sense of historic contribution, and draft letters and comments competed for center stage. Some proposals contained bitter diatribes asserting the client was innocent and being hounded from office. Others attacked the press, others attacked the lack of support from the President, or Speaker Carl Albert, etc. After interminable bickering, I put forward my proposal. I shamelessly take full credit for submitting the winning concept: delete all editorializing. My draft read as follows:

> The Honorable Henry A. Kissinger
> The Secretary of State
> Washington, D.C.,20520
>
> Dear Mr. Secretary:
> I hereby resign the Office of Vice President of the United States, effective immediately.
>
> Sincerely,
> s/

That's the letter Vice President Agnew signed and submitted the next day. (Ten months later, Richard Nixon's resignation letter bore the same text.)

We took a similar minimalist approach in the Vice President's courtesy letter to President Nixon:

> The Honorable Richard M. Nixon
> The President of the United States
> Washington, D.C. 20500
> My Dear Mr. President:

I have today resigned the Office of Vice President of the United States pursuant to the provisions of 3 U.S.C. Sec. 20. A copy of the instrument of resignation is enclosed.

I deem it appropriate on this occasion to thank you for the support which you have given me, and to express through you to the American people my eternal gratitude for their confidence in twice electing me to be Vice President. I have concluded that, painful as it is to me personally, it is in the best interests of the Nation that I now relinquish that office.

Respectfully,
Spiro T. Agnew

It was a painful deal for all on our side, but it made sense for the country and the client, and before he resigned, the Vice President sent me a photograph with a note of thanks.

"4, Marty London, – quick, aggressive, courageous – a lawyer who serves his client with total dedication. I am proud to count him a friend.

[signature]

"To Marty London, – quick, aggressive, courageous – a lawyer who serves his client with total dedication."

Spiro T. Agnew

Now the final act of the drama: the actual plea and resignation. On Wednesday, October 10, 1973, the defense lawyers arrived at the federal courthouse in Baltimore five minutes in advance of the 2 p.m. start time. We had been assigned to a particularly large courtroom and the gallery was filled to capacity. In front of the rail were two lawyers' tables, the far one occupied by a team of publishers' lawyers. They were highly exercised. Motion papers, printed cases, and written outlines covered every inch of their table surface. Blood pressures were up. They actually sneered at us when we entered the courtroom and occupied the near table.

In most cases, I have usually enjoyed cordial relationships with adversary counsel. But self-anointed "First

Amendment Lawyers" (my definition: those who earn their
fees by working for publishers) are a breed apart. Some are
decent company at lectures and organized Bar meetings, but
many tend toward fundamentalism. They get their wisdom
and instructions in two-way conversations directly with
James Madison. They arrogate to themselves the exclusive
knowledge as to the reach of The Amendment. They do
not recognize any competing interest, be it privacy, coun-
terterrorism, or the rights of citizens to a fair trial. Judge
Hoffman's charge to the grand jury mentioning the need to
resolve the conflict between First Amendment and Sixth
Amendment rights was, to them, apostasy.

Judge Hoffman's hearing notice issued the day before,
had been intentionally vague, and these lawyers reasonably assumed the hearing was about their motions to quash
our subpoenas. When the marshals, without explanation,
insisted they pick up their papers, leave the table, and repair
to seats or standing room behind the rail, they were furious. But the marshals were court officers, and the lawyers
prudently retreated as they glared at us with animosity and
confusion. The angry buzz in the courtroom was instantly
stilled when new players arrived to occupy the table from
which the publishers' lawyers had just been evicted: the
Attorney General of the United States, attended by his cote-
rie of prosecutors. Jaws dropped at 2:01 p.m. when the Vice
President of the United States joined us at our table. (Was I
nervous because he was a minute late? You betcha.)

Judge Hoffman took the bench and announced:

> Once this hearing begins, no one will be permitted
> to leave, so if you need to depart, do so now. There
> will be no disturbance or outcries of any kind. If
> so, the marshals have been instructed to take you
> into custody.

No one stirred.

Counsel identified themselves, a waiver of indictment signed by Messrs. Agnew, Topkis, and London, was handed up to the Court, as was the Information charging the tax count. Jay offered up the *nolo* plea, Judd Best was in the clerk's office on the phone with the Office of the Secretary of State and confirmed that the Vice President's letter of resignation had been delivered, Richardson and Agnew made the statements we had so painfully negotiated in the preceding days and weeks, and the judge said he accepted the plea and sentenced the defendant to a fine of $10,000 and probation.

In short, the scripted proceedings played exactly as agreed, and 40 minutes after we arrived, just seven days after the Judge ordered depositions of the government and the press, we departed the building accompanying our client, the former Vice President of the United States.

Two days later, my all-time favorite political cartoon, by Paul Conrad, appeared in the *Los Angeles Times*:

"Pot, Wine, Beer, and Sex"

*I*n *1964, the Surgeon General of the United States declared that smoking cigarettes was a serious health hazard, and the "Smoking and Health Fifty-Years War" began. Skirmishes still flare up today, but in the 1970s, pitched battles were a regular occurrence in courts, government agencies, and in the media. While there were many general criticisms of the industry, one broadcaster's specific attack on my client led to a litigation that stunned the national media and its legal representatives. The result shouldn't have surprised them, but the First Amendment crowd sometimes talks only amongst themselves.*

✦

In 1975, the Brown & Williamson Tobacco Corporation was using the Ted Bates agency to advertise and promote its Viceroy brand of cigarettes. When B&W put them on notice that it was unhappy with its work, Bates hired a marketing research consultant, MARC Research, to develop a theme that Bates could recommend to its client for a new advertising campaign. MARC suggested to Bates that B&W adopt an advertising campaign that related Viceroy to "illicit pleasure," more particularly, to "pot, wine, beer, and sex."

It would be difficult to imagine a more inappropriate and useless proposal, but Bates nevertheless passed the MARC report on to B&W management. B&W not only rejected the "pot, wine, beer, and sex" strategy, it fired Bates!

The rejected MARC document was interred in the files of B&W for years, until the FTC, flexing its muscles in the anti-tobacco wars, served a blunderbuss subpoena on B&W seeking its marketing and advertising documents. The document demand was so broad that B&W was required to employ an over-the-road tractor-trailer truck to deliver the tons of responsive paper. Buried in that mountain of dross was the rejected MARC report. But it was not dead, just napping, and, in time, it became the subject of a significant libel case.

After years of paging through the mountain of junk, the FTC staff published a report on what it found, including, a reference to the MARC report. The staff report also referred to a B&W six-month test advertising campaign that showed young adults adhering to "a free and easy hedonistic lifestyle." The most damning example of the test campaign that CBS could come up with at trial was a print advertisement photograph of a smiling, age 25-30 woman, wearing a knee-length dress, standing calf-deep in a public fountain, smoking a Viceroy cigarette, with a smile on her face, while her boyfriend, on dry land, smiled back. That's it. There was nothing in the FTC report suggesting B&W had ever adopted a "pot, wine, beer, and sex" campaign, or even considered doing such a thing. Nothing, there or elsewhere.

In 1981, Walter Jacobson was the 10 p.m. nightly news co-anchor for Chicago's CBS-owned television station,

WBBM. He had held that post for ten years, and it was said that Walter Jacobson was to Chicago what Walter Cronkite was to the United States. Five nights a week, after delivering the news from his anchor desk, Jacobson would hustle to another part of the newsroom, sit at a different desk, and deliver a *Walter Jacobson Perspective*. Each Perspective was replayed the next day as part of the early evening news broadcast. As the Seventh Circuit Court of Appeals later put it:

> [Jacobson] was touted by CBS as someone who "pulls no punches," "lays it on the line." According to the [CBS] ads, he is a journalist "who will make you angry. Or make you cheer." . . . When he delivered his Perspective on November 11, 1981, he made the Brown & Williamson Tobacco Corporation very angry.

The WBBM promos for Jacobson's November 11, 1981 Perspective were explicit: "How the tobacco industry hooks children . . . tonight at 10:00."

Jacobson's broadcast essay had two parts. The first dealt with the tobacco industry in general, accused various brands of giving free cigarettes to teenagers, and referred to other examples of what Jacobson said were marketing attempts "to addict the children to poison." The second part was all about Viceroy.

I copy here the specific defamation. The quote below is from one of the several court decisions in this case. (While Jacobson spoke, a current Viceroy ad showing two packs of Viceroy cigarettes, a golf ball, and a golf club were on the screen. I have no idea of the relevance of those objects, beyond the name Viceroy). Jacobson, in a sneering tone, delivered this report:

The cigarette business insists, in fact it will swear up and down in public, it is not selling cigarettes to children; that if children are smoking, (which they are, more than ever before), it is not the fault of the cigarette business. "Who knows whose fault it is," says the cigarette business. That's what Viceroy is saying. "Who knows whose fault it is that children are smoking? It's not ours."

Well, there is a confidential report on cigarette advertising in the files of the federal government right now, a Viceroy advertising. The Viceroy strategy for attracting young people (starters they are called) to smoking– **FOR THE YOUNG SMOKER .... A CIGARETTE FALLS INTO THE SAME CATEGORY WITH WINE, BEER, SHAVING OR WEARING A BRA . . .** says the Viceroy strategy . . . Therefore, "an attempt should be made," says Viceroy, "**TO PRESENT THE CIGARETTE AS AN INITIATION INTO THE ADULT WORLD, to . . . PRESENT THE CIGARETTE AS AN ILLICIT PLEASURE . . . A BASIC SYMBOL OF GROWING-UP,**" . . . *"An attempt should be made," says the Viceroy slicksters, "TO RELATE THE CIGARETTE TO POT, WINE, BEER, AND SEX.* **DO NOT COMMUNICATE HEALTH OR HEALTH-RELATED POINTS.**" That's the strategy of the cigarette-slicksters, the cigarette business which is insisting in public . . . "we are not selling cigarettes to children."

THEY'RE NOT SLICKSTERS, THEY'RE LIARS.

The Perspective aired a total of four times, and its substance was picked up and reported by the *Saturday Evening Post* magazine.

B&W was outraged. The FTC staff report never suggested B&W had adopted MARC's ridiculous "pot, wine, beer, and sex" strategy. In fact, prior to the broadcast, Jacobson's research assistant, Michael Radutsky, had called the company, and Thomas Humber, B&W's public relations officer, explicitly told him **the company had not only consigned the MARC report to its dead file, but it had fired Bates,** *there were no pot, wine, beer, or sex advertisements, and there never had been.* **Humber warned Radutsky that,** *any suggestion to the contrary would be libelous*.

The tobacco company engaged eminent Chicago counsel and sued Jacobson and CBS for libel, asserting the Perspective was false, the company had never used a pot, wine, beer, and sex campaign, or even considered doing so, and Jacobson knew it. Jacobson and CBS, in turn, engaged *their* eminent Chicago counsel and the battle royal was on.

Jacobson and CBS asked the federal court to dismiss the complaint on various legal grounds, the principal one being that the First Amendment immunized the broadcast from legal attack. The District Judge promptly granted their motion and dismissed the case without even writing an opinion, saying only that he was dismissing the complaint "for the reasons set forth in the defendants' memoranda." And he added, "to deny this motion would unduly restrict the freedom of the press and the right of a journalist to express opinions freely."

Within days of that decision, I received a call from Ernest Pepples, Vice President and General Counsel of B&W. I'd done some work for Ernie in the past, and he said, "Marty, we want you and your team to write the appeal brief and argue the appeal to the Seventh Circuit." I said, "Sure."

Lew Clayton worked with me on the brief. We argued that B&W was entitled to prove the Perspective was knowingly false and the First Amendment does not protect knowingly false defamatory statements. The defendants countered that the District Court's decision was correct because: i) B&W's complaint failed to meet technical pleading requirements; and ii) the Perspective was a "fair summary" of a government report and therefore enjoyed a First Amendment privilege from attack.

The Seventh Circuit Court reinstated B&W's complaint. The eminent Chief Judge Richard A. Posner wrote the unanimous opinion. The court found: i) a detailed analysis of the complaint showed it adequately met pleading standards, and ii) whether or not Jacobson's rant was a fair summary of the FTC staff report was a question of fact, and therefore a jury question, as was the question of knowing falsity. The case was reassigned to a different district judge, Walter Hart, for discovery and trial before a jury.

I called Ernie Pepples to applaud his victory. (Rifkind's Rule: when reporting a successful result to a client, you said, "Congratulations, you won," and when reporting a loss, you said, "I am sorry, I lost.") Ernie, was, of course, pleased, and, in his soft drawl, offered up an unexpected assignment. "Marty, now please go to Chicago and try the case." I said, "Ernie, thank you. I am flattered. You know I love trying cases, but are you sure this is such a good idea? Chicago has a reputation of being a big city with small town attitudes towards 'foreigners.' Do you really think the best way for a Kentucky tobacco company to assault a Chicago TV hero represented by a Chicago lawyer, is to employ me, a New York lawyer, to represent it?" He laughed and said, "Yup."

Hey, I didn't make my legal career by turning down clients. Done.

After losing the appeal, CBS changed counsel, and our adversary for the trial was Tom Morsch, the very competent head of litigation at the eminent Chicago firm, Sidley & Austin. That firm was headed by the distinguished former chairman of the FCC, Newton Minow, who sat on the board of CBS.

Lew and I went off to Chicago to take depositions – Lew took the deposition of Jacobson's research assistant, Michael Radutsky, and I deposed Jacobson. The parties exchanged documents. There were lots of disagreements, and the pre-trial discovery phase took years to complete.

The Trial

The District Court sat on a high floor of the Dirksen Federal Office Building in downtown Chicago. On the first day of trial, camera crews were set up in the lobby, and as we entered the building, I recall saying to Clayton, "Wow, there must be a big-time case going on here." We soon learned we were it. Because of Jacobson's prominence in Chicago, and the unbelievable impudence of a tobacco company not only to sue Walter for libel for an anti-cigarette rant, but to use a New York lawyer to prosecute the cause, the Chicago press was fascinated by the case, and covered it extensively.

Before the trial began, we had a trial management conference with Judge Hart. He ruled, among other things, that we were to start out with an eight-person jury. We could afford to lose up to two members and still get a valid verdict, but none of the eight were alternates, i.e., they would all deliberate, and we would need unanimity to get a verdict. Unlike many other federal judges, he permitted the lawyers to talk directly to the prospective jurors during the selection process. Finally, he directed that each side would have 30 minutes for opening statements. Whoa. I protested. I said I had to tell a full story up front so the jurors could understand where each piece of evidence fit in the larger picture. I had the burden of proof here, which, given the First Amendment hurdle I had to clear, was substantial, and I needed an hour and a half. He said, "Mr. London, you cannot do that. You will put them to sleep." I said, "Well, Judge, I guess that is on me. My risk, my failure. That's what I want. That's what I need, not a minute less." He reluctantly agreed. Some years later, I was told that Judge Hart taught a trial practice class in a local law school, and used my opening as an example of trial craftsmanship. He said it was the best opening he had ever heard. I sure hope that story is true.

The judge also ruled that the trial would be bifurcated, i.e., we would first try the liability question, and only if the jury ruled for the plaintiff on that issue, would we next attack the issue of damages. That was somewhat to the defendants' advantage because it meant we would not be able to get CBS's financials before the jury on the first go-round, but it simplified things for us – we could focus all our energies on the liability question.

It became immediately clear that I had been correct in predicting an appeal to local bias, but I had underestimated how consistently CBS would play that card. The network had hired a press relations flack to cover the trial and attend every session. It was apparent that the goal of its publicity campaign was to spin this trial away from the merits and to emphasize three themes: i) the big, bad tobacco company was attempting to chill the free speech of *Chicago media*; ii) the big, bad tobacco company's big, bad lawyer was from *New York*; and iii) the big, bad New York lawyer was *intimidating the helpless Chicagoans*. It was as if a CBS marketing strategist had concluded this approach would divert the jurors' attention from the facts of the case. From the beginning, I thought the CBS strategy had much in common with the MARC strategy – they were both dumb. I believed CBS was insulting the jurors' intelligence, but hey, CBS didn't consult me.

The CBS strategy was employed in court and out. During the *voir dire*, when Tom Morsch had his opportunity to question prospective jurors, he chatted with them about his familiarity with the neighborhoods where they lived and worked, where Tom's wife worked, etc. He made it eminently clear he and his wife were as local as local can be. Frankly I thought all that bullshit was unnecessary – Morsch's accent was as clearly that of a native Chicagoan as mine was of a native New Yorker. When I spoke to the jurors, I confronted the issue directly. I inquired whether they would hold my status as an outsider against me. They assured me they would not. We ended up with eight Chicago men and women of mixed ethnicity: **two of the jurors had obviously Polish names, and two had obviously Hispanic names**.

The single most outrageous in-court effort to pander to local bias occurred during the CBS counsel's examination of Jacobson's research assistant, Michael Radutsky. Morsch's questioning of him began with the customary inquiry into the usual background stuff, and when asked about his education, Radutsky volunteered **he wanted to study journalism in college** *because he thought the local media did not pay enough attention to Chicago's Polish and Hispanic populations*! How bush league could these guys get? I exploded out of my chair and objected. Judge Hart immediately sent the jury out, told Radutsky to keep his seat, and ordered counsel into the robing room. "Okay, Mr. London, now that there is no jury here, let's hear what you have to say." I told him I thought the witness's extraneous remarks about Polish and Hispanic populations were an outrageous and specific effort to play to the ethnic bias of at least four of the eight jurors, and was unconscionable misconduct. I wanted the witness to be harshly reprimanded, and I wanted that done in front of the jury. The judge nodded, and turned to my adversary: "Mr. Morsch, was this planned? Did you know the witness was going to say that?" Morsch fessed up, and told the judge that yes, he knew the Polish and Hispanic references were going to come out on direct because that had been part of Radutsky's planned testimony at his prep the night before, which was, of course, after the jury had been selected. The judge then scolded Morsch, said jury impartiality was the cornerstone of the judicial process, and he wanted no more such episodes. I said something to the effect of, "Judge, that does me no good in here. Say that again – out there." Judge Hart agreed he would give a harsh jury instruction when we got back in the courtroom.

But by the time His Honor had re-ascended to the bench and the jury was back in the box, he had cooled down, and he gave a mild instruction to the jury about deciding the case on the merits. I was unhappy, but would have more to say on the matter shortly.

When the Radutsky direct was over, the judge asked if I wanted a break before starting my cross. I politely declined. I did not want the witness to step down and talk to his lawyer. I wanted to hammer home to the jurors that the witness and the defendants had insulted them by assuming they would be receptive to an appeal to ethnic bias. So before I got to the substance of Radutsky's role in the defamation, I went back to his remarks about wanting to be a journalist to serve the Polish and Hispanic communities in Chicago. I asked him whether those remarks were part of his planned testimony, rehearsed with the CBS lawyers. **"No," he said,**

he had not discussed that with anyone. I was counting on that. Standing in the middle of the well, I said, in the clearest of tones so no one in the courtroom could miss a word:

> Your Honor, I call upon Mr. Morsch to do his ethical duty to inform the court that his witness has just given false testimony.

Chaos! Morsch, instantly on his feet, shouted his objection. The gallery, filled to the brim with local press, buzzed and chattered. Clayton told me afterwards that he said to one of the people at our table, "Holy Shit, what do we do now? London is going to jail!"

Judge Hart banged the gavel, sent the jury out again, ordered counsel back into the robing room, and I sat there awaiting the axe. I knew of no specific legal precedent that defined Morsch's ethical duty in these circumstances, but my objection sounded right to me at the time, and I went with it. The judge was fair, and the substance of our conversation was this:

> Hart: Look fellas, ok, let's get on to the evidence.
>
> London, I am not going to sanction you for what you did out there because I owed you one. I told you earlier I was going to give a harsh instruction after the Radutsky comments, but instead I gave a soft one. But I am telling you now, you have spent your credit. We are even. Got that, Mr. London?
>
> London: Yes, sir, Your Honor!

The substantive testimony given by Radutsky, earlier extracted by Lew Clayton in the deposition process, was this: he had come upon the FTC report after reading an article in a Louisville newspaper. He called the newspaper, got the FTC report, called B&W and spoke to Humber, who denied B&W had ever adopted the MARC report, told him they had never run a pot, wine, beer and sex advertisement, etc. At Jacobson's request, Radutsky looked for Viceroy pot, wine, beer, and sex ads, could find none, and so informed Jacobson. Radutsky testified he made contemporaneous interview notes, made extensive notations on his copy of the ten-page FTC staff report, drafted an 18-page proposed script for the Perspective which set out "both sides of the issue", including the B&W denial, and made six additional copies of the balanced script. But in discovery, CBS did not and could not produce any of those documents.

Why?

Because, Radutsky admitted, **after B&W sued, he destroyed all his contemporaneous notes, he destroyed five of the ten pages of the FTC report – the pages containing his notations on the MARC report – and he destroyed 15 pages of his 18- page proposed "both-sides-of-the-issue" script. And the six additional copies of that script that Radutsky distributed to newsroom personnel had disappeared entirely!**

Why did he destroy the documents that were at the heart of this case? And significantly, only the key parts of some documents? It was, he said, part of a "general house-cleaning," and he insisted he did it during the six-day window between the dismissal of the complaint and the filing of B&W's Notice of Appeal. He conceded his document destruction violated a written CBS policy, which he said he had not read. The incredulity of his explanation for his document destruction was exacerbated by his admission that at the time he destroyed his own documents, **he also destroyed Walter Jacobson's copies of the key documents, even though at the time he "cleaned up" Jacobson's desk,**

Radutsky no longer worked for Jacobson because he had been promoted to be producer of the 5 p.m. news program. Furthermore, Radutsky's desk was then on the other side of the room from Jacobson's. I did not see how anybody could believe there was a reason to destroy those key documents, in whole or in part, other than the concern that they would reveal a truth CBS wanted to hide – they had aired a program they knew was false.

CBS played the *"big bad New York lawyer* card" heavily during the Radutsky testimony. I questioned him extensively about the details of his document destruction. In a misguided effort to move the jury's attention off his bad-faith conduct, CBS pivoted to the claim that I had intimidated Radutsky. It was a full court press: after the cross-examination of Radutsky about his destruction of the documents – I mean, I didn't make this up, he did destroy obviously relevant documents under circumstances that were indefensible – Morsch took to the airwaves. He defended his witness in front of the assembled camera crews in the lobby of the building. But not on the merits. Instead he used his 60-second sound bite to make a personal attack *on me – and where I was from!* He said, and I quote:

> I think this thing is tremendously intimidating. We have a young researcher here, one of the best researchers we have ever had at Channel 2 in the history of the station. And he is up there being browbeaten by Mr. London. **He has a lot of maneuvers he apparently learned in New York and he's brought them out here to try them out in Chicago.**

Subtle, huh?

By now, the Chicago press was super-obsessed with this case. The local media fascination increased day by day. It was over the top, and, I thought, fueled by CBS. Their press officer saw to it that Jacobson had pungent comments following the prepared line of the day. He and Morsch gave daily press conferences and their pitch appeared on 5 p.m., 6 p.m., and 10 p.m. television news reports (which, by the way, rarely failed to describe me as B&W's *"New York* attorney.") The case was monitored closely by four local TV stations, as well as the newspapers. In the beginning, when Lew Clayton and I were approached by the press, we simply said, "No comment." When Ernie Pepples asked me why he saw only their side on the tube, I told him my practice was to not engage with the press during trial. He said, "Look, Marty, I understand, but if the other side is doing it, you gotta do it too." Fair enough, and thereafter, on the elevator coming down to the lobby at the end of each court session, Lew and I would discuss what our sound bite would be for the day. The PR team of London-Clayton at work.

I thought the most super-heated press exaggeration came from the television news anchor who, on the day I cross-examined Jacobson, opened his broadcast with,

> "Just as Reagan met Gorbachev today, Walter Jacobson met Martin London!"

We sat around in the hotel that night and laughed hard at that one.

The cross of Jacobson led to one of those ancillary anecdotes that sticks in the memory. One night, when I was working in my room preparing for that cross, I needed to refer to an exhibit that I had left in court, and I sent Phil White, a first-year associate, to the courthouse with a key to our exhibit closet to get it for me. Phil, dressed in jeans, t-shirt and sneakers, ran to the Dirksen Federal Building, went up to the trial floor and was promptly arrested by the

U.S. Marshal Service! He had no i.d., no proof of who he was and what he was doing there, and they locked him in a cell. They did allow him a phone call, and he wisely used it to call Aubrey Holder, our case manager, who by now was well-known to the marshals. Aubrey got up, got dressed, and sprung Phil – and my exhibit.

Jacobson turned out to be our best witness. A master television personality, the media king of Chicago, he knew his craft in and out. But now, in court, he was playing ball on my home turf, not his, and he made the mistake so many business executives make – he thought he could outsmart trial lawyers at their own game.

We did not need Jacobson's testimony to prove falsity. There could be no serious doubt that on its face the Perspective falsely accused Viceroy of *currently* using the pot, wine, beer, and sex theme in its advertising. The Perspective spoke in the present tense: "Viceroy says," and it was about "the Viceroy advertising," "the Viceroy strategy," and "says the Viceroy slicksters." On cross, Jacobson was forced to admit as much.

Though CBS could not realistically overcome the overwhelming evidence that the program was both defamatory and false, they still had another available defense. They asserted that Walter Jacobson lacked "actual malice," i.e., he didn't *know* his words were false when he uttered them.

Permit this historical note. The Founders were aware that public attitudes were inclined to bend to and fro with the political winds, and therefore made it impossible *casually* to change the bedrock structural rules of our republic. Article V of The Constitution provides a detailed set of requirements for Constitutional amendment: two thirds of both houses of Congress or of State Conventions must propose, and three quarters of the States must approve any changes. **There are no exceptions.**

In 1787, when the Founders wrote the Constitution, and in 1789, when they drafted the First Amendment, a libel victim needed to prove only that the defendant published a defamatory statement about him that was false. Ignoring Article V, in 1964, the Supreme Court amended the Constitution by grafting onto it a new First Amendment addendum: when the maligned victim is a public official, the Constitution requires him to prove that not only is the defamation false, but that *the defamer knew it was false when he published it, or at least had serious doubts about its truth and nevertheless published it with a reckless disregard for whether it was false or not.* In that classic "hard-cases-make-bad-law" decision reversing an Alabama court decision finding *The New York Times* liable for an advertisement sponsored by civil rights leaders, the Supremes labelled this newly-manufactured requirement "actual malice." The holding has since metastasized to include non-public-official citizens who have thrust themselves into the vortex of public debate, corporations that advertise to the public, and a growing array of other victims.

And to add to the plaintiff's burden, a subsequent Supreme Court decision required defamation victims to prove actual malice by "clear and convincing evidence." No more 51-49 "preponderance of the evidence," the normal standard for proving something in most civil cases. Therefore, if our jury found that Jacobson really *thought* what he was saying were true, *even if it were false,* he wins. Indeed, he wins on the actual malice issue even if he didn't know one way or the other if his statement were true, but had no suspicion it was wrong! Finally, even if the jury is uncertain about what he believed, Jacobson wins, because we would have failed to carry our burden to prove *by clear and convincing evidence* that he published with actual malice.

Actual malice is a state of mind. How do you prove that? Two ways: direct evidence and circumstantial evidence. Naturally enough, defendants took the first route, and we relied on both.

While it was our burden to prove actual malice, defendants chose to add to that burden by introducing direct evidence of Jacobson's *lack* of actual malice, and Tom Morsch asked him to tell the jury what his state of mind was when he wrote the Perspective. **Jacobson testified that when he wrote the script for the Perspective, he "believed" it was true, and he believed it was a fair summary of the FTC report.** He swore that at the time he composed the piece, he specifically remembered examining a list of documents, including the Radutsky outline, the sample "balanced" script, the FTC report, and some newspaper clips. He testified he remembered specific conversations with Radutsky about making sure the information was accurate, and he was careful about the need to look at all the documents. He reflected on all the work Radutsky had done. He told the jury he did all this work before he wrote the Perspective so he could carefully and prudently *"make a decision as to which side was telling the truth."* **He testified about what he "intended" to inform his audience when he "sat down to write" his script.**

I was astonished. What were they thinking? Did these guys think they could put this witness on the stand, he could look at the jury with those baby blues, and say whatever he wanted, in his best TV anchor voice, and the jury would swallow it hook, line, and sinker while we sat there at our table like deer caught in the headlights? I mean, really, did they think that all people who had New York accents were stupid?

The total destruction of Jacobson's credibility was at hand. When we reached the point on cross when it was time to pull the lever that opened the trapdoor under Jacobson's witness chair, I asked the set-up questions:

> London: **Isn't it true that you really have no recollection at all of what you thought about in preparation for this script? Isn't that a fact?**

> Jacobson: **Absolutely untrue, Mr. London.**

> London: **You don't remember what you thought when you wrote that script, do you?**

> Jacobson: *How do you know what I don't remember?* **I do remember . . . I thought about every word on this script, every line, every fact.**

Without asking another question, I read into evidence his testimony at his pretrial deposition, at the beginning of which he acknowledged he i) recognized he was under oath, ii) had prepared for the deposition by looking at documents his lawyer showed him, and iii) had refreshed his recollection about the matter as best he could. This is what he said at the deposition:

> London: I just want to know if you have a recollection whether in 1981, when you called the manufacturers of Viceroy cigarettes liars, you were attempting to be objective?

> Jacobson: *I don't know now what I was thinking when I wrote that three and a half years ago.*

> London: Can you recall whether when you wrote the November 11, 1981 script, you were trying fairly to present both sides of the question?

Jacobson*: I don't remember what I was thinking when I wrote that script. It's hard to remember three and half years ago.*

London: **You don't remember what was on your mind?**

Jacobson*: Right.*

London: You do remember writing the script, though?

Jacobson*: I don't remember writing it. I do see it.*

London: **You don't remember writing it?**

Jacobson*: Yes, I mean – I don't remember sitting at my typewriter, what I was thinking and how my hands were working. I see the script. It has a date. I wrote it, obviously, and I remember being involved in a series of reports on that subject.*

It doesn't get much better than that. I turned to Judge Hart and said I had no more questions. Jacobson was toast. Taken together, Radutsky's bad-faith document destruction and Jacobson's false testimony under oath gave us solid evidence of actual malice. And I think Walter dug himself into a deeper hole, when, on redirect, he attempted to explain away the earlier sworn deposition testimony by contrasting it with his trial preparation. He said this time his memory had been refreshed "by a whole team of lawyers." Ha, I'll bet.

We had one more delicious piece of evidence – the icing on the cake.

Buried deep in the CBS document production, was a single sheet of paper setting out suggested elements to be included in programs broadcast during sweeps periods, i.e., when audience measurements were taken. The document said programs should include elements that are sensational, and confrontational. The Perspective was delivered during a sweeps period, and we thought this was powerful circumstantial evidence on the question of actual malice. But the document was an "orphan." No names were on it, no origin was revealed, and no CBS employee was willing to say he or she had ever seen it before, no less authored or used it. But it was in CBS's files and there was a dispute over whether it was admissible. The judge reserved ruling, and that night I called my pal Stephen Gillers, who had worked with me at Paul, Weiss, and was an NYU Law School professor who taught evidence. He gave me the winning argument. "Look, it is admissible because it is there in their files. It is not hearsay. You don't want to prove the contents are true, you just want to prove the document is in the files available to CBS personnel. It's a tiny piece of evidence, – just a single brick in a large wall you are building." I liked physical, mechanical analogies. It worked, Hart let the document in, and I think it helped to inform the jury of the real motive for the sensationalism reflected in the Perspective broadcast.

I was constantly amazed at the media attention to this trial. While I was not nearly as famous in Chicago as Walter, my stock was rising. An incident that made me laugh involved my sister-in-law Karen Galvin, who lives in Indiana in a town that is a virtual suburb of Chicago. I had arranged for her to get a seat at the summations, and driving to court that day, Karen stopped at her local gas station. While filling the tank, the attendant chatted with his regular customer, "Hi, Karen, how are you? Where are you off to today?" When she told him she was going to the Walter Jacobson trial summations because her brother-in-law was the lawyer who represented the tobacco company, the attendant was blown away. "Marty London? Oh my God, Karen, you know Marty London?"

Summations

I had two goals. First, I reminded the jurors that they had promised me during jury selection that they would decide this case on the basis of the evidence they heard from the witnesses, not on the basis of what cities my client and I hail from, and I was demanding payment on that promissory note now.

Second, our toughest job was to show that not only was the Perspective false, but it was delivered with actual malice. Proving an adversary's state of mind is a heavy burden – it's pushing a big rock up a steep hill. I talked to the jury about the clearly-not-credible testimony given by Jacobson and Radutsky. Jacobson's deposition testimony totally rebutted his trial testimony, and Radutsky's bad-faith destruction of relevant documents was powerful circumstantial evidence that gave rise to an inference he destroyed them because he knew they would reveal a painful truth, and hurt CBS's case.

I described what circumstantial evidence was, and gave an example of its persuasive power. It can frequently be more convincing than direct evidence. When judges define circumstantial evidence to juries, they frequently use the wet umbrella analogy: you are in a windowless room, and people arrive from outside, carrying dripping umbrellas. Those conditions amount to strong circumstantial evidence that it's raining outside.

But I thought the wet umbrella analogy was a bit sterile, and I developed a cookie jar scenario. My sister-in-law Karen was not the only family member in attendance at the summations. My wife Pinks, along with the kids (Stephanie was 11 and Robert was 8) also came, and were sitting in the second row, not far from the jury. Karen, Pinks and the kids all share the same gene pool – blond hair, blue eyes, and they are stunning. The children were simply angelic, in looks and demeanor. Before my summation, we all had lunch in the courthouse cafeteria. (Yes, I knew jurors ate there too).

As I began my explanation of the nature of circumstantial evidence, I glanced at the two shining young faces in the second row, then back to the jury:

> Now I go to the kitchen just before dinner, and I see the top is off the cookie jar, I see crumbs on the counter top, and I see a chocolate chip stuck to Robert's cheek. I have no *direct* evidence that Robert has stolen a cookie, but I can rely on the powerful *circumstantial evidence* to infer that Robert has indeed done just that. He denies the theft. His sister Stephanie will surely provide direct testimony to support him, but I am justified in rejecting that testimony because she is hardly an impartial witness and will always stick up for her little brother. This demonstrates the power of circumstantial evidence, and you can rely on it.

The bit brought a smile to everyone's face, but I think it also made an important point: just as they would be justified in rejecting Robert and Stephanie's denials in the hypothetical I described, the jurors would be more than justified in rejecting Jacobson's and Radutsky's denials, and inferring from the circumstantial evidence of the document destruction and the unreliability of the Jacobson and Radutsky testimony, that defendants knew the documents were harmful to their case, and that Jacobson published his essay with actual malice.

Morsch's summation reviewed the evidence he thought was favorable to his clients, and he emphasized a by-now familiar theme: the big bad tobacco company and the big bad New York lawyer had come in here to shut down the Chicago media. "It's all about chilling the media," he said. "We have people in *this town, (Uh, which town is that again, Tom?)* who when they see hypocrisy, have the guts to stand up and say something about it!"

The Verdict

The Judge charged the jury and sent them out to deliberate. He submitted three questions on a verdict form:

> 1. Was the Perspective substantially false? If "no," you don't have to deliberate further. If "yes," go to the next question.

> 2. If the answer to question # 1, is "yes," did defendants know it was false or publish it with reckless disregard of whether it was false or not? If the answer is "no," no further deliberation is necessary. If "yes," go to question # 3.

> 3. If the answer to question # 2 was "yes," was the Perspective a fair summary of a government report?

The judge said we need not hang around, we could go back to our hotel and the court clerk would call when the jury had a question or a verdict. We packed up our briefcases, locked up the exhibits, and walked the five blocks back to our rooms at the University Club. I had just dropped my bag in my room and was reaching to take off my tie, when the phone rang. After two hours of deliberation, the jury had reached a verdict.

We took our seats in the courtroom. No matter how intensely I examined the jurors' faces, I couldn't divine a clue. The judge asked them if they had reached a verdict, and the foreman said, "Yes."

Was the program false? "Yes." Was it published with actual malice? "Yes," again. And, "No," it was *not* a fair summary of a government report.

The big, bad New York lawyers had overcome formidable legal and other obstacles and won a major victory for their big, bad tobacco company client.

The verdict came down on a Wednesday and the judge sent the jury home and told them to come back to court on Monday for the damage phase. He asked us to go back to New York, and please explore with CBS headquarters if we could find a way to settle the case and avoid the damage trial and any appeals. And he directed the defendants to turn over their financial information so the jury could hear evidence on our request for punitive damages, if necessary.

The Walter Jacobson daily press conference in the courthouse lobby that afternoon was a mob scene. The Chicago journalists were surprised by the verdict. (I was not.) It seemed as if every camera, every reporter's notebook in the city, were in that scrum. Clayton and I stood on the outskirts of the crowd, straining to hear what was being said. Jacobson basically told the press the jurors made a mistake, he did nothing wrong, this was all the fault of the bully New York lawyer, blah, blah, blah. And then we heard, clear as a bell, a reporter ask, "Walter, would you do anything different today?" I believe Jacobson's bravado response ultimately cost his employer millions, "No, I wouldn't. I wouldn't do anything different at all." We rushed back to our quarters to catch that on the 5 o'clock news and make sure the VCR was running. We checked and found that the WBBM station manager was saying the same thing on the radio – they had done nothing wrong, and would do the same thing again!

We flew back to New York City the next morning and complied with the judge's request; we tried to settle the case, but our cordial conversations with CBS's General Counsel failed to produce an agreement. It was my sense that CBS feared a settlement payment to us would open the libel floodgates, and they were going to bet all their chips on a successful appeal. More than 70% of plaintiff libel verdicts were ultimately reversed, and they thought they had a better shot than most.

The Damages Trial

We flew back to Chicago. On Monday, we were going to ask the jury for $17.1 million dollars for compensatory and punitive damages. The former was designed to compensate our client for injury to its reputation, and the latter award was to punish defendants in order to deter future misconduct. Our compensatory damage claim was entirely for "presumed" damages, i.e., a general injury to reputation. We sought no out-of-pocket damages for lost sales, or other specific or special damages. We wrote our calculations on a big sheet of paper that we set up on an easel before the jury: 2.5 million people saw the program on WBBM, and 2 million read about it in the *Saturday Evening Post* magazine. We arbitrarily hit upon the number $2.50 per TV viewer and $1 per magazine reader, a demand of $7 million. Add a $10 million punitive damages request against CBS, and $100,000 against Walter Jacobson, you get $17.1 million.

As to our claim for compensatory damages, Morsch's argument was, in substance, "Don't give them any compensatory damages because they basically have no reputation to injure. What kind of a reputation does a company that sells cigarettes have? How good is the reputation of a company that must put a health warning on its product? And they haven't lost a nickel."

But our jaws dropped when he opposed our request for punitive damages by telling the jurors that their verdict was itself punishment enough. He argued, **"Your verdict has sent a resounding message to us – to Walter Jacobson and to CBS and to the news media, and to the *City of Chicago*!"** For all their supposed communications expertise, these defendants totally underestimated their audience. They treated the jurors as if they were five years old, and they continued to play to presumed prejudices to boot. What did "the City of Chicago" have to do with this? Chicago didn't libel anybody, Jacobson did. Are they really the same thing? Get a new line, guys, this one doesn't work. Never did.

And as to the claim that the jury verdict "sent a message" to Jacobson, it was perfectly clear that Jacobson wasn't home when it was delivered. **Morsch urged the jury to award no punitive damages because Jacobson and CBS were already "well deterred."** Was this a dream? *"Deterred"? "Well deterred?"* Jacobson was the opposite of deterred. **He said he would do the same thing again tomorrow; he wouldn't change a thing.** Is that what "deterred" means in Chicago-speak?"

To demolish the "deterred" argument, we offered in evidence the video of Jacobson's post-verdict statement to the press that he "would do the same thing again tomorrow. He wouldn't do anything different." I was astonished when Morsch objected to my playing the tape. What could be more relevant? Morsch had argued Jacobson was deterred, but *Jacobson told the press he was not deterred and would do it again.* When the judge asked Morsch for the grounds of his objection, Tom said that ***to put in evidence a statement Walter Jacobson made to the press and that was broadcast to the public would violate***

Jacobson's First Amendment rights! I was standing in the well just in front of the jury when I heard him announce the basis for his objection, and I involuntarily flipped my pen high into the air. (Happily I caught it on the way down.) That was the single most absurd objection I had ever heard in a courtroom. When I flipped the pen in the air, Clayton whispered to our colleagues, "Oh, shit, he's done it again. This time he's really going to jail." But Judge Hart simply said, "Overruled," and we played the tape.

Beyond Walter's taped statement to the press, our damage case was brief. Lew Clayton put on the station manager and confronted him with the "we would do the same thing tomorrow" audio tape from his radio appearance. Alisa Shudofsky, a third-year associate did a nice job with a Viceroy district manager who told the jury about the distress the defamatory program caused his staff. The judge charged the jury, sent them out, and we went back to our rooms at the University Club to await the jury verdict. Again, we had barely arrived when the call came in from the clerk.

After less than two hours of deliberation, the jury gave us $3 million in compensatory damages, $2 million in punitive damages against CBS, and $50,000 in punitive damages against Walter Jacobson. Walter went downstairs, stood in front of the cameras, and, surprise, surprise, railed against me!

We did not get to speak to any jurors after the verdict, but the press did. One of the TV stations that night broadcast an interview with a juror who remarked:

> The evidence was overwhelming against the defendants – overwhelming – and I don't see how any jury could have arrived at any other verdict than we did.

We were too tired to fly home that night, and the team celebrated with Scotch and a steak at the Pump Room, and got the first good night's sleep in a long time. The next morning, as we walked through the airport, we saw that the entire front page of the *Chicago Sun-Times* was devoted to the verdict. The large type headline read, "Jacobson Rips Bully Lawyer," and included a picture of Walter. On the jump was a picture of me. The caption was the best endorsement a lawyer could want;

> "I would like to have Marty London as my lawyer if I were trying to get away with something," says Walter Jacobson.

Those pages are on my office wall.

Post-Trial

In a post-trial decision, Judge Hart affirmed the jury verdict as being consistent with the evidence. But he held, as a matter of law, we were not entitled to *any* presumed damages, and he cut our award from $5 million to $2 million.

The Appeal

For its appeal to the Seventh Circuit, CBS again chose new counsel, the distinguished Cameron DeVore of the Davis, Wright firm in Seattle. We cross-appealed from Hart's decision rejecting our compensatory damage claim.

What was the job of this Circuit Court on this appeal?

After all, the unanimous jury had found the facts as to
CBS's culpability: the program was defamatory, false, published with actual malice, and it was not a fair report of a
government document. Aside from our cross-appeal on the
presumed damage question, what was left for these three
judges to do? Lots. In fact, everything!

The Twentieth Century Fund is a non-profit, non-parti-
san "think tank" dedicated to the "timely analysis of economic policy, foreign affairs, and domestic political issues."
They publish thoughtful essays on these issues in a series
ironically entitled PERSPECTIVES ON THE NEWS. In 1993
I was invited to write a paper about libel. My piece was
entitled "The Myth of the Muzzled Media," and in a section I called "Special Jury-Verdict Nullification Rules for
Publishers," I argued that the publishers had succeeded
in dramatically changing the libel law to their benefit. To
the "actual malice" standard established in *New York Times*
v. *Sullivan* in 1964, the Supremes had been persuaded in
1968 to add the onerous "clear and convincing" standard,
and then, in a 1984 decision ("*Bose*"), the Court created the
remarkable "independent assessment" requirement. The
Court ruled that even when a jury unanimously finds *actual
malice* by *clear and convincing evidence,* appellate judges
are nevertheless required to make their own *independent
assessment* of the evidence on the actual malice finding.
This requirement was manufactured by the Supreme Court
out of whole cloth. Nothing in the Constitution supports
this dramatic expansion of the rights of defamers. I wrote:

> It is startling that the *Bose* ruling was not met with
> the lawyerly equivalent of rioting in the streets. Jury
> supremacy has *always* been an accepted part of our
> constitutional scheme. When a jury sits, judges do

not assess evidence; only the jury can find the facts. Even powerful appellate judges are not authorized to weigh the evidence and decide how they would have voted as a juror. Judges lack that power even when a jury verdict deprives a citizen of his most valuable right – his liberty.

But in *Bose*, the Supreme Court decided that publishers and their editorial employees faced with civil tort claims are entitled to more appellate consideration than that given to a citizen given a prison sentence or a company like Texaco seeking reversal of an $11 billion breach of contract verdict. Defendants who lose actual malice libel verdicts now have the *exclusive* right to demand that the appellate court "independently assess" the evidence earlier weighed by the jury.

It is not clear precisely what "independent assessment" means. Is it a surface look at what the jury has done, searching for obvious jury mistakes? Does the reviewing court give deference to the jury findings, in that the jurors saw and heard the witnesses and therefore are the best judges of their credibility? Not in this case. In this appeal, the Seventh Circuit opted to take, *for the purposes of this case*, the most extreme interpretation of the "independent assessment" standard. They undertook a **"wide ranging appellate review with little or no deference to the jury's findings, of all aspects of the case, including falsity and opinion."**

In other words, the court basically threw out the jury verdict, and re-tried the entire case on the stenographic record made in the trial court. Now we had a new trial, before a new jury, consisting of three sophisticated appellate judges. Somehow, the Seventh Amendment command that "no fact tried by a jury shall be otherwise re-examined in any Court of the United States" got lost in a cloud of cigarette smoke.

The key issue was *actual malice*. Falsity was a given, but Jacobson's state of mind when he wrote that piece was paramount. Even discarding his contradictory trial testimony, we were left with his pre-trial testimony that he didn't remember *anything*. That might not meet the *clear and convincing* test. We needed to show he *knew* his broadcast was false, and the key evidence in that regard was the document destruction that leads inexorably to the inference the defense knew the documents would harm their case by showing actual malice. I urged in my new "summation" to this learned three-person jury that Radutsky's explanation that his document destruction was just part of a general housecleaning, was simply not credible. It follows that because the document destruction was in bad faith, we were entitled to an inference that they destroyed the documents because they knew they would show they knew their broadcast was false.

In the course of making that argument, I told the three appellate judges, "Your Honors, every time I think about this subject, I cannot clear my mind of the image of Michael Radutsky, producer of the 5 p.m. news, wearing a little apron tied at the waist, holding a feather duster in his hand, going about the newsroom 'doing some housecleaning' by tearing out selected pages of important documents and destroying them." I got a chuckle from the bench. It is an enduring image.

The appellate court began its detailed 24-page opinion with this unusual introduction:

> The attitude of most knowledgeable and disinterested persons toward the tobacco industry is certainly negative, at least it has been negative for the last decade. In such an atmosphere, it becomes difficult to imagine how a tobacco company can

be libeled. The bashing of the industry by government and private groups has become a virtual cottage industry. This case, however, demonstrates that general bum raps against the whole industry are different from specific accusations of skullduggery by a specific company or person. And this case involves some very specific statements against a very specific company in the tobacco industry.

After their independent examination of the trial record, the three appellate judges, using the same adverb as the juror interviewed on television, unanimously concluded that the evidence *"overwhelmingly supports the inference that Radutsky destroyed the documents in bad faith,"* and **the bad faith destruction was "the most compelling evidence of actual malice."**

And, of course, there was also the evidence of Jacobson's contradictory testimony about his state of mind. The court quoted, word for word, the section of my cross of Jacobson in which I used his deposition to prove that his trial testimony on the question of actual malice was simply not believable.

To conclude its review, the three appellate judges found Jacobson's Perspective was not protected opinion, but was a false statement of fact, and was not a fair summary of the FTC staff report. The court noted that the *Bose* standard did not require it "to believe the unbelievable and to accept the untenable."

The unanimous opinion not only affirmed the judgment of liability, it reversed Judge Hart and restored $1 million in presumed damages, so that the final verdict stood at $3.05 million.

The court's final paragraph was almost a statement of regret for the need to affirm:

One of the most important functions of the court system in the United States is to protect the freedom of the press. . . . After conducting [our] review, it is unfortunate that we are forced to conclude that this case does not involve freedom of the press. Rather, it is one in which there is clear and convincing evidence that a local television journalist acted with actual malice when he made false statements about the Brown & Williamson Tobacco Corporation. Because false statements made with actual malice are not protected by the First Amendment, this court is required to affirm the district court's finding that Jacobson and CBS libeled Brown & Williamson.

A year later, on my birthday, the Supreme Court denied CBS's petition for certiorari. The case was over. At the time, it was the largest federal libel verdict ever sustained on appeal. CBS sent a check.

Postscript

1. Years after the trial, I learned that Judge Hart's parents owned a small newspaper somewhere in Illinois. Wow. Had I known that before trial, I might have considered asking him to recuse himself. How lucky I didn't know. While I did not agree with Hart's legal ruling on the damages question, he gave us an absolutely fair trial and I enjoyed being in his courtroom.

2. In 2012, Jacobson wrote a book. I guess I should not be surprised that even after the unanimous jury verdict, the opinion by the District Judge, the unanimous opinion of the three-judge Court of Appeals, and the denial of certiorari by the Supreme Court, Walter was still unable or unwilling to face reality, and 25 years later, in a chapter devoted to this case, he explained it all away:

I've imagined the scenario a thousand times – a meeting in a wood paneled, marble-floored, liquor-cabineted corporate conference room; two or three tobacco big shots, salt-and-pepper hair, gray suits, white shirts, rep tries, and (fake) gold cuff links. A scotch in a hand of each. . . .

"That little fucker in Chicago," I imagine one saying to another. "Let's nail him." Which is precisely what they do. They hire Martin London, one of the toughest, smartest, most aggressive corporate lawyers in the country, onetime counsel to Jacqueline Kennedy Onassis, and to Spiro Agnew, vice president of the United States under Richard Nixon, who resigned when convicted of federal tax evasion.

(When I informed Ernie Pepples of these laughable remarks, and asked him if he was one of the "big shots" in the that room, he responded, "Scotch? Fake gold? That's Kentucky bourbon and those cufflinks are made from hand-carved ivory from African elephant tusks!")

Walter concluded with a repetition of his front-page rant after the trial verdict:

> "Martin London is an angry, flamboyant bully who was brought in here to intimidate me, and he convinced the jury of eight people with his histrionics in court that I did something I did not do."

So, do I sue for libel, or send Walter a thank-you note?

Before Bridgegate:
New Jersey Hustle

In my practice and my lecturing, I often opposed the First Amendment Fundamentalists, and argued to courts and audiences that The Amendment was not nearly as broad as some thought it was. On the other hand, when my client's cause required me to argue for a broad reach of his First Amendment rights, I did so with vigor. I needed to establish that "make no law abridging the freedom of speech" means the government cannot punish, civilly or criminally, opinion speech that is substantively inconsistent, or incentivized by financial gain. When it comes to speech, "Greed is good" – or at least it's okay. Moreover, The Amendment covers not only paid-for speech, it also protects the paid-for decision to stop speaking. When a Chris Christie predecessor U.S. Attorney for the District of New Jersey, along with a sitting federal judge who had held that office before his elevation to the bench, didn't see it that way, we had to teach them what James Madison was thinking when he drafted The Amendment – or at least what he would have been thinking had he thought about Nat Serota.

✦

Fort Lee, New Jersey, can't get a break. Located at the western terminus of the George Washington Bridge, the Borough was named after General Charles Lee, who was found guilty of cowardice, incompetence, and failure to obey orders while serving in the Continental Army under General Washington. Lee's command, and the place of his disgrace, was the area of New Jersey now bearing his name. Why anyone would name a town after a disgraced military figure is an interesting question, but not the subject of *this* story.

Fast forward to 2014, and the national press was obsessed with "Bridgegate." Two members of New Jersey Governor Chris Christie's administration were convicted by the U.S. Attorney for the District of New Jersey in connection with a scheme to strangle traffic on the George Washington Bridge by closing some of the access lanes in Fort Lee. Why did Christie's people do this? The press and Mayor of Fort Lee speculated that the traffic clogs were designed to punish the Democratic mayor of the Borough, because he had refused to support Christie's bid for re-election. The traffic clog would not only frustrate the mayor's constituents, it would hinder the advancement of a proposed billion-dollar project favored by him – a real estate development on land immediately adjacent to the access lanes.

The scandal is cited as one of the reasons Mr. Christie, an early supporter of Mr. Trump, was denied a spot on the Trump ticket, or even a place in the Trump cabinet.

My connection to that real estate parcel dates back to 1974 – a story that morphed into a saga involving reputed Mafia figures, New York real estate moguls, a former Mayor of Fort Lee, two of Chris Christie's U.S. Attorney predecessors, and Nathan L. Serota, a Long Island shopping center developer who became ensnared in a criminal case involving all the above. It was a nerve-wracking drama that might reasonably be called "New Jersey Hustle."

In 1971, a developer named Arthur Sutton acquired the real estate parcel in question, and proposed a vast mixed-use development project. To get the necessary permits, Sutton and his partners (Investors Funding Corporation, headed by New York real estate mogul Norman Dansker) needed significant zoning changes from the Fort Lee authorities. But local opposition was vigorous, and one of the most outspoken opponents was Nathan Serota. Real estate development was Nat's meat. Brooklyn born, he started out as a ticket seller for the New York Central Railroad, but when a relative asked Nat to supervise construction of a one-family home in the borough, Nat discovered his milieu. One project led to another and another, Nat gradually became a substantial developer, and ultimately the guy who "invented" the notion of massive Long Island shopping centers. Unlike some others in that occupation, Nat never forgot his roots. He was, for his entire life, a plain-talking, no-bullshit, mensch.

In 1974, Nat and Vivian Serota lived in Fort Lee, N.J., where he had been honored by being appointed as an unpaid member of the Fort Lee Parking Authority, the municipal body that collected the quarters from the Borough-owned parking meters. The Serotas lived in an expensive condominium apartment building adjacent to the Sutton-IFC proposed construction project. They enjoyed a magnificent view of the New York City skyline.

Because the proposed new construction would, without doubt, degrade the Serotas' tranquility, their view, and the value of their investment, Nat went to work to protect his home and family by exercising his First Amendment rights to block the project by opposing the requested zoning changes. He attended Borough Council meetings with his real estate lawyer and voiced objections to the changes, organized and funded a slate of candidates opposed to the project, paid for advertisements in the local press, funded citizen's groups who sued to stop the project, and was otherwise, as Nat would put it, a very effective pain in the ass. His advocacy no doubt contributed to the desired result: the Council denied the requested changes.

Sutton and the IFC crowd did not go away. They owed a lot of money to New York banks and desperately needed to monetize this project. After being turned down by Borough authorities, they reapplied with modified plans, and the dance started anew. But this time, new partners had taken to the floor, to wit, Valentine Electric Company, co-owned by Andrew Valentine and Joey Diaco. The company had a long-time reputed connection to New Jersey organized crime figures. Former Valentine partner Joey "Boy" Boiardo, and employee Joseph Biancone, had been prosecuted for extortion.

The new approach to get approval for the project began when Valentine partner Diaco approached Sutton and asked, "Would your people give Valentine Electric the contract to do the electric work for the new complex if we could eliminate Serota's opposition and get Mayor Burt Ross's approval of the project?" Sutton and IFC's Dansker said "Yes," and the hustle was on.

"Joey D" next approached Serota: Would he drop his opposition to the project if he didn't live across the street from it anymore? And if the answer to that question was "Yes," would Nat agree to sell his apartment and move? Nat was nobody's fool. He said "Yes" and "Yes." It was win,

win for the Serotas. Nat could eliminate the risk the project would be an aesthetic and financial thorn in his side, and at the same time make a profit on the sale of his apartment.

And Vivian had been on his case about moving to Manhattan. So Nat did what any sensible businessman would do, he went to his real estate lawyer at a prestigious New York City law firm (no, not mine, there are, believe it or not, a few others that meet that description), and the excellent lawyers there drafted the contract. It provided, in plain English, that Nat was selling his apartment (for a fixed price that was in excess of its market value), and he would stop his campaign against the project.

Nat was told nothing about the second leg of the transaction – Diaco's approaches to Mayor Burt Ross. After several meetings and telephone calls with the mayor, "Joey D" ultimately offered Ross a $500,000 cash bribe for his support of the project. But Ross was "playing" Diaco – the Mayor was reporting those conversations to the U.S. attorney from the beginning, and Diaco, Valentine, and the Sutton-IFC participants were in the soup when Joey delivered a suitcase with a $25,000 cash down payment to Ross at a Fort Lee diner chock full of donut-eating FBI agents. Ross was wired, and the sound quality was excellent. The mayor took the suitcase to the bathroom to count the cash, and entertained his FBI listeners with his off-key rendition of the Depression-era hit song, "We're in the money, we're in the money . . . ."

Shortly thereafter, U.S. Attorney Jonathan Goldstein asked Nat to testify before a federal grand jury. Serota, having no premonition of what was going on, said "sure," and did so.

Within days, Goldstein obtained a grand jury indictment charging the Valentine defendants, the IFC defendants, *and Nat Serota*, with three felony counts:

I. Conspiracy to bribe Ross and Serota,
II. Actually bribing Ross, and
III. Actually bribing Serota.

The day after the indictment came down, I got a call from Nat's real estate lawyer, "Uh, Marty, one of our clients has a problem. Do you have time to take on a new matter?" In 47 years, I rarely said "No" to that question.

When Serota walked into my office with his lawyer a few days later, I thought immediately of a character from *Guys and Dolls*. Dressed in business attire, sans necktie, Nat wore large tinted glasses, carried a leather purse, and sported a diamond stud earring twice the size of a pencil eraser. He told me his story in unvarnished English. (Every word was later proved to be true.) With an embarrassed smile, Nat asked, "So, will you defend me?"

You bet I would. Unless I was missing something, I thought there was a chance, albeit slim, we could dispose of this case by persuading the prosecutor he had leaped too far, too fast. And if, as was likely, we failed in that endeavor, I hoped we would do better with pre-trial motions addressed to the court. As far as I could see, if the facts were as Nat presented them, he had done nothing that anybody else wouldn't have done in similar circumstances. If somebody wanted to build a garbage disposal plant next to my home, I would do exactly what Nat did: fight like hell to kill the project, and if, in the end, I proved to be such a nuisance that they offered to buy my house for more than it was worth, I'd sell. Who wouldn't? And Nat's honorific Parking Authority membership had nothing to do with the project and nothing to do with the case.

I knew nothing about the other characters in this play, and what I learned in the following days was not encouraging.

Despite his large and capable staff, newly appointed U.S. Attorney Jonathan Goldstein was going to try this case himself. Not a good sign. The head of the office doesn't put his reputation on the line unless he is confident of a highly publicized victory. Further, the case was assigned to District Judge Frederick Lacey, who had held Goldstein's job three years earlier. Lacey had a fearsome reputation. New Jersey lawyers described him as rabidly pro-prosecution, rigidly uncompromising, a harsh sentencer, and extremely bright. He took pride in his record of never having been reversed. Uh-oh.

My effort at pre-trial disposition of the charges failed. There was nothing I could say to Goldstein that he didn't know, and he wasn't backing off an inch. In court, we sought a pre-trial dismissal via our legal arguments. The profit on the sale of Serota's apartment was not "bribery" in any sense of the word, private citizen Serota had an absolute First Amendment right to modify his political advocacy at any time for *any* reason, and his position as an unpaid member of the Parking Authority was irrelevant to the project. Judge Lacey was no more receptive than U.S. Attorney Goldstein. We were going to trial, a place where sometimes bad things happen.

Lacey's disposition was not sweetened when, before trial, defendants moved to recuse him for bias. During his tenure as U.S. Attorney, Lacey had made public comments tying defendant Valentine Electric to organized crime. He had twice subpoenaed defendant Diaco before grand juries asking about his connection to Valentine Electric, and it was Lacey who prosecuted Valentine personnel Boiardo and Biancone. Sounds open and shut, huh? Why didn't Lacey step aside from the git-go? There was no shortage of federal judges in the District who could handle this case. I cannot imagine any other federal judge who, under these facts, would not have simply turned the case over to someone else. But Lacey not only failed to pass up the case on his own, he denied defendants' motion.

The pre-trial publicity in Fort Lee and Newark was overwhelming. The suitcase full of cash, the singing Mayor, the size of the project, the involvement of the New York real estate moguls and alleged organized crime figures, combined to make sensational copy. When the defendants moved for a change of venue, i.e., to move the trial to a place far removed from the media hype, Lacey outsmarted the defendants; he ordered us all to Trenton, New Jersey, 60 miles south of Newark, to pick a jury from that "vicinage." He denied the lawyers any opportunity directly to question the panel of 100 prospective jurors, and only at the end of the one-day marathon session did he tell the selected jurors to go home, pack a bag, and that federal marshals would the next day transport them to a motel in the Newark area where they would be sequestered for the duration of the trial. More uh-ohs.

The Trial

We knew there would be no evidence that Serota knew of the Ross bribery, and we needed to show the jury a clear and visible separation from the IFC-Valentine defendants. The effort started with the not-so-trivial question of counsel tables in the courtroom. In some courtrooms, the prosecution (or the plaintiff in a civil case) sits at the table closer to the jury, and the defendants sit at a table farther removed from the jury. In other courtrooms, as in this case, the prosecution sat at a table closer to the judge, and defendants in a row behind. My concern was that with eight defendants, many of them having two lawyers each, there could be as many as sixteen plus people sitting at defendants' long table, and I did not want the jury to see us as part of the "bribery crowd." I adamantly refused to sit at the same table as the IFC-Valentine defendants. At first, Lacey was unhelpful but ultimately relented. The IFC-Valentine defendants sat at one long table facing the judge, and at the far end of that table, we had our own table, perpendicular to theirs, the bottom of an inverted letter "L." Hey, no stone unturned. As it worked out, the fact that our "L" leg put us closer to the judge's bench played a role in the ensuing drama.

The trial evidence covered three main points:

1. Mayor Ross told the story of the Diaco bribe. The prosecution played the tapes and showed the jury the $25,000 in cash, now neatly encapsulated in sealed transparent plastic packages. Over defendants' vigorous objection, the judge allowed the prosecutor to permit the jurors physically to handle the cash bundles. How do you cross-examine that? We had no questions for Ross; he didn't lay a glove on Serota. The Mayor was an excellent witness and clearly enjoyed himself immensely. Frankly, a bit theatrical for my taste, but I thought the jury liked him.

2. Arthur Sutton had turned state's evidence and was allowed to plead guilty to a misdemeanor. His testimony tied the IFC defendants to the bribery scheme. He did not lay a glove on Serota.

3. The prosecution put in evidence the profitable sale contract drawn by Serota's lawyer, which provided that he would cease his opposition to the project, and they put in evidence proof that Serota was a member of the Fort Lee Parking Authority.

Now came the crunch. At the end of the prosecution's case, lawyers for each of the defendants moved to dismiss the three-count indictment. While defense lawyers always do this, they rarely succeed, and, for the most part, do not expect to do so. After all, the facts are for the jury to decide, not the judge, so the only two things left to argue on the motion are i) points of law that, for the most part, had been previously hashed out in pre-trial motions, and ii) questions of sufficiency of the evidence, i.e., have the prosecutors submitted enough evidence so that a sentient juror could find the defendant guilty? It is not up to the judge to render his opinion as to how he would vote, or to weigh the evidence. It doesn't matter whether the judge thinks the scales are at 60-40 or 70-30, only whether there is enough evidence upon which a reasonable juror could rely to find the defendant guilty. If there is, the defendant's motion must be denied.

But for Serota, this motion was not just a throw-away exercise. I had been preparing my argument for days. I really believed that even Frederick Lacey could and would see that there was no evidence Nat Serota was in any way involved in the Ross bribery (Counts I and II) and that Serota's lawyer-documented sale of his apartment and consequent withdrawal from the political scene (Count III) was not bribery but was behavior absolutely protected by the First Amendment.

The jury was excused for the day. Lacey listened to the arguments made by counsel for each of the eight defendants, then listened to prosecutor Goldstein, and then said, "Motions denied. Tomorrow, defendants will put in whatever evidence they choose, and then we'll have summations." Onto the scrap heap went my arguments, and, I thought, the rule of law.

No defendant planned to testify, only to submit some documentary evidence. The next morning, as the defense lawyers gathered in their room to talk about the order of the document presentation, there was a knock on the door, and in walked Lacey's courtroom deputy. He announced, "The judge has given the jury the morning off. He wants Mr. London, *and Mr. London only*, to re-argue his motion to dismiss!"

Could it be I had misjudged the man? When we got back to the courtroom, I gave it my all. I was brilliant, I was earnest, I replayed yesterday's effort with urgency. And most important, I was right – again. Lacey was a tough adversary and gave ground grudgingly. After listening to me, then to Goldstein, he ruled that because there was *no evidence* that Serota participated or even knew about the bribery of Ross, he was dismissing Counts I (conspiracy to bribe Ross and Serota) and II (actually bribing Ross). But Lacey made clear he was *dismissing those counts only as to Serota. They remained in the case as to the other defendants.* And he refused to dismiss Count III, the charge that Serota was the *recipient* of a bribe by reason of his written agreement to sell his apartment at a premium and cease his opposition to the real estate project. That count, he said, was going to the jury.

His ruling added yet another reason Count III had to be dismissed. First, as I had argued, Nat's change of advocacy was, pure and simple, a perfectly legal transaction, and any interpretation of a bribery statute that declared that conduct to be illegal would offend the First Amendment. The prosecutor's frequent reference to Nat's service on the Parking Authority was a red herring and should have nothing to do with this case because there were no facts tying that position to the rejection of the zoning variances for the project. None.

Second, Serota now faced an insurmountable barrier to a fair trial: the jury could not reasonably be expected to

differentiate between the colorful, and damning, cash bribe
evidence against the IFC-Valentine defendants, and the dramatically different story of the sale of Serota's apartment.
There were now two different alleged "bribes" in the case
and two different alleged "bribees" (Ross in one instance,
Serota in the other), and while all the other defendants
were still charged with bribing both Ross and Serota, it was
now clear Serota had nothing to do with the Ross bribery
attempt **though both their names *remained as bribees* in
Count I of the indictment**. And though evidence of guilt
on Counts I and II was not admissible as to Serota, he was
still in the case and subject to jury confusion. But Lacey
had gone as far as he was willing to go, and he kept Serota
in the case on the single count alleging he accepted a bribe
by agreeing to sell his apartment at a profit and to cease his
campaign against the bridge parcel project.

Summations

The judge set a schedule that we saw as calculated to
the prosecutor's advantage.

Though all federal district courts are established by
the same statute, local rules of practice differ, often taking
on the coloration of state practices. In many jurisdictions,
the summations follow the order of the trial evidence: the
prosecution goes first, setting out in some detail the evidence and legal principles upon which it urges conviction.
Then the defense, having heard the prosecution's case in
chief, gets to argue its case, showing why the elements of
the prosecution's summation do not lead to conviction, and
reminding the jury of evidence favoring acquittal. Last, the
prosecution gets one more shot in which the prosecutor is
limited to rebutting the arguments advanced by the defendant's lawyers. While that sequence is obviously to the

prosecutor's advantage in that he gets the last word, at least the defendant gets a fair opportunity to listen to the government's case in chief and take a shot at it.

But the local New Jersey practice turned logic on its head. The *defendants, who have no burden of proof,* sum up first, only guessing at what the prosecutor will say. When they sit down, that's it, they never get to speak to the jury again. No rebuttal for them. Then the prosecutor sums up. He rebuts the arguments made by the defendants, points to other evidence he favors, and makes old and new arguments while we sit there like mummies.

Lacey's schedule was wicked. The final week of the trial was the week before Easter. The judge insisted that all defendants complete their summations on Thursday. The government summation and Court's charge would follow on Friday morning and the jury could deliberate that afternoon, on Good Friday. If the jury did not reach a verdict that day, the Trenton residents could spend the Easter weekend in their Newark motel.

A trial judge has great discretion to organize the mechanics of the proceedings, even down to establishing bathroom and lunch breaks. Lacey drove us hard on Thursday. He pushed the defendants to hurry. It was clear to all of us that his motive was to finish all the defendants' summations on Thursday, so that the only thing the jury heard on Friday, the day they started their deliberations, was the government summation and Lacey's charge. My summation was the last one of defendants' speeches. It came at the end of a long day. In that context, I made a decision that still bothers me 40 years later.

I have been in courtrooms my entire professional life, and pay careful attention to my personal needs. I have learned by experience that on court days, I must limit myself to one cup of coffee in the morning. That's it for the day. I don't need the stimulation, but I do need to concentrate with all my brain power on *everything* going on in the courtroom. Trial law is full of "gotchas." If the other side oversteps its boundaries, or the judge makes a mistake harmful to my client's interest, I must object immediately. If I don't, the trial or appellate court may later say that even if the error was to my client's disadvantage, I may be deemed to have waived it by having failed to speak up and object on the spot. In the courtroom, I need to focus keenly on everything being said. The last thing I need is to be distracted by a full bladder!

But the intensity of the summation schedule threw me off stride and I broke one of my cardinal trial-lawyer rules. I call it *The Prophylactic Pee Rule*. It is simply this: Go every chance you get, whether you have the urge or not. Always walk into court with an empty bladder because you can never be sure when you will have the next opportunity to drain it.

The inevitable happened. In the rush to complete defense summations by the end of Thursday, Lacey skipped a recess. When my turn to sum up came, I asked the judge for a five-minute break. He said "No." Not only was I distressed at that ruling, I could see the same reaction on the faces of some of the jurors. But I was a good soldier, it was Lacey's courtroom, not mine, and I approached the jury and began my summation. Actually, I did not have a lot to say. I needed to remind them that my case was now different from the case against the other defendants, that Serota was not involved in the Ross bribery, that he had engaged in what he and his real estate lawyer thought was just another business transaction, and if there were any reasonable doubt in their minds about whether his conduct was a felony, the law required them to acquit. I don't think my entire piece lasted more than 30-40 minutes. But was the jury paying attention? No, they certainly were not. Several were wiggling in their seats, trying to catch the court deputy's eye while I was speaking. Never have I had that experience before, and on this occasion, I was arguing for my client's freedom! In the middle of my summation, a juror finally caught the deputy's eye, beckoned him to the jury box, whispered to him, and the deputy then climbed to Lacey's throne, whispered to the judge, whereupon Lacey banged the gavel once and announced, "Everybody stay exactly where you are. Juror number 3 may be excused for two minutes!" When juror number six anxiously raised her hand, Lacey said, "Okay, you can go too. Nobody else." I caught the judge's eye, "Your Honor, me too, please. It's right across the hall." Unbelievably, Lacey said, "No, Mr. London, you stand just where you are!"

For decades after that incident, I have tortured myself over the question of whether I should have just said, "I am sorry, Judge, I cannot stand here any longer," and walked out the door. What result? Contempt? A night in jail? Excoriation in front of the jury? Would the jury have loved me if as a result of my walking out he let them all take a break? Or would they have resented me for delaying the end of a brutally long day, and maybe prolonging their imprisonment? Was my staying there an act of cowardice before a bully, or an act of respect for judicial authority? I have replayed this scenario again and again. It is perhaps the only courtroom decision I have ever made of which I am ashamed.

In the end, I stayed because I concluded that this was not about me, it's not my case, it's Serota's case, and I thought less harm would likely come to him if I remained than if I left. Was I right? Were the jurors who did not get a bathroom break bothered to the extent that it adversely affected their focus on my summation? I guess I will never know. We were barred by New Jersey court rule from interviewing jurors after verdict. Would I do it differently today? Yeah, I would.

Trial lawyers generally agree that jurors resent it when you interrupt your adversary's summation. Only the most egregious errors usually prompt an objection. It's a dilemma; you want to avoid pissing off the jury and making them think you are trying to prevent your adversary from spelling out your weaknesses. That argues for silence. But when the other side makes a material error that could hurt your client, you either object or risk losing the claim because of the waiver rule. Goldstein followed form; he did not say one word during all the defense summations.

But when the prosecutor summed up the following morning, my fears were realized. Lacey's decision to keep Serota in the case on one count generated a pile-up of error and confusion. At our insistence, the judge had instructed Goldstein that his summation must not only differentiate between the conspiracies, he had to specify which bits of evidence the jury could consider against which defendants. Impossible, you say? That's what we said, too. The important thing was to be sure that when Goldstein summarized the evidence relating to the Ross/Serota conspiracy charge in Count I, and the actual Ross bribery charged in Count II, he made it clear to the jury each time that those facts could be used only against the IFC-Valentine defendants and not against Serota because he had been dismissed from those counts.

I think Goldstein did try to obey the judge's admonition to make the necessary distinctions, but the task proved to be impossible. Again and again, Goldstein's summation failed to separate out which evidence was admissible against Serota and which was not. The eggs were already scrambled.

The result was each time he tied "the defendants" to a piece of evidence in Counts I or II of the indictment, I objected and insisted he differentiate among the defendants, and the two alleged "bribes." The judge agreed each time I objected, but after a while, he just said something like, "Yes, the jury is so instructed." Confusion reigned.

At a recess after summations and before the judge's charge to the jury, I was standing in the corridor when a short grey-haired woman, wearing a long fur coat, angrily approached me. I had often seen her in the courtroom but had no idea who she was. "Mr. London," she called out while steaming toward me, "I am Jonathan Goldstein's mother and I am furious at your behavior. You ought to be ashamed of yourself. I know your partner Simon Rifkind and am calling him right now to complain about you. My son never interrupted your summation. Not once. But you interrupted him 12 times! Shame on you!" I bowed my head and apologized to Mrs. Goldstein.

The Judge's Charge to the Jury

While determining the facts is the exclusive province of the jury, instructing as to the law is the exclusive province of the judge. Preparation of the judge's charge is an effort that begins even before the trial starts. Lots of people on both sides of the case are involved. We look for every conceivable legal precedent that supports a request that the judge use specific language helpful to our client. For our team, my colleague Max Gitter took on this assignment and did a brilliant job.

One of the standard elements in a criminal case is the "reasonable doubt" charge. The judge must explain to the jury that they can convict only if they have unanimously concluded the prosecution has proved the defendant's guilt *beyond a reasonable doubt.* Lawyers and judges have written books on the meaning of this phrase, and we submitted pages and pages of language requests expounding on that element. At the charge conference, the judge told us he accepted our requests and would use the language we had submitted.

Two courtroom details came into play here.

First, throughout the trial, the parties had ordered "Daily Copy." We wanted promptly to read the transcript of each day's proceedings to see if there was something there that could help us the next day. We usually received the copy the same evening. Given the technology of the '70s, that could be accomplished only by having two stenographers alternate in twenty-minute shifts, so that while one was in the courtroom tapping the keys on his stenotype machine, the other reporter was in the back room typing out his notes to create the trial transcript.

Second, Lacey had written out his charge in longhand before he read it to the jury. To assist the court reporters, he had placed each page up on the bench ledge after he read it to the jury, so that the reporter ending his shift could take the stack of pages on his way back to type up the transcript. The judge's hand-written pages would be helpful in deciphering the reporter's steno notes.

As he had agreed to do, the judge read to the jury our requested reasonable-doubt language. But while the rest of his charge was delivered at a normal pace, Lacey raced through the reasonable-doubt section as if he were trying to win a speed-reading contest. His words were barely discernible to us, and we had submitted them! We were shocked.

When he finished reading the charge, the judge followed the required procedure: he sent the jury out, and asked counsel if they had any objection. I turned to Max and poked him hard in the ribs, the high-tech courtroom move I learned from Rifkind. "Max," I said, "Ya gotta object!" Max whispered, "Yeah, but what should I say?" I was furious. I could take no more of this judge's manifest pro-prosecution bias, and responded in a voice loud enough so that Lacey was sure to hear, **"Max, tell him to say it again, *this time with feeling*."** Because of the position of our "L" table – close to the bench and facing the other lawyers and their clients, not only Lacey, but every other person in the well, heard every word I said. By the time Max stood up, Lacey's face was already progressing from beet red to purple. Max later confessed he thought for sure he would spend the night in jail, but though he used more respectful language than mine, he did ask for a reread. Lacey reacted with fury. For the first time in the trial, he lost his composure. He raised his voice and accused us of making a "personal attack." He was right about that. After all, *he* was the one who did it. No surprise, he refused to read that section of the charge again. We had made our record but I was not sure what to do with it. How do you prove something like that to an appellate court?

We got an answer to that question right after the judge sent the jury out to deliberate, and counsel retired to their room to commiserate. Once again, a knock on the door, but this time it was the head court reporter. He asked Max and me to step outside and he led us down a half flight of steps. When we reached the landing and had absolute privacy, he said:

> Mr. London, you are absolutely right. I have been a court reporter in this courthouse for 12 years and I have *never* heard such speed-reading of a portion

of a charge. I can prove what he did. You saw, as Lacey finished reading a page, he put it on the ledge so we could pick up the pages on our way out? Well, to maintain order, the reporter going off shift marks each batch of pages with the time of his pick-up. *Those time notations show that the reasonable-doubt portion of the charge was read at 2-3 times the speed of the rest of the charge.* If you need it, Mr. London, I can supply the evidence for your appeal.

Holy shit!

The Verdict

Goldstein and Lacey successfully stuck Serota to that big ball of tar that was the Ross bribery. After that pair finished their oral presentations on Friday morning, the jury, came back the same day with a verdict of all defendants guilty on all counts, and they got to go back to Trenton and spend Easter Sunday with their families.

All lawyers hate to lose. But losing a criminal case when you know in your gut that your client did nothing wrong, and that the case was a total miscarriage of justice *that you let happen,* is the worst. When the verdict came in that Friday, I was bereft. How could I have failed to protect an innocent client? I was full of "shoulda's." I shoulda done this, I shoulda done that. Maybe I shoulda been a plumber.

Sleep evaded me that night. No amount of alcohol put me under. I was despondent.

Saturday morning, at 10 a.m., my home phone rang. I had a wicked headache. It was Nat Serota. "London, get up, shower, shave, and dress! Vivian and I are picking you up in the Rolls at noon, and we are going for a champagne lunch!" I said, "Nat, what are you smoking? You just got convicted of a federal felony and for sure that sonofabitch is going to give you the five-year max!" Nat, bless him, responded, "Fuck em, Marty. I did nothing wrong, and you're gonna get me off! We'll be at your door in two hours. Be ready." And he hung up.

Sentencing

Lacey was every bit the avenging angel I had predicted. The maximum penalty for each count in the indictment was five years. The judge had discretion to give less, but not more. In the case of multiple counts, he had the discretion to make the sentences concurrent (all served at the same time), or consecutive (each one served after the other.)

Our adversary-on-the-bench gave each of the IFC-Valentine individuals the maximum 5 years in prison on each of the three counts, to be served consecutively. In other words, he sentenced each of them to fifteen years in federal prison.

Nat Serota had no criminal record. He never had so much as a parking ticket. He had nothing to do with bribery of the Mayor. But as we stood before him, Lacey seethed. He called Nat "greedy" because he changed his position for money. I will never forget it. "Mr. Serota, I can't give you the fifteen years I gave the other defendants. I *would* have done so if I hadn't been *required* to dismiss those first two counts against you. But on the one you are guilty of, the sentence is five years."

I argued Nat's appeal in February, 1976. We raised a number of arguments about the legal unfairness to Serota in the way the trial was conducted. After much internal discussion, we omitted the speed-reading objection. We thought we had strong legal arguments and wanted to avoid overkill, marked by a personal attack on the trial judge. Most appellate judges were once District Court judges, and they still wear the same uniform. Besides, after poring over the trial record, I was more convinced than ever that Point I of our brief was a winner. It was the basic assertion we made from day one: what Nat did was not bribery. The First Amendment entitled him to modify his public advocacy for a fee. That was not corrupt. He was not a public official involved in the request for variances. He was a private citizen and did nothing wrong. I pounded on that point for most of the 20 minutes allotted to me for oral argument.

I was encouraged when one of the judges asked John Barry, who argued for the U.S. Attorney's office, whether there was any evidence in the record suggesting that Serota's position on the Parking Authority had anything to do with the plan to develop this property. I held my breath, fearing an obfuscation, but Barry was a straight shooter, and said, "No, Your Honor, there is not."

June 2nd of that year found me in New York's Hospital for Special Surgery with another herniated disk. (Tension related? Nah.) At that time, the prescribed treatment, short of surgery, was for the patient to lie on his back with ankle cuffs attached to sand-bag weighted ropes that ran over pulleys at the foot of the bed. They called it "traction," and though it sounds like a medieval torture, it was really not so awful, but I was miserable.

At 10 p.m., I heard a commotion in the normally quiet hospital corridor. An exasperated nurse was threatening to call security if the intruders did not leave at once. "Visiting hours were over an hour ago," she said at a very un-hospital-like volume setting. "You must leave. NOW." I had no doubt to whom she was speaking. Nat's voice was unmistakable. He was telling her that I was his lawyer, his mission this evening was "a confidential legal matter, an *emergency!*" and he had to speak to me at once. She did not relent, but there are no locks on hospital doors and Nat just barged into my room, Vivian in his wake. For this urgent legal conference, Nat's briefcase was a shopping bag. The diamond stud I had barred from the courtroom was back in his ear. I sat up as far as my tethers would permit, the three of us hugged and kissed and cried, and out of the shopping bag came a bottle of champagne and three stemware glasses. That's how we celebrated his appellate victory.

The Third Circuit Court of Appeals had that day unanimously reversed Nat's conviction. It held that our "vigorously" advanced assertions were correct. Nat had violated no law. The profitable sale of his apartment and his agreement to stop opposing the adjacent real estate development were in all respects legal activity. His conduct was not "bribery" in any sense of the word. Any interpretation of New Jersey law that criminalized Serota's paid-for agreement to abandon his opposition to the construction project would violate the First Amendment. The overly broad theory advanced by the prosecution and embraced by Lacey was unconstitutional. Nat was a private citizen. He had abrogated no official duty. His position as a member of the Parking Authority had nothing whatsoever to do with the IFC project. While the court did not use the words "red herring," that concept was implicit in its opinion.

While many jury conviction reversals result in an order for a new trial, there was nothing to retry here. There were no facts in dispute. The legality of Nat's conduct was unquestionable, and the appellate judges unanimously directed Lacey to enter a *judgment of acquittal*. For Nat Serota, vindication was complete and final.

Postscript

1. Because we were able to knock out the lone surviving Serota count, two of the three counts against the other defendants were also dismissed because they relied, in whole or in part, on the alleged "bribery" of Serota. Accordingly, the other defendants' sentences were reduced from fifteen years to five years. Subsequent legal motions addressed to other district judges (made by appellate counsel for the other defendants – not me) further materially reduced the Lacey-imposed sentences.

2. Years later, on a day when I was back in the New Jersey federal courthouse on another case, I was greeted warmly by the court stenographer. "Mr. London, nice to see you again. You should know that people in the courthouse still talk about how you guys stood up to Lacey. Congratulations." On a separate occasion, Gitter had a similar experience.

3. I had separate post-trial chance encounters with Jonathan Goldstein and Frederick Lacey. I ran into Goldstein in Newark Airport as we were each delivering children to flights out west for some summer activity. We chatted amiably for about 20 minutes. We did not talk about the case. Goldstein left the U.S. Attorney's office and had gone over to the "dark side," defending clients facing criminal charges.

   On another occasion, I was attending a legal conference, and during the cocktail hour found myself uncomfortably chatting one-on-one with Lacey, who had resigned from the bench, and joined a law firm. I was on my best behavior, and we neither talked about the case, nor shared our opinions of each other. Our conversation was civil but stilted. I was immensely relieved when I saw Peter Fleming approach. Peter was a big guy, big smile, a universally well-liked, gregarious member of the white-collar criminal defense bar. We exchanged greetings, and Peter turned to Lacey, and with an ear-to-ear grin on his face, said, "Well, Fred, Marty sure beat ya, didn't he!" Fleming laughed and said again, "He beat ya, Fred." Lacey didn't say a word. He glared at Fleming, turned on his heel, and walked away.

4. In 2008, *The New York Times* published a court filing that listed the names of those who had lost money in the Bernard Madoff Ponzi scheme. Nat Serota called me at once. "Marty, I just saw your name in the paper. I don't mean to pry into your affairs, but are you going to be okay?" I told him I was luckier than many. My losses were painful but not catastrophic. He said, "OK, darling, glad to hear that. I just want you to know I am here if you ever need me."

Where do you find clients like that?

"A Time to Kill": Threats, and the First Amendment

Threats are not protected speech. While the First Amendment does not say so explicitly, our legal history makes that clear. But while it is undoubtedly a crime to threaten the President or a provider of legal abortion services, there can be room for disagreement as to whether a specific combination of words, uttered in a particular context, is an illegal threat or protected opinion. That can be a triable case.

In the early '90s, the country endured a series of murders of physicians who provided legal abortions to their patients. A group of anti-choice fanatics in Portland, Oregon, by various means, voiced their support of the murderers and encouraged and facilitated others to kill physicians. Did the particular speech pattern they employed constitute illegal threats and intimidation, or was it an exercise of their First Amendment rights? Even the ACLU, a fervent supporter of both a woman's right to choose and an expansive view of the First Amendment, was torn by the issue. We weren't. On behalf of physicians and clinics targeted by the supporters of violence, and under the leadership of Paul, Weiss's Maria Vullo, the firm sued the bad guys. I am proud my law firm did that, and especially proud I was part of that trial team.

✦

Meet Sam. Ten years old, crew cut, short hair, big eyes, freckles, shy smile, built like a diminutive middle line-backer, Sam's idea of bundling up for cold weather was to add a second tee shirt. A Norman Rockwell natural. But Sam had an uncharacteristic wariness that set him apart from his contemporaries.

You see, Sam knew things that other 10-year-old American kids did not know. He knew he must be extra-attentive to his surroundings, of people and cars in his vicinity, of unusual circumstances, because there were people out there who wanted his parents dead. Sam could not go to school on the bus; waiting on a street corner or in front of his house with his parents was too dangerous. He could not be seen standing at a specific place on a predictable timetable. Sam was also taught contingency plans no child should be required to learn; if he heard gunshots in or about his home, Sam was to go to the safest place in the house, the bathtub, and lie there until told "all clear."

Why is that? Sam's father was neither a Colombian drug lord, nor a Mafia Don. He was a physician who had served in the U.S. Army in Vietnam as a medic in an advanced infantry battalion and won medals for bravery. In fact, both of Sam's parents were physicians who provided gynecological and obstetric services, from taking pap smears to delivering babies. And they also provided safe, legal abortions to women who wanted or needed that procedure. Sam's parents wore armored vests when traveling to and from work, and were our clients.

Our physician client #3, Bob, stopped performing abortions because of the violence inflicted on doctors and clinics, but one day he was asked to perform an abortion on an AIDS patient whose life was endangered by her pregnancy. He did so, and eight days later, a shotgun blast ripped into his home. The experience reinforced his belief that his work was important and he resumed helping women who wanted legal abortions. He was thereafter accompanied by law enforcement bodyguards when traveling, and used an alias lest his name be found on an airline computer. Bob flew to several cities each week because of the lack of abortion providers in seven states. He was the last person to board every plane and the first person to get off. After the shotgun blast, he regularly wore his armored vest. When traveling with his family, they went in separate cars.

Physician client #4 was Warren, of Boulder, Colorado. He too traveled frequently to provide abortion services in areas where no other physician was willing to do so. He employed disguises, and wearing his armored vest, traveled with three federal marshals at all times.

What frightened these good people?

In 1993, anti-choice extremists circulated a "**WANTED**" poster of Dr. David Gunn, an abortion provider in Pensacola, Florida. The poster evoked the "Wanted, Dead or Alive" meme of the Wild West era. As with later posters, Dr. Gunn's poster had the word **WANTED** across the top, a photograph of him in the center, with the addresses of his home and office. On March 10, 1993, shortly after the distribution of that poster, Dr. Gunn was shot in the back and killed outside his Pensacola clinic. His murderer, an anti-abortion demonstrator by the name of Michael Griffin, was applauded by an Oregon-based splinter group of anti-abortion extremists.

Because of that group's refusal to renounce violence, it was ultimately shunned by Operation Rescue and other established anti-choice organizations. The splinter group then formed its own organization, the American Coalition of Life Activists (ACLA), which, along with eleven individuals, applauded the murder of physicians and petitioned for release of their murderers.

After Dr. Gunn was killed, a **WANTED** poster targeting abortion provider Dr. George Patterson appeared in Mobile, Alabama. Several months later, he too was shot to death. Then one Shelley Shannon of Oregon, shot and attempted to kill Dr. George Tiller, an abortion provider from Kansas, after his name, photograph, and personal information were published by the defendants in their house organ, *Life Advocate Magazine*. Shannon had copies of the magazine in her car when she was arrested. She testified that she used them to identify Dr. Tiller so she could shoot him. (Dr. Tiller was wounded but survived Shannon's attack, only to be later murdered by another anti-abortion activist while the doctor was serving as an usher at his church's Sunday services. The Tiller murder followed anti-abortion activist James Kopp's killing of Dr. Barnett Slepian upon the latter's return from a synagogue memorial service for his father).

Dr. Gunn's replacement at the Pensacola clinic was Dr. John Bayard Britton. Activists who applauded Dr. Gunn's murder monitored the clinic and photographed Britton's arrivals and departures. One of those photographs found its way onto a Britton **WANTED** poster and soon thereafter, an anti-choice activist named Paul Hill killed Dr. Britton and his 73-year-old unarmed escort, James Barrett, and wounded Mr. Barrett's wife, June. Knowing that Dr. Britton wore a bulletproof vest, Hill approached

Dr. Britton's vehicle with a shotgun, and from a distance of three feet, shot him in the head.

The ACLA group vigorously applauded the murders and solicited signatures on petitions urging acquittal of the killers on the ground the killings were justified.

In January 1995, defendants issued their own **WANTED** poster. They upped the ante. Apparently unhappy with single posters, they held a press conference in Washington, D.C. on the 22nd anniversary of *Roe* v. *Wade,* and exhibited to the media a three-foot by five-foot billboard-type multi-physician **WANTED** poster, **The "Deadly Dozen" List.** At the top, in bold six-inch letters was the word "**GUILTY**." In the center were the names and home addresses of **thirteen abortion providers**, three of whom were to become our clients. Below their names, also in bold, was the word "**REWARD**."

The publication of the Deadly Dozen List received nationwide media publicity. It also received attention from the Justice Department, which dispatched FBI agents to visit the thirteen physicians on the list to inform them that a serious threat had been made against their lives by people who not only advocated murdering physicians, but were known to have associated with others who had been convicted of the murder of physicians and the bombing of clinics. The physicians were offered round-the-clock federal marshal protection and were advised to take immediate precautions, including wearing armored vests, reinforcing their homes and offices with steel doors and bulletproof glass, adopting disguises, altering their routes to and from work, informing schools to take extra precaution with respect to their children, and various other security measures.

The defendants' publications noted with satisfaction the fear that "rippled through the ranks" of abortion providers when the Deadly Dozen **WANTED** poster was published. Obviously pleased with the fear-inducing effects of the publication of the Deadly Dozen hit list, defendants republished it, including home addresses, in the next issue of their magazine, the front cover of which featured a picture of the Grim Reaper, with a skeleton face, black hood, and scythe.

Several months later, the defendants held a conclave in St. Louis, Missouri, where they again published the Deadly Dozen List, along with three additional old-style **WANTED** posters of physicians. Those doctors were immediately contacted by federal law enforcement authorities, given warnings their lives were in jeopardy, and they too were offered around-the-clock protection by federal marshals. Two of the three newly postered physicians promptly stopped providing abortion services. The third continued his work and ultimately became our client.

In January 1996, defendants held a news conference where they published what they called the *Nuremberg Files* (they equated these physicians with the Nazis) – a large poster board, dripping with blood, that contained the photographs and extensive personal data of more abortion providers. Doctors who had been killed were listed with their names crossed out, and those wounded were greyed out. They also produced a box of files said to contain the personal details of approximately 30 abortion providers throughout the United States. A video clip of one of these files showed that the defendants had gathered not only photographs of Sam's father but personal information about his family, photographs of his home, and other information gleaned from surveillance. The site also listed, among pictures of what purported to be fetal remains and dripping blood, the names of judges who had presided over cases in which anti-abortion activists had been enjoined, the names of law enforcement officials who had investigated anti-abortion violence, and the names of pro-choice activists.

The extremists succeeded in frightening physicians. Many stopped performing abortions. Who wouldn't be afraid? Their intimidators were dedicated supporters of convicted murderers, bombers, and arsonists who shared the "I-don't-have-to-obey-the-law-because-God-tells-me-I'm-right" view of the social contract.

So many physicians had stopped performing legal abortions because of fear of injury to self and family, there were no physicians providing legal abortion services in more than 80 percent of the counties in the United States of America. In those places, the terrorists had effectively trumped *Roe* v. *Wade*. The Supreme Court's decisions are meaningless if citizens do not have the option to utilize the rights granted to them by the Constitution.

How did this come to pass? Where were the great defenders of women's rights? Where were the medical profession, the law enforcement agencies, the organized bar, while this was happening? Doing too little, too late, that's where. Are our liberties subject to cancellation by violent extremists who assert they have the *right to* kill physicians and to bomb clinics? By their publication of hit lists and **WANTED** posters with names, home and work addresses and other personal data, these people asserted they had the *right* to threaten violence. ISIS-like, they proclaimed they were "authorized" by God to encourage atrocities. But the ACLA group asserted an additional defense for their conduct, a defense that other jihadists lacked. These extremists claimed a right to terrorize others that was backed not only by God, but by the First Amendment.

The Portland Lawsuit:

In Oregon in 1995, four physicians and two Planned Parenthood clinics, sued ACLA and eleven of its planners and managers. The lawsuit was entitled *Planned Parenthood of the Columbia/Willamette, Inc., et. al.* v. *American Coalition of Life Activists, et. al.* and was tried in federal district court in Portland.

The claim was based on two federal statutes: (1) the Freedom of Access to Clinic Entrances Act (FACE), 18 USC §248 (*threat of force* used to intimidate or interfere with the supplying of reproductive health services), and (2) the Racketeer Influenced Corrupt Organizations Act (RICO), 18 USC §1961, et seq., the predicate acts for which were violations of the Hobbs Act, 18 USC §1951 (*threat of force* in an attempt to deprive plaintiffs of their property). The defendants were two organizations and ten individuals, who, we alleged, together published the threats.

The central question in the trial was whether the defendants' speech constituted a "true threat." A threat may be explicit or implicit, and any set of words possibly conveying a threat must be viewed with a focus on the environment in which it is made. A group of beer drinkers making jokes about shooting the President may be boors, but not felons. Telling someone, "I'm gonna get you" could be an athletic challenge, a sexual quip, or a warning of murderous intent. It all depends on the context, the backstory. The pertinent legal definition was:

> A statement is a true threat when a reasonable person making the statement would foresee that the statement would be interpreted by those to whom it is communicated as a serious expression of an intent to bodily harm or assault.

It was going to be up to the jury in this trial to decide this question:

> **In an atmosphere where a *poster/murder pattern* is unambiguously established, and where the publisher of a new poster knows that physicians clearly recognize existing posters as threats, is a new poster a threat?**

The architect and lead lawyer for the plaintiffs was Maria Vullo, who was a senior associate at Paul, Weiss when she filed the lawsuit. Maria crafted the legal basis of the complaint, drafted the pleading, managed the discovery, successfully opposed defendants' motions to dismiss and for summary judgment, and otherwise organized all aspects of our side of the bitterly contested litigation. A phalanx of Paul, Weiss associates pitched in to help. The firm was fully committed to this *pro bono* effort. We collected no fees from any of the clients.

Lawyers rarely take discovery of people on death row or serving long prison terms. Paul Hill, who shot and killed Dr. Britton, Michael Griffin, who shot and killed Dr. Gunn, and Shelley Shannon, who bombed ten clinics and shot Dr. Tiller five times, were all deposed by the Paul, Weiss team. Basically, the fundamentalists were of the view that killing doctors who performed abortions was justified. Defendant Michael Bray, who wore a clergyman's collar, said he believed God was on his side, because the Bible says "There is a time to kill." In fact, one of the defendant's lawyers had published a tract setting out the legal basis for that theory!

Maria was in the midst of trial prep when I popped into her room in late 1998. I had observed the course of the litigation for three years and fully supported the cause emotionally and intellectually, but had made no concrete contribution. Though I was heavily engaged in a large variety of matters for which I was the responsible partner, I felt the need physically to do something for the cause, as well as the obligation to help Maria personally. I had worked with her before, and was aware of the heavy burden this case imposed on her. I thought maybe there was a chore I could do – perhaps take a deposition, edit a brief, something of that order, to help relieve some of the strain. Sitting in her visitor's chair, I asked Maria if there was anything I could do to lighten her load. To my surprise, she said, "Marty, our trial is scheduled to start in three months. Will you come out to Portland and try this case with me?" Whoa! That certainly was not what I had in mind when I walked in, but I love trying cases, and especially ones as important as this one. I said, "Are you kidding? Sure! Just let me check my calendar." I did, moved some stuff around, and signed on.

Over the course of the next several months, we worked out who would do what. I had a lot more experience than she, but this was Maria's case, she was the lead lawyer, and had an encyclopedic knowledge of the facts and the pertinent law. We divided up the responsibilities: we would split the witnesses, she would do the opening and the principal close, and I would do the rebuttal close. Our other principal lawyer was Carol Bernick, a partner of Davis, Wright, Tremaine in Portland. (Yup, the same firm that had been my opposing counsel in CBS's appeal of the *B&W* v. *CBS* verdict). A crew of Paul, Weiss associates and paralegals went to Portland in support.

During the trial, our clients continued to wear their armored vests at all times, and were driven to and from court in a U.S. Marshal's van. We were offered the same opportunity but opted to walk the few blocks from our hotel to the courthouse. The notion of all that security was simply too oppressive, too much of a surrender to the bad guys. We were standing up for important rights in that courtroom and wouldn't give in to the intimidation. It all came out okay, though I confess I was creeped out on our first night in Portland. While we were having dinner in the ground floor hotel dining room in front of a floor-to-ceiling window, I kept seeing the same vehicle, old, rusted, dented fender, drive slowly back and forth in front of the hotel. On the fifth pass, I was ready to dive under the table. Creepy, creepy, creepy. And the mid-trial 4 a.m. walk down eight flights of stairs when the hotel fire alarm sounded and the hotel had to be evacuated was no lark either. We were told that a smoky, wet log in the lobby fireplace had triggered the alarm. True? Happenstance? Perhaps, perhaps not. I had slept through the fire alarm, but my good teammates, on the way down, realized I was absent, and came back for me, and I rushed out. Did I feel a little exposed standing on that sidewalk swaddled in my hotel bathrobe and slippers? Yes, I did.

A light note in an otherwise dark drama: Maria's multimedia opening statement was superb, a presentation using exhibits, video, charts, PowerPoint, the whole deal. We had a run-through at Carol Bernick's law firm on the day before the start of the trial, and the mock jury consisted of anyone in the office who could spare the time to listen. When Maria was finished, the audience sat open-mouthed at the awe-inspiring performance, and when asked if they had any comments or recommendations, only one person spoke up. A young, very serious Portland lawyer, said in all seriousness, "Ugh, Ms. Vullo, could you do something about your New York accent?"

Jury selection had its challenges. Given the atmosphere, the trial judge ruled the jurors would remain anonymous.

Each prospective juror was asked to fill out a detailed questionnaire that asked personal questions about politics and religion. We ended up with four men and four women, ages 26 to 66, including a postal worker, a computer programmer, a dental hygienist, some retirees, etc. When asked about their political leanings, one said "liberal," one said "conservative," and six chose "middle of the road." Six of the eight were Catholic.

The trial judge was as experienced and fair-minded as any I have encountered. Judge Robert Jones had been a Republican state legislator, a state court judge, and a member of the Oregon Supreme Court before he was appointed to the federal bench by George H. W. Bush. With 35 years of experience on the bench, Jones ran a tight ship. He was smart, totally in control of his court, and as hardworking as any of us.

At the start, he instructed the panel of prospective jurors that this case *was not about abortion*, which was a legal procedure. What the jury needed to decide was whether the defendants' statements and conduct amounted to "true threats," to be defined as he instructed. Nevertheless, at the defendants' request, the prospective jurors had been asked if they, or any member of their family, had any personal experience with abortion. To my surprise, of the eight panel members we ended up with, one woman had had an abortion, and one older gentleman had vigorously opposed his daughter's decision to have an abortion, but reluctantly concluded it was her call, not his. (When I expressed surprise to one of our clients that 25% of the group had a personal connection to abortion, he told me that someone has had an abortion in 33% of American families).

The trial got off to a unique start. Maria gave her opening, and the first lawyer up for the defendant pointed to her and said, "That woman is a liar." I objected so loudly that everyone at both tables jumped. And relations went downhill from there.

In the well of the courtroom, there was an icy wall separating the tables. These defendants and their lawyers were proponents of violence and murder. They admitted as much. Not one of the people at defendants' table was marginally approachable. After all, they had direct two-way communication with God, and were persuaded they were doing His work.

The defendants had a paralegal who was right out of an Alfred Hitchcock movie. One day, just before the judge and jury came into the courtroom, the paralegal stormed over to our area and confronted one of the physicians sitting in a chair behind us. Voices were raised. I jumped up and physically put myself between our client and the Norman Bates character and, using my best New York vernacular, told him where he could go. I did not whisper. The lawyers from the opposing table ran over, and we were on the verge of a major brawl. The courtroom stenographer (who, we had concluded, was NOT on our side) had run back to the robing room and said I-don't-know-what to the judge, who hurried out, mounted the bench, banged his gavel, put all of us back in our seats, and then proceeded to excoriate *me*. I wasn't about to accuse his stenographer of making a biased report, so I accepted the tongue-lashing. What would have happened if he had not come out when he did, I dunno. What instigated the confrontation? The assholes decided to serve a subpoena on the doctor. He had been sitting in that chair every day of the trial, and if they wanted to call him as a witness, they could have just called him. Or they could have given the subpoena to us, or asked the judge to get his agreement to testify when they called him, etc., etc. Instead, they had that creep physically confront the doc. I think they got some sort of pleasure in frightening the crap out of him. All sleaze, all the time.

Each of our clients testified how they reacted when the FBI and the federal marshals told them their lives were in danger from these credible threats. They told the jury the details of their security precautions, and the fear they lived with every day after the defendants added their names and addresses to the list of prospective *poster/murder* victims. The testimony took up three weeks.

On every available occasion, the defendants argued the First Amendment to the jury, and the judge permitted it, though we thought he should not have done so because it is not a jury question, it's a question of law, and is therefore the exclusive province of the judge. Aside from their approval of violence, defendants linked their free speech jury arguments to their engagement in legal, nonviolent picketing. In an effort to get the jury to take their eyes off the ball, defendants hammered on this free speech theme over and over again. But they were undone, really, by one of the unforeseen star witnesses of the trial. Doctor Abraham Anderson, who was not a plaintiff, came in from Alabama to take the witness stand for us. A gentle soul (who physically resembled, in appearance and manner only, the former Republican candidate for President, Dr. Ben Carson), Dr. Anderson captivated the courtroom with his simple narrative. The soft-spoken physician testified that he had been hectored by picketing at his home and his office, but continued offering abortion services to his needy patients, until he was threatened by a **WANTED** poster bearing his photograph and personal information, and then he reluctantly quit providing abortions. I can best describe his testimony by quoting from my rebuttal summation:

There has been a lot of talk during this defense presentation, about peaceful picketing, about non-violent protest. Who would criticize Abraham Anderson? Do you remember Dr. Abraham Anderson? Will anybody forget the sight of that gentle man sitting there on that witness stand, reaching into his pocket, and holding up the yellow **WANTED** poster of him that had been made by defendant David Crane. Can anyone forget Abraham Anderson saying, in his soft, gentle voice, "Well, I felt that my life was threatened, because I was aware of the fact that some months earlier, Dr. Gunn, in Florida, had been shot and killed after some similar posters were circulated, and I was terrified. Not just for me, but for my family." And he went on, "I had fear for the life of my wife and children and fear for my life, and I didn't want to be sacrificial."

And then on cross, [a defendant's lawyer] asked him if he was being paid by Planned Parenthood for his lost earnings in coming to tell you his story. And he said, "No, and if they offered, I wouldn't accept it."

Now, who among you could say that Dr. Anderson's fear, after defendant Crane's wanted poster, was not reasonable? Is there a voice in the room who would mock Abraham Anderson, as defendants have mocked these plaintiffs, by saying, to Abraham Anderson, "Well, have you ever been physically assaulted, Dr. Anderson? Did you ever call up the defendant, Mr. Crane, and ask him to please stop?" Is Abraham Anderson's fear less real, less valid, less important, because, before the threatening **WANTED** poster, his office may have been picketed peacefully? Does that make the threat any less gut wrenching? Is his fear less choking because there may have been a nonviolent protest in front of his house? What has that got to do with it? Nothing. And that's why there's so much attention, in this trial, being paid to nonviolent protest, because it has nothing to do with threats that cause fear of bodily harm. Nothing whatsoever. The ice water in Dr. Abraham Anderson's belly, the ice water of fear didn't go away because there had been a peaceful picket the week before. He feared for his life, and he feared for his family, and he quit, as so many other physicians have done – as these plaintiff physicians refuse to do, at great sacrifice to their safety.

The defendants could not deny their conduct caused the plaintiffs to fear for their lives – conduct, we asserted, that was absolutely barred by federal statute. Indeed, when I cross-examined one of the defendants, Andrew Burnett, and asked him if he could not see that the pattern of posters followed by murders would intimidate the physicians who were so targeted, Burnett agreed:

"If I were an abortionist, I would be afraid."

That admission was highlighted in the closing statements, and later in the definitive appellate court decision as well.

The last thing these defendants wanted was a verdict. They saw it coming, and repeatedly moved for a mistrial. Any ground would do. One of the serious and at the same time humorous grounds was a surprising loss of temper by the gentlemanly Judge Jones. Maria was crossing defendant Monica Miller, and caught her in a prior inconsistent statement. The witness tried to evade, but could not escape the trap she had placed herself in, and in response to Maria's question about whether, in light of the inconsistency, her trial testimony was *truthful*, the following colloquy ensued:

> Witness: I am not sure what you mean by "truthful."

> The Court: Truthful means truthful! Telling the truth! This is not a Clinton deposition!

The courtroom exploded with laughter. It was a great tension release, but a surprising breach of judicial composure in front of the jury. Jones denied the mistrial motions, apologized in open court, and even offered defendants the opportunity to recall the witness for additional direct testimony. They declined. No harm, no foul.

Another mistrial motion was generated when one of our stalwart docs refused to respond to a cross-examiner's question that referred to him as an "abortionist." He said he would not answer any question containing that word. It was not a medical term. It was a slur that evoked images of old men wearing filthy gowns, using coat hangers to perform abortions. Defendants' counsel did not repeat the word in the continued cross of that witness, but nevertheless used it every other chance they could. They were so relentless that mid-trial, juror number seven sent a note to the judge asking him to please tell the defendants and their lawyers to stop using the word; it offended her and interfered with her ability fairly to appraise the evidence. Defendants howled, asking again for a mistrial. No soap. The judge did give the jury a careful instruction on deciding only on the basis of the evidence. I was sorry the juror wrote the note. I thought from the beginning that defendants' continued insults worked against them with all the jurors, but defendants and their lawyers were so filled with righteous venom, they could not see that.

After three weeks of testimony and argument, the judge charged the jury. His instructions were lengthy and detailed as to what constituted a true threat under the law, and what the elements of the FACE and RICO statutes were. He sent them out to deliberate with a lengthy verdict form that required them to answer YES or NO to three preliminary questions. The jury form read:

1. Is the "Deadly Dozen" poster a true threat by one or more of the defendants to bodily harm, assault, or kill any of the plaintiffs?

2. Is the other poster in the case a true threat by one or more of the defendants to bodily harm, assault, or kill any of the plaintiffs?

3. Are the Nuremberg files a true threat by one or more of the defendants to bodily harm, assault, or kill any of the plaintiffs?

If the answer to any of these questions was YES, they were next to turn to a 15-page matrix of questions involving assignment of compensatory and punitive damages for each plaintiff on account of each defendant's conduct in violation of each of the FACE and RICO statutes.

Waiting for jury verdicts can be torture. This one was as bad as it gets. The jury was out for almost five full days. The judge had optimistically typed the date "January __, 1999" at the bottom of the verdict form. When it came back signed, "Presiding Juror # 14", the word "January" had been stricken and replaced with "Feb." (Who was "Presiding Juror #14" remains a mystery to this day. The handwriting, I think, suggests a woman, but it's a 60-40 question).

But there was no question about the unambiguous message the jury sent to these defendants and to the community at large. The jurors checked YES to each of the first three questions, and then meticulously filled out the complicated appendix calculating and deciding compensatory and punitive damage awards in favor of each of the four doctors and six clinics against each of the defendants. It was worth the wait. The total damages came to $109 million, the largest jury verdict in the history of the State of Oregon. The verdict received front-page treatment.

In subsequent proceedings, Judge Jones enjoined the defendants from any more postering and threats. Violation of his order would be criminal contempt.

But two years later, a panel of three conservative judges of the Ninth Circuit did what we feared that particular trio would do. In a decision we thought motivated by abortion politics, not First Amendment jurisprudence, they voted to reverse the judgment and dismiss the complaint. They said that in their view, the First Amendment required, that to qualify as a true threat, the words had to indicate that *the speaker* himself was the one who would do the killing. The Court opined that,

> **Merely encouraging or making it more likely that others would carry out . . . the gruesome mission was constitutionally protected speech!**

I am cynical enough to wonder what those judges' First Amendment views would be today in this hypothetical situation. Assume ISIS jihadists publish a series of **WANTED** posters targeting outspoken anti-ISIS activists, each of whom is thereafter murdered by a person or persons unknown, in a serial poster/murder pattern. Following upon their voting to affirm a conviction of an alleged ISIS terrorist, our three Ninth Circuit judges become the targets of **WANTED** posters supplying *their* home addresses, the names of *their* wives and children, the location of *their* children's schools, the place and time of school bus stop locations, etc.

Would they vote to protect *that* speech?

One year later, an *en banc* court of Ninth Circuit judges reversed, and reinstated the jury verdict. The vote for reinstatement among the judges who had not been part of the previous reversal was 6-3. Ultimately the punitive damage figure was reduced (as if we really expected to collect any material part of $109 million!) but the injunction remains.

Actually, the case went to the Ninth Circuit three times. Maria, by this time a significant partner at Paul, Weiss, carried all three arguments.

The reinstatement decision contained a bit of personal vindication. In my rebuttal summation, I had discussed the importance of "context" in determining what words or conduct constituted a "true threat." I had argued:

> You know, there was a matter once in which somebody parked a yellow Ryder truck out in front of an abortion facility. I can hear defendants' lawyers say, "Well, it was a legal truck. It was on a legal street. It had legal license plates, it had legal insurance. What's the problem?"
>
> Well, the problem is, if, months before, a yellow Ryder truck took on great significance because it was the vehicle used to bomb the Oklahoma City Government Building, then the sight of that yellow Ryder truck, in that context, becomes a dramatic threat.

While there was no objection during my argument, two days later, while the jury was deliberating, defendants made their final mistrial motion. They said my argument was inflammatory and employed facts not in the record. While I was pretty confident there was no merit to that claim, I was uncomfortable awaiting Jones's ruling. I could not bear the thought that I might have uttered words that sunk our ship after this long voyage. Judge Jones relieved my anxiety by promptly ruling my argument was just that, argument. He denied the motion. I was especially happy to see this sentence in the *en banc* court opinion:

> The posters are a true threat because like Ryder
> trucks or burning crosses, they connote something
> they do not literally say, yet both the actor and the
> recipient get the message.

Defendants applied for certiorari to the Supremes,
who, before voting, asked the United States Solicitor
General to submit his views on whether the Justices
should review the Ninth Circuit *en banc* decision. The
S.G. recommended against review, and the defendants
failed to muster the four votes necessary to grant their
petition. The case was over.

There were times during trial when the testimony
of doctors who feared not only for their own safety,
but for that of their families as well, brought me to
tears. Some of those physicians stopped performing
abortions, and others, like our clients, stuck with it out
of obligation to the women they served. I was moved
by both groups.

But the most emotional moment for me occurred
after the trial. One of the things I had said in my
summation was:

> Defendant's counsel talked about freedom. That's
> what we want. Our clients want freedom from fear.
> They want the freedom of a parent to hug his child
> without worrying that he's standing in front of a
> window or that he can't feel the beating of his child's
> heart through the bulletproof vest he's wearing.

The excerpt was published back at the firm, and the
day after the verdict was announced, while we were preparing to depart Portland, I received this email from a
Paul, Weiss associate:

To: Martin London
From: [Deleted]
Subject: My Dad, "The Abortionist"

My parents called me crying last night. My father felt personally vindicated by the verdict.

From one of the kids who was drilled in how to avoid the windows, Thank You.

Part II:

PRO BONO PUBLICO:
FOR THE
PUBLIC GOOD

"Crackpots and Left-wingers:" The Roy Cohn Disbarment

In 1988, the American Bar Association passed a resolution urging lawyers and law firms to devote 50 hours a year to pro bono services, either directly serving impecunious clients, "or other public service activities that . . . improve the legal system or the legal profession."

Long before that, Paul, Weiss lawyers were encouraged to do that much, and more. I did. In the years prior to my pro bono work on the Portland abortion case, I devoted thousands of hours to other pro bono stuff, including my efforts to rid the bar of unethical lawyers, and the bench of incompetent or corrupt judges.

✦

At one time, every sentient adult in the United States knew Roy Cohn's name and reputation. As chief counsel to the *Red Scare* witch hunt managed by the disgraced U.S. Senator Joseph McCarthy of the Senate Investigations Committee, Cohn used his power and influence to try to force the United States Army to let his good friend G. David Schine escape the draft. And when Schine was drafted anyway, and the Army refused to give him a commission for which he was not qualified, Cohn brazenly threatened that if Pvt. Schine did not get special privileges while in basic training, Cohn would "wreck the Army." This resulted in the extraordinary 1954 spectacle of nationally televised gavel-to-gavel coverage of the Army-McCarthy hearings, in which, among other things, the McCarthy-Cohn team introduced a doctored photograph and a counterfeit FBI letter. The public exposure of the committee's abusive style destroyed McCarthy's career, but seemed to enhance Cohn's.

Cohn went on to build a highly visible and apparently successful career at the New York Bar. It was years before the pile-up of fraud, ethical misconduct, and perjury brought him down. During his reign, he represented powerful people, from mobsters to millionaires. His father had been a politically connected judge, and Roy had high-up political connections of his own, including at the White House.

But none of that is the reason I remember getting a telephone call from him when I was a young lawyer at my first job. Cohn was adversary counsel on some matter I no longer recall, and our conversation was right out of a comedy routine. He called me, and after only a minute or so of introductory chatter, Cohn said "I am hanging up now. I am calling from my car phone!" And in a beep, he was gone. A car phone! My first ever call from such a thing. I had heard of them, but had never seen or experienced one. Ah, technology, what would they think of next?

My next contact with Roy Cohn came almost 20 years later, and we were adversaries of a different sort.

New York State's judiciary is divided into four geographic departments, each headed by an intermediate

appellate court. In addition to hearing appeals from infe-
rior courts within their jurisdiction, the Appellate Divisions
are charged with a number of administrative functions, one
of which is the discipline of lawyers. The First Judicial
Department was responsible for the counties of New York
(Manhattan) and the Bronx, where more than 40,000 lawyers were registered.

Each Appellate Division Department is required to
appoint a Disciplinary Committee of lawyers and lay-
persons to hear allegations of lawyers' ethical violations,
and make preliminary inquiries and determinations. If
the matter were serious enough to suggest possible public censure, suspension or disbarment, the committee is
obliged to petition the court for appropriate action. Three
of the Appellate Divisions complied by selecting their
own Committees. All the departments had full-time staff
to handle their caseloads.

Uniquely, the First Department court designated the
Grievance Committee of the prestigious Bar Association of
the City of New York, as its official Departmental Disciplinary
Committee. That process, however, ended in 1980, with
an unseemly dispute between the Bar Association and the
court. The issue arose when the court's Presiding Justice,
Francis "Tim" Murphy, sent the President of the City Bar
the names of two lawyers he suggested be included in
the next appointment cycle of the 30-person Committee.
Remarkably, the P.J.'s suggestion was met with resistance.
The Association's leadership saw it as "interference" with
"their" disciplinary function, and the Chair of the Grievance
Committee resigned in high dudgeon. Murphy was accused
by some as trying to "cronyize" the disciplinary function
and, after some public wrangling, the Bar Association with-
drew from the process altogether. The P.J. snuffed out the

incipient brouhaha by appointing his two recommendations, plus all the surviving members of the old Bar Association Grievance Committee, to be the court's newly-constituted Departmental Disciplinary Committee. As the replacement Chair of the new Committee, he appointed a lawyer who could hardly qualify as a Murphy "crony" because the new guy was somebody Justice Murphy had never met.

I had been active in Bar Association affairs, and done other pro bono work, but never had any contact with Justice Murphy. If I had ever argued a case before a First Department five-judge panel that included him, I didn't remember it. So when I got a call asking me to come down and see the man, I had no idea what he wanted. I was astonished when he asked me to be Chairman of the newly constituted Departmental Disciplinary Committee. I said I would be honored to serve.

Aside from the large committee of lawyers and a few lay persons of which I was now the head, I was also now the *de facto* managing partner of a medium-sized law firm consisting of a staff of ten lawyers, plus paralegals and secretaries. They did the important work of receiving complaints, investigating them, and making recommenda-tions to the Committee Chair and the staff Chief Counsel, as to how the Disciplinary Committee should proceed in each matter. In the more serious instances, these lawyers tried cases before a committee-appointed hearing panel or a court-appointed referee.

My first step in my new job was to meet the staff and its Chief Counsel, view the premises, and familiarize myself with how, and by whom the work was done. At Paul, Weiss, I was a partner of a well-run law firm, I was active in its administration, and knew something about running a law office.

What I saw on my early visits to the DDC office was appalling. The staff was overwhelmed by the work, and as a result, was marginally guilty of malpractice for neglecting the affairs of its clients, i.e., the court and the public. Forget computers that were just coming into office use – the staff was using manual typewriters! Case management systems consisted of lawyers typing cryptic one or two line entries on index cards. Not quite the quill pen era, but close. Complaints against lawyers were addressed months, and in some cases years after they were received. The Grievance Committee of the Bar Association had been an honorable group of well-meaning lawyers, but its leadership had ignored its administrative responsibilities.

The biggest shock on my introductory tour came when the Chief Counsel took me into his office, opened the deep bottom drawer of his desk, pointed to several fat red file pockets, and said, "You think we are slow? See those folders? They are cases that are so big, so important, we cannot do anything with them. Nothing. These respondents are well-known lawyers in this city, have effective counsel, and the cases are so time consuming, that if we attended to these matters, we would not be able to do much else."

My Chief Counsel had it backwards; those cases were *more* important than the others. I did what any sentient managing partner would do. First, I asked the Chief Counsel to resign, effective thirty days hence, and after an intense search in the interim, I replaced him with Michael Gentile, an experienced felony prosecutor from the Brooklyn District Attorney's office. Second, I went to see the Presiding Justice, told him of my findings, and asked for two things: i) a budget that would enable me to hire more people and equip them with up-to-date office equipment; and ii) the right to recruit members of the bar to volunteer their services as temporary staff members so I could attack those "bottom drawer" folders. The P.J. said "Yes," and "Yes," and we went after the "elites."

One of those bottom drawer folders had Roy Cohn's name on it. When I read that file, I was stunned. There were three serious complaints, two of which were *three years old*. The third complaint had been brought to the Committee's attention earlier that year, but described an egregious abuse of a client that had persisted for 15 years! (A fourth count against Cohn developed in 1982, two years after my appointment, when, in the course of applying for admission to the District of Columbia Bar, he denied, *under oath*, the existence of these three outstanding complaints).

The First Department's courtroom is a magnificent structure. The roof is a gorgeous stained glass dome. At the bottom, the circumference has a double band inscribed with the names of the justices who have graced that bench. The "Cohn" listed there was Roy's father, who sat on that court until 1955. In 1982, as Chairman of the DDC, I signed a petition asking the justices sitting in that room to disbar Justice Cohn's son on two of the four counts.

Those two counts were based on court decisions that had earlier adjudicated Cohn's conduct as fraudulent: a federal court judgment finding Cohn liable for escrow fraud, and a Florida court decision concluding that he had deceived an elderly client. Because those judgments were final, it was our contention that no additional proof was necessary. The Appellate Division disagreed and ruled that Cohn should have the opportunity to challenge those holdings, and it directed that a Committee Hearing Panel be appointed to hold fact-finding hearings. I appointed a seven-member panel that took evidence during the 20-month period from March 3, 1984 to October 30, 1985. It heard charges based on the two court decisions that were the subject of the first petition, and two other counts that had not earlier been adjudicated. The Panel heard 48 witnesses, examined 170 exhibits, and presided over the taking of 2,445 pages of testimony. It found Cohn guilty of three of the four charged counts, and recommended he be disbarred.

My two-year appointment as DDC chair was scheduled to expire in 1982, and the Presiding Justice asked me to accept appointment to an additional three-year term. I accepted. A lot of work remained to be done in reorganizing and refitting the Committee staff. In 1985, as my second term of office was nearing expiration, the P.J. asked me to serve yet another three-year term. I thanked him for the court's confidence in me, but I asked him to let me go; the Committee and the staff were then functioning efficiently, and the strain on my law practice was unrelenting. I did, however, ask a favor. In my five years on the job, we had disposed of all but one of the "bottom drawer" cases, and I wanted to see the last one through to its conclusion. Would the Court agree to appoint me to continue as "Acting Chair" with respect to that remaining case? Justice Murphy obliged, and the second petition I signed on behalf of the DDC asked the Court to disbar Cohn on the basis of the four discrete charges. The pleading bore this footnote below my signature:

> Pursuant to this Court's Order dated November 21, 1984, the Committee's former Chairman Martin London is Acting Chairman of the Departmental Disciplinary Committee for the First Judicial Department with respect to this proceeding.

Cohn was represented by eminent, indeed nationally distinguished counsel: Harold "Ace" Tyler, and Mike Mukasey, of the New York City firm of Patterson, Belknap,

Webb & Tyler. Tyler was a former Deputy United States Attorney General and a former federal judge, and Mukasey went on to become Chief Judge of the Southern District of New York and thereafter was appointed the Attorney General of the United States. Their effective advocacy on behalf of their client not only forced us to file two petitions, but to make an unprecedented total of six trips to the Appellate Division before procuring a final order concluding the matter.

What did Cohn do? The court reviewed the four counts:

The Schlesinger Note:

Cohn's law firm, Saxe, Bacon & Bolan, had been retained by Mrs. Iva Schlesinger in connection with her divorce from her wealthy South African husband. While much of the work had been done by her previous counsel, Cohn and Bolan concluded the matter in 1965, and under the terms of the separation agreement, her husband paid the Cohn firm's fee of $60,000 in full payment for all services it had rendered to Mrs. Schlesinger in connection with the divorce. Four months later, Cohn needed money, took a check from Mrs. Schlesinger's checkbook, made it out to himself in the amount of $100,000, marked it "loan," and flew to Paris where he met his client and asked her to sign it. She demurred and asked for collateral, but he talked her out of it and she signed the check. He gave her a 90-day promissory note in that amount that also referred to the "loan." For the next *seventeen years*, he evaded her numerous demands for payment. In the ten years before she sued, there were more than 20 documents passing between the parties in which Cohn acknowledged the "loan." He even made a number of partial payments, reducing the principal balance to

$60,000, but that amount remained unpaid. Remarkably, when Mrs. Schlesinger finally sued, Cohn defended by swearing *there was no "loan,"* that the $100,000 was actually an advance payment against future legal services for which his firm could provide no documentary evidence because it did not keep time records, retainer documents, or similar records. In both the Schlesinger litigation in the New York Supreme Court and before the DDC hearing panel, Cohn repeatedly swore that the $100,000 was some sort of "loose arrangement" involving payment for past and future legal services, despite i) all the correspondence in his own hand calling this a "loan," ii) the partial payments he made on the loan, and iii) the lack of any written evidence supporting his "retainer against future services" claim. The Hearing Panel rejected Cohn's absurd explanation. So did the Appellate Division. Basically, the court branded Cohn a perjurer. Noting that he had finally repaid the loan only after Mrs. Schlesinger sued and obtained a judgment, and even then, he satisfied that judgment only after we petitioned for his disbarment, the five-judge court unanimously held that Cohn violated his ethical duties by taking advantage of his client, and that:

> After 10 1/2 years of declaring and acknowledging the transaction to be a loan, [Cohn's] disavowal of such characterization of the transaction, under oath in legal proceedings before the Supreme Court, was untruthful.

"Untruthful" is a fudge word. It is designed to soften the sound, but not the meaning, of "a lie." For some reason, courts frequently find the words "lie," "liar," "perjury," and "perjurer," to be ungentlemanly. But if the shoe fits . . .

The Pied Piper Saga

In 1971, the Securities and Exchange Commission brought a fraud action against the Pied Piper Yacht Company and obtained an order freezing its assets to protect the public investors. The company retained Cohn, who negotiated an escrow agreement for certain assets, including two ships, with Cohn's firm as the escrowee. The agreement was approved by Judge Palmieri of the Southern District federal court.

But Cohn and his partners violated the escrow, and ultimately paid much of the escrowed assets to themselves. The bizarre story involves an escrowed ship that sank while chartered by Cohn to his own firm, and a lawyer named Manley who, one year out of law school, and not a member of the bar, handled a series of court appearances as Cohn's alleged "partner in charge of corporate work." He "dropped out of sight" in Texas, and was "unavailable" to testify in the disbarment proceedings.

Judge Palmieri found Cohn to be in contempt for his blatant violations of the escrow order, and entered a judgment against him and his partners for $219,000, plus interest, costs, and fees. Cohn defended himself before the Disciplinary Committee Hearing Panel and in papers to the Appellate Division by spinning an explanation that the court found to be "incredible" (another familiar fudge word), and the charge against Cohn was sustained.

The Rosenstiel Codicil

Lewis S. Rosenstiel was a multimillionaire philanthropist, and founder of Schenley Distillers. In the Fall of 1975, he was 84 years old, had suffered a debilitating stroke, and had diabetes, high blood pressure, prostate cancer, and "assorted heart and blood disorders." He was effectively blind in one eye, had limited vision in the other, and had symptoms of Alzheimer's disease. When corresponding with his personal attorney Maurice Greenbaum, Rosenstiel required him to read aloud any pertinent documents because of his failing eyesight.

Mr. Rosenstiel entered Miami's Mount Sinai hospital in September, 1976, and never left. He died there four months later. His will had been prepared by Mr. Greenbaum in 1970, and, among other provisions, named Greenbaum and a local Miami bank as executors of his estate and trustees of the trust established in the will. Greenbaum was also trustee of another trust established outside the will.

According to the testimony of hospital personnel, Cohn and his companion David Tackett arrived at the hospital on the night of December 5th, six weeks before Rosenstiel died. They told Rosenstiel's personal attendant they had just come from the airport and asked about Rosenstiel's condition. The attendant told them there was "no change" and the patient was "critical." Nevertheless, they dropped their bags in the corridor and went to Rosenstiel's bedside where they tried to get him to sign a one-page document, but the heavily sedated patient was "almost comatose" and "completely out of it." Cohn took Rosenstiel's hand and tried to get him to sign, but the patient "couldn't move his hand if he tried."

Cohn and Tackett returned the next morning. They ignored the nurses and aides who told them there was an outstanding doctor's order that no business be transacted with the patient, and Cohn assured them that the one-page document he wanted Rosenstiel to sign was just to clear up a small matter with the "Suzie case," i.e., the concluded matrimonial litigation Cohn had earlier handled for Rosenstiel. Cohn was overheard saying to the patient, "Lew,

this is to terminate the affairs of Suzie." The nurse refused
to let Cohn proceed, and refused his request to summon
a notary public as a witness. When she went off to summon the hospital administrator, Cohn said he would have
Tackett witness the signature, and Rosenstiel's medical aide
heard Cohn say, "We will help you sign, Lew." The "signed"
document bears what the Appellate Division later described
as "a number of squiggly lines which in no way resemble
any letters of the alphabet." As Cohn and Tackett left the
hospital room with the "signed" paper, they encountered
the hospital administrator and told him they had been "just
visiting" and "weren't here to get anything signed."

The one-page document had nothing to do with "Suzie."
*It was an amendment to Rosenstiel's will appointing Roy Cohn
as an additional executor of the sizable Rosenstiel estate.* It
also appointed as co-executor one James Finkelstein, whose
family members later submitted some $4.4 million in claims
against the Rosenstiel estate.

In Florida probate proceedings, several of Rosenstiel's
physicians testified their patient lacked the mental competence to make any decisions about business matters
of importance. One physician said the patient was in "a
primitive state bordering on discoordination." Another
said a brain scan two months before Cohn's bedside visit
"revealed marked brain atrophy or senility . . . consistent
with Alzheimer's disease which would cause diminished
comprehension and awareness of surroundings." The
Florida court ultimately struck down the codicil and found
that Cohn had misrepresented the nature of the document
to his client.

Ten years later, when those facts were reviewed by the
DDC Hearing Panel, the charge of unethical conduct was
not sustained. Based largely on testimony of Cohn's partner

Bolan that had been excluded from the Florida proceedings because of evidentiary rulings, the Hearing Panel said it could find no reason for Cohn to have acted in a surreptitious or fraudulent manner. I rejected that conclusion, as did Mike Gentile, and on behalf of the DDC, we petitioned the Appellate Division to find otherwise.

And it did. After examining all the evidence adduced in the Florida and New York hearings, the Appellate Division found Cohn's conduct to be "particularly reprehensible." As to Cohn's testimony that the evidence supplied by the disinterested hospital personnel was "manufactured out of whole cloth," the court found Cohn's claim "strained credulity." Once again, the court found Cohn to be a liar:

> [W]e find [Cohn's] testimony with regard to the events in the hospital on December 6, 1975 to have been [wait for it, wait for it] *untruthful*, misleading, and evidence of highly unprofessional conduct for an attorney-at-law.
>
> Accordingly, we reject the recommendation of the Hearing Panel and hereby sustain [the Rosenstiel] charge.

The Washington D.C. Bar Application

The fourth count in the Cohn proceeding was a charge of perjury in connection with his sworn application for membership in the D.C. bar. Nobody ever accused Cohn of being timid. In July, 1982, while the Schlesinger, Pied Piper, and Rosenstiel complaints were pending, Cohn's application for bar admission read, in part:

> 8. Are any charges or complaints now pending concerning your conduct as an attorney, or as a member of any profession, or as a holder of any public office?

Astonishingly, Cohn answered "No."

The second part of the question asked,

> If so, state the name, and address of the authority in possession of the record thereof.

Having answered "No" to the first part of the question, Cohn should have left the second part blank, but he nevertheless answered:

> Except usual crackpot complaint letters following media appearances, etc.

The Appellate Division found this sworn statement was *"untruthful,"* and rejected Cohn's defense that he just didn't think of the pending complaints because of the Committee's delay in prosecuting them. The court was kind enough to say the charges in the petition I had signed were "certainly much more than usual crackpot complaint letters."

That was not the only lie on Cohn's D.C. Bar application. Question 16 asked:

> Have you ever been adjudged liable in a civil action or proceeding involving a claim of fraud, conversion, breach of fiduciary duty or legal malpractice?

Cohn answered "No."

The Appellate Division said this too was false because in the Pied Piper case, the district judge had found that Cohn and his firm had repeatedly and flagrantly violated the court's escrow order by converting the escrow funds, and ruled that Cohn and each of his partners were individually liable for the entire amount of the conversion. That federal court order clearly required Cohn to answer "Yes" to the question.

And in the matter of the Rosenstiel codicil, the Appellate Division ruled that because the Florida Probate court found that Cohn misrepresented to the decedent, Lewis S. Rosenstiel, the nature, content and purpose of the document that he offered to Mr. Rosenstiel for execution, [the Florida court] order thus constituted a decree of liability against respondent involving "fraud . . . breach of fiduciary duty or legal malpractice."

> [Cohn's] failure, under oath, to disclose these adverse court findings and rulings on his bar application was inexcusable and constituted professional misconduct. The Charge is sustained.

The Appellate Division concluded:

> We find the evidence so compelling on each of these four charges as to leave us no recourse but to order disbarment. Accordingly, respondent should be disbarred, and his name stricken from the roll of attorneys authorized to practice law in this State.

The degree of Cohn's celebrity status was marked by i) the two-inch high letters of the front page of the *New York Daily News* on June 24, 1986: "ROY COHN DISBARRED." There was also an astonishing parade of 36 character witnesses who had attested to "Respondent's good character" and were willing to swear that "Respondent possesses the highest [degree of] integrity." Among the recognizable names among those witnesses were Ms. Barbara Walters and Mr. Donald Trump.

A year before the court's disbarment decision, Cohn explained away the disciplinary charges pending against him in an interview with a reporter from the *Washington Post*. He said that his accusers [i.e., London, Gentile, and the DDC staff] were:

[S]imply left wingers, deadbeats, and a bunch of yo-yos just out to smear me up. . . . What McCarthy was accused of practicing is actually being practiced against me.

Lesson learned. On some cats, the stripes never change.

MANHATTAN ★ ★ ★ ★ SPORTS FINAL

YANKS GET BACK AT BOSOX, 11-3
See Sports

DAILY◎NEWS

35¢   NEW YORK'S PICTURE NEWSPAPER®   Tuesday, June 24, 1986

ROY COHN
DISBARRED

Story on page 3

SANIT MEN WALK OUT OVER FELLOW WORKER

FEAR OF AIDS Striking sanitation workers gather across from garage at Park Ave. and E. 131st St. yesterday to continue protest against return to work of co-worker Levy Wallace (photo right), who they believe has AIDS. **Page 7**

Judging the Judges

John Adams enshrined in the 1780 Massachusetts Constitution the concept of "a government of laws, not of men." That notion is at the heart of the Constitution adopted by the thirteen colonies seven years later, and we remain so proud of it, we have erected statues of blindfolded "Lady Justice" holding balance scales, and we have inscribed over our courthouse entrances the promise of "Equal Justice Under Law," (the latter being an acceptable redundancy.) The weakness in this conceit is the answer to the question, "Who decides what is 'Justice' in any given case?" The equality of our justice is only as good as the wisdom, knowledge, temperament, and good faith of our judges. And it's important to remember that while the blindfolded Lady holds scales in her left hand, she holds a sword in her right. Her power is awesome. When the judge becomes an instrument of injustice, whether willingly or otherwise, it is vital we do something. I did what I could.

✦

Justice Wilfrid Waltemade:

"The Ten Worst Judges in New York" was the cover article in the October 16, 1972 edition of *New York Magazine*.
The piece caused an uproar in certain quarters. Judges are
high priests in the New York legal community. In the state
court system, they are avatars of reigning political power.
While technically "elected," New York judges are, for all
practical purposes, appointed by the political bosses in
their county.

The Jack Newfield piece was based upon his interviews
with lawyers and judges to whom he had promised anonymity,
and like all news reports based on unnamed sources, its accu-
racy can fairly be called into question for that reason. Moreover,
it is considered bad form, if not a breach of judicial ethics, for a
judge to engage in public debate about political or other issues,
and that makes it difficult for them to defend themselves to the
press and the public. At least so goes the argument.

Enter the prestigious Bar Association of the City of New
York. Its leadership declared that it was the duty of the organized bar to do for the judges what they could not do for
themselves, and President Orville H. Schell, Jr. directed the
relevant Association committees to make an independent
investigation of Newfield's charges. This was not to be a
whitewash – the instructions were to "tell it like it is." I was
then a member of the Association committee covering the
Supreme Court of New York County, on which Mr. Justice
Wilfred Waltemade sat. (New York's Supreme Court con-
sists of two levels, a trial court and the Appellate Division.
Supreme Court judges are "Justices." The state's highest
court, the Court of Appeals, is populated by "Judges"). I was
appointed to head an investigation of the article's allegations about Justice Waltemade, who was then in the elev-
enth year of his fourteen-year term.

Newfield's criticism of Waltemade was harsh. The judge often sat in the Matrimonial Part, and in 1972, a New York couple who wanted a consensual divorce was required to engage in a ritualized procedure – after a separation agreement was signed, the plaintiff sued for divorce on the grounds of "cruelty," the defendant defaulted, and the plaintiff went before the judge and swore to a *prima facie* case. Because there was no opposition, it was a "mill," and to speed things up, the court clerk would hand lawyers a form listing the questions to ask and what answers the plaintiff should give to satisfy statutory requirements. The process should take no more than 5 or 10 minutes for each case. But Newfield reported that with Waltemade on the bench:

> It's like visiting an insane asylum. Waltemade screams at the top of his lungs at litigants, lawyers, and even court clerks. He seems totally irrational, the most visibly unstable Supreme Court Justice in the city. He destroys the dignity of the law.

First step, I interviewed the judge. We had a polite conversation in his chambers, and he denied Newfield's allegations. Now the hard part. The only way to find out what really went on in his courtroom was to inquire of the lawyers who were there, but that presented two problems. *First*, lawyers are not eager to go on the record saying bad things about judges before whom they might someday reappear. They even reasonably fear harsh treatment from other judges who might look unkindly upon a lawyer who publicly attacked a member of their exclusive club, and, as a result, the most I could expect to get was a few more not-for-attribution reports. *Second*, while all courtroom testimony is stenographically recorded, matrimonial records are sealed and were not available to me.

When word got out that I was running this inquiry, I received a game-changing telephone call. In 1972, the four Appellate Divisions had the power to admonish or censure judges within their jurisdiction. In extreme cases of misconduct, the Presiding Justice had the power to convene the Court on the Judiciary, a statewide panel headed by the Chief Judge of the Court of Appeals, New York's highest court. That tribunal had the power to remove a judge. Key to the First Department's judicial discipline function was its Judiciary Relations Committee, a group consisting of five judges, two lawyers, and a lay person. The Committee was charged with looking into complaints of judicial misconduct, and then making recommendations to the P.J. Prior to my inquiry, their work had never resulted in a public censure or a reference to the Court on the Judiciary.

The Committee's chief of staff was a lawyer named Gerald Stern (no relation to my partner of the same name), a hard-working straight arrow who was later named Administrator of the New York State Commission on Judicial Conduct when that body was established by constitutional amendment in 1975. When my Waltemade inquiry became known to the Bar, Stern called, introduced himself, and said we had a confluence of interest. His Committee had received a complaint about Waltemade, and he offered up a Christmas present. Would I share my findings with his Committee if the court entered an order giving me access to the sealed matrimonial files of the uncontested Matrimonial Part presided over by Waltemade? That was an easy question to answer. I enlisted my partner Cameron Clark and we went to work on the bushel of transcripts Stern delivered to us.

Getting lawyers to talk to us was now a lot easier. With our new status, we were given work space in the courthouse.

It was only two small carrels in the basement, opposite the staff's lockers and bathrooms, but they had telephones, and when we called lawyers, we could honestly say, "Hi, I am calling from the Appellate Division, on behalf of the Court's Judiciary Relations Committee, to inquire about your experiences before Justice Waltemade on [date]. I have the transcript of your appearance if your memory needs refreshment." What a difference a badge makes.

Our findings were stunning. Newfield was on target, but he was like the blind man who felt only the tail of the elephant. He had no idea how large the creature was.

Waltemade made proceedings before him a shambles. He interrupted the simple scripted testimony with lengthy inquiries that witnesses, especially women, found humiliating. Many were reduced to tears. Just a few examples suffice to paint the picture of this man who demeaned the title "Justice."

In one case, a young woman, a college graduate, seeking no alimony, was subjected to a 20-page barrage of impertinent and leering questions: Where was she living? Alone? How could she afford her $126 monthly rental? When the witness said she planned to move to Hawaii and seek work there, Waltemade said, "As a hula dancer, or what?" When the witness answered that she was a fabric designer, the judge admonished, "In Hawaii, you have to look for work too, you know, you can't stay on the beach all day, do you know that?"

In another case, plaintiff was an airline stewardess, suing for an uncontested divorce on the basis of cruelty. The judge took over the questioning: "Do you live with other stewardesses? *Is it true what they say about stewardesses?* Show me where your husband hit you, show me where he touched you."

And then there was the young man who, in passing, referred to the Philippines as an American "colony." The remark, of course, had nothing to do with the case but the judge went off the deep end, saying that was a "Communist line," and harangued the witness for pages and pages on the subject. He later forced the witness to recant and withdraw the comment!

All these digressions, and dozens of others, consumed court time, humiliated witnesses, frustrated lawyers, and were a great disservice to all involved. Lawyers told us that litigants waiting for their cases to be called, upon observing Waltemade's treatment of those who took the stand, fled the courtroom and abandoned their opportunity to be heard. Lawyers, upon learning who was presiding, adjourned their matters. In the matrimonial bar, there was a prevailing epidemic of "Waltemade Flu." The judge exhibited symptoms of imbalance. He was a disgrace to the bench, and though we sought no psychiatric testimony, the instance where the judge turned to the stars and stripes on the staff to the side of the bench and said, "You're a grand old flag, a high-flying flag, and forever in peace may you wave," actually frightened many of those present. As did an outburst when he saw someone open the door in the back of the courtroom, and apparently recognizing he was in the wrong place, close the door and depart. Waltemade went off the deep end, and railed against "The Peekers, the Peekers, they are always peeking at me!" Scary. Newfield's description of his court being like "an insane asylum" was right on the money.

And I said so in my report to the Bar Association and the Judiciary Relations Committee. The latter group then decided, fairly enough, that the judge was entitled to the opportunity to contest those extreme findings, and for the

first time in its existence, the Committee ordered an evidentiary hearing – before all seven members!

The three-week trial played out in the Appellate
Division's second floor judges' conference room.
Waltemade was defended by the gruff former First
Department Justice James B.M. McNally, who had retired
from the bench just months before our hearing. McNally
was tough, smart, and scrupulous.

(Several years later, I got a call from him at home, and
quaked, but he called to tell me he had been asked for his
opinion respecting my candidacy for Fellowship in the
American College of Trial Lawyers, and he wanted me to
know he gave me an unqualified endorsement.)

There were seven judges in the hearing room. Cameron
Clark and I were surrounded. When I addressed the chair,
it often sounded something like this: "Judge, I object to
Judge McNally's characterization of Judge Waltemade's testimony," etc. It was hard being the only kids on the block
who were not members of the club.

The eight-member panel unanimously sustained the
charges of misconduct, but were evenly split on the remedy: four members thought Waltemade should be censured,
and four thought he should be brought before the Court on
the Judiciary, which had the power to remove him.

The Committee's determination was advisory. Only the
Presiding Justice had the power to submit the charges to
the Court on the Judiciary and P.J. Owen McGivern refused
to do so. But Chief Judge Charles Breitel of the Court of
Appeals, who was also the Chief Judge of the Court on the
Judiciary, received the record and the briefs from what was
said to be an "anonymous source" (it wasn't me, I swear!),
and he convened the Court on the Judiciary on his own
motion. To dispel any notion of bias and to declare its

independence from the Appellate Division's committee, the Court appointed its own counsel to investigate anew, and to draw up a new set of charges, if appropriate. This was, in my view, a colossal waste of time and energy, but given the constitutional scheme at that time, there was no avoiding a new trial on the same evidence, plus any additional evidence my successor, Michael Armstrong (an excellent lawyer) could develop.

After another plenary hearing, the Court on the Judiciary, citing the evidence garnered in the "extensive investigation" done by Cameron and me, as well as additional charges proven by Mike Armstrong, concluded the facts justified removal, but inasmuch as the respondent's term of office was about to expire in a few months, and he said he did not plan to run again, the punishment was limited to public censure. The same political bosses who put Waltemade on the bench in the first place immediately thereafter thumbed their nose at the Court, as did Waltemade, and they tried to nominate him for a new fourteen-year term, but the condemnation was too great, and the Democratic convention turned him down.

Justice Frank Vaccaro:

The Waltemade matter had a significant impact, and by 1976, the judicial discipline scheme in New York State had changed. A permanent State Commission had been created and charged with the duty to investigate and bring charges against judges when that was appropriate. Brooklyn Supreme Court Justice Frank Vaccaro was one the early targets of the Commission. He was charged with numerous counts of perjury and related sins, and The Court on the Judiciary directed a trial of the charges before a Referee, and it appointed Bronx Supreme Court Justice Joseph DiFede to preside at the hearing.

Gerry Stern called me again. "Marty, our staff is overwhelmed. Will you try this case for us?"

Here we go again, *London* v. *The Bench*. At least this judge sat in Brooklyn, where my practice seldom took me. I learned early on that Manhattan lawyers often would not appear there without "local counsel." And the Vaccaro case was a clear demonstration of the wisdom of that advice. The facts were enough to sicken a naive person.

There were eleven perjury and misconduct charges against Vaccaro, and the three-week public trial yielded a verdict of "guilty" on four of them. The "not guilty" counts were perjury charges, which, in my view, had been clearly sustained at trial. I don't want to whine about the built-in bias of trying a judge in front of another judge; that method of discipline is prevalent among lawyers, doctors, and other professions. But it appeared to me that getting a judge to sustain charges against a colleague was an almost insurmountable obstacle. Finding the judge guilty of perjury would surely have required his removal from the bench, so the result was, in my opinion, fashioned to avoid that result.

I had no experience before Justice DiFede, but I sure did know Justice Vaccaro's lawyer – once again I was dealing with Al Julien, my adversary in the Jackie Onassis case.

The Brooklyn law firm of Gerberbaum, Garson & Goldberg had frequently appeared before Mr. Justice Vaccaro. Named partner Gerald Garson, a powerful Brooklyn politician who later became a judge (as did his wife and his brother), was a long-time friend of Frank Vaccaro.

Garson was involved in three of the four sustained charges. The first two related to a vacation at Kutsher's Country Club in the Catskills. Garson, on behalf of Gerberbaum, Garson & Goldberg, treated Justice and Mrs.

Vaccaro to a weekend there. To avoid a written record of this gross violation of legal and judicial ethics, *Vaccaro hid his identity by registering under the name of Garson's partner, Louis Goldberg*! Before the Judicial Conduct Commission, and again in the trial I prosecuted, the judge tried to explain that away by testifying that upon arrival at the hotel, he was exhausted from changing a flat tire on the way up, and he sat in the lobby resting, while others attended to the registration details. He swore that when he had to sign the hotel register, he signed Goldberg's name because he wasn't really thinking. (Huh*?) He insisted he did not intend to deceive anybody into believing he was Goldberg.*

Would *anybody* believe that?

The absurdity of his testimony was enhanced on cross-examination. If he did not intend to deceive anybody into believing he was Goldberg, could he please explain to the court why *his wife also used the name "Goldberg" when she signed spa and other hotel chits*? Ahh, he could not. I thought a finding of perjury was open and shut. I was naive.

That's not all. The clincher, I believed, was a number of long distance telephone calls made that weekend from his room, to a telephone number in area code 914. All outside calls were made through the hotel switchboard, and those records showed that the calls were made by somebody who identified himself as "Mr. Goldberg." The judge swore he did not make those calls, and he had no idea of the identity of the "Mr. Goldberg" who made the calls *from his room!* Moreover, he swore the 914 telephone number was unfamiliar to him and he had no idea whose number it was. His entire story collapsed when I confronted him with a reverse telephone directory that showed the number *belonged to the judge's sister-in-law!* Only then did the witness surrender and "remember" it was indeed he who made the calls, and that he used the name Goldberg to do so. Open and shut, right? His earlier testimony was a lie, right? Not so fast. Referee DiFede found Vaccaro *did not attempt to deceive or lie under oath*! Instead, DiFede concluded that Justice Vaccaro had *"an incredibly bad memory."* I think the Referee missed the irony of his finding. "Incredibly" means "not credible," "not believable," "not truthful."

Instead of the obviously appropriate perjury finding, DiFede twisted himself into a pretzel and concluded that "although Respondent may not have intended to conceal his identity, he did create the objective impression on the records of the hotel that he was Louis Goldberg, which was injudicious and in violation of the Canons of Judicial Ethics."

Whuh?

The hotel registration incident yielded a verdict of misconduct on two counts: i) accepting a gift from a lawyer who had cases before the judge, and ii) registering under a false name.

The third sustained count was also based on misconduct involving Garson. Years earlier, Garson had been sued in Small Claims Court by a fuel oil dealer for non-payment of his heating oil bill of several hundred dollars. Vaccaro was then sitting on the lower level Civil Court, and was obliged to take his turn presiding over the "night court" where claimants could get "justice" without the expense of hiring lawyers. Garson repeatedly adjourned the matter until his friend Vaccaro cycled onto the Small Claims Part, then insisted on a trial. Judge Vaccaro himself undertook a withering cross-examination of the hapless heating oil merchant who must have thought he had stumbled into a world of Martians, or more pertinently, a scene from Kafka. Of course, neither Vaccaro nor Garson revealed their close friendship, and the matter was concluded with Garson paying the beleaguered tradesman $106.81. In some respects, I found the transcript of that "trial" more sickening than the other charges.

The fourth sustained count involved *Vaccaro presiding over settlements of cases in which his law clerk's law partner was counsel!* He did not deny doing so.

The Court on the Judiciary concluded:

> We find no evidence in this record of corruption . . . or of a repeated and unrelenting display of non-judicial temperament (see Matter of Waltemade). Accordingly, removal is unwarranted . . . and Respondent is suspended for six months without pay.

In some matters, you take what you can get.

The story is not complete without mentioning some interesting subsequent developments of which I was only an observer.

Four years later, lawyer Julien and Justice DiFede were back in the same courtroom, only this time, *Julien was defending DiFede,* **against charges that DiFede accepted gifts from a lawyer who regularly appeared before him!** The charges were sustained, and the judge was publicly admonished.

Four years after that, Gerald Garson was admonished by Brooklyn's Second Department Disciplinary committee for his involvement in the Kutsher's Country Club incident with Vaccaro.

Nevertheless, thirteen years later, in 1997, the same Gerald Garson was selected by the Brooklyn Democratic leadership to be their candidate for an open seat on the Supreme Court! He was, of course, elected to a fourteen-year term, but his time on the bench was cut short upon his commencement of a stretch in state prison after a conviction for accepting bribes to fix divorce cases. His marketing turned out to be too effective. A woman approached his "fixer" when she heard that for $5,000 she could fix her divorce case pending before Garson, but the "fixer" told her she was too late, the judge had already been hired by her husband! The scorned client reported the matter to the Brooklyn District Attorney's office, which wired Garson's chambers. He was sentenced to three to ten years in the penitentiary.

The New York Times nailed it with its comment about the Garson conviction:

> It was news that confirmed every sneaking suspicion, every paranoid fantasy, of anyone who had ever felt wronged in a divorce court.

Sometimes I am not so proud to be a lawyer.

Part III:
NATIONAL POLITICS

Trumping Trump

"The rich have a very low threshold for pain."
Donald Trump (Christmastime, 1985)

In his successful campaign for the Presidency in 2016, Mr. Trump's track record was such that some in the Republican Party leadership abandoned ship. The candidate's language and demeanor raised questions not only about his competence and integrity, but his psychological blueprint as well. If he really were a bully, as so many of his detractors claimed, was that a characteristic recently acquired as a result of his successful television reality show, or had it been "baked in" well before that?

A litigation I handled long before Trump's TV turn supplies an answer that does not surprise. A wealthy businessman can often impose his will on commercial adversaries who lack the wherewithal to get what's coming to them. But for those who can hold on long enough to get to a court, the result is not only satisfying to the client, but makes the *successful lawyer feel good about his craft. Bullying some-times doesn't work against judges, or against adversaries who can persist long enough to get a judge to hear the case.*

✦

Two weeks before Christmas, 1985, my friend Rick Fischbein came to see me with a tale that still makes me shudder. Rick was the managing partner of a small, successful New York City law firm when he got a call from his bank informing him that they were freezing his firm's account because he and his partners were being sued in federal court for 105 million dollars. The civil complaint alleged the firm had violated the federal statute that made it a crime to "participate in the conduct of an enterprise's affairs through a pattern of racketeering activity." Yup, Rick and his partners were accused of violating the federal statute enacted to rein in the mob – RICO, which stands for Racketeer Influenced and Corrupt Organizations. The same day he got the call from the bank, Rick and his partners read about the civil complaint in the *New York Post* – three days before they were served with the document. That brings new sting to "Honey, today I had a bad day at the office."

What was this about? The Fischbein firm often defended the rights of tenants. They were very good at what they did, and they had been retained by the occupants of an apartment house recently acquired by a company owned by Donald Trump (hereinafter "Trump"), which applied to demolish the building. In an effort to safeguard the tenants' right to remain in their homes, the Fischbein firm attempted to thwart the demolition by instituting a series of state court proceedings and complaints to administrative agencies. None of this was unprecedented lawyering. It was, then and now, a reasonably common pattern employed by other lawyers in similar situations. Indeed, the complaint specifically alleged that the defendant lawyers had used similar "tactics" as their "*modus operandi*" in other proceedings on behalf of other tenant groups against other landlords.

But none of those other landlords accused the tenants' lawyers of violating the RICO statute by means of their zealous lawyering on behalf of their clients.

The foundational allegation of the Trump pleading shows just how far Trump was willing to go to crush the tenants by crippling their lawyers. The pleading, as described by the District Court judge,

> [A]lleges that the [Fischbein] law firm engaged in the course of proscribed conduct through the enterprises of the New York courts, the DHCR [NY State Department of Housing], and the Corporation Counsel. ***This presents the question of whether a defendant can violate RICO by participating as a mere litigant in a court system or before an administrative agency.*** [Emphasis mine.]

Trump basically alleged that by petitioning for judicial and administrative action to bar the demolition of the building, the defendants had used the New York courts and administrative agencies as a RICO enterprise, ***despite the lack of any allegation that anyone in the court system or any administrative agency had been corrupted, or had done anything other than receive and lawfully act upon the pleadings and petitions filed by Fischbein on behalf of his clients.*** (In fact, up to the time when the Trump lawsuit was commenced, the courts had denied all of the Fischbein motions!)

Promptly after we obtained a copy of Trump's complaint, we secured an immediate court conference with

Judge Whitman Knapp, the federal judge to whom the case had been assigned. He granted our request for an expedited schedule for our planned motion to dismiss the complaint for legal insufficiency.

We also sought permission to move, under a federal procedural rule, to sanction Trump and his lawyer and require them to pay my clients' legal fees. We had two grounds for that latter motion: i) Trump's claim was frivolous, and ii) the case was instituted for an improper purpose; it was not brought to gain recompense in connection with an injury incurred by reason of defendants' wrongful conduct, but was motivated by plaintiff's desire to malign and intimidate the tenants' lawyers in order to gain an unfair advantage in Trump's legal dispute with Fischbein's clients.

The judge agreed to an early hearing of our motion to dismiss, but our motion for sanctions would be held in abeyance until after his decision on the merits, and that of any appeals court. The schedule was tight; the complaint had been served on my clients on December 16th, we had a conference with the judge on December 20th, we worked over the Christmas holiday and filed and served our motion to dismiss the complaint on December 26th. Trump amended his complaint on December 30th, and the court heard a lengthy argument on our motion to dismiss the amended complaint on January 10th. On January 23rd, a little over one month after the complaint was filed and first reported on in the *New York Post*, the District Court handed down an opinion that included a detailed discussion of each of Trump's allegations of "racketeering activity" and concluded that *even assuming every fact Trump pleaded were true, there was no legal basis for the RICO charge.* The court dismissed the complaint "with prejudice." That means it cannot be repleaded, amended, whatever. It was done. Cooked.

There were two bases for Judge Knapp's decision. First, he ruled there was no RICO enterprise. On the question of "whether a defendant can violate RICO by participating as a mere litigant in a court system or before an administrative body," the court noted there was no allegation that anyone in the courts or administrative agencies had been corrupted or had engaged in any wrongdoing, and he therefore concluded:

> Mere use of the courts as a litigant does not satisfy the [RICO] requirement that the defendant . . . "participate in the conduct" of the court's affairs. Therefore, a litigant cannot transform the court system into an illegal enterprise **absent some complicity with an employee of that court** . . . [emphasis mine.]

Second, as an independent ground for dismissal, the judge examined each of the acts allegedly constituting "racketeering activity." One of them was Trump's allegation that Fischbein partner Herman Badillo, who had what the court described as a "tenuous" association with a member of the Housing Department, told Trump that the proceedings in that agency were "rigged." (We didn't know then how much Mr. Trump was inclined to rely on that word). Badillo called the allegation "absurd," but the court found that even if that allegation and *everything else* in the complaint were *true*, plaintiff's allegations did not meet the statutory test for "a pattern of racketeering activity."

Of course, Trump appealed. Hey, it's only legal fees for him – more pressure on the little guy. At the argument in the Second Circuit Court of Appeals, I offered up a bit of humor. Though the harm inflicted on my client by the pendency of this claim was hardly a trifling matter, I opened with, "Your Honors, I argue today with some trepidation, lest I later find that in urging my clients' cause before this tribunal, I am accused of participating in a RICO enterprise." I don't recall any of the three judges chuckling, but I did get a few quick smiles.

The Court of Appeals didn't waste any time. On April 25, 1986, just four and a half months after Trump filed his complaint, the appellate court unanimously affirmed the dismissal of Trump's RICO complaint "for the reasons stated in the district court opinion," and sent the case back to the district court to decide the pending motion for sanctions against both Trump and his lawyer.

Now my turn at bat. Yogi got it right, it wasn't over till it was *over*. Back in the District Court, we supplemented our motion for monetary sanctions. We pointed out that now *all four federal judges* who had examined this pleading had concluded it was barren of legal sufficiency. That was not a close question – the claim was clearly not "warranted by existing law or a good faith argument for extension, modification or reversal of existing law." It was patently frivolous, and on that ground alone, we were entitled to sanctions.

But, belt and suspenders, we again pressed our second basis for sanctions: the lawsuit was instituted for improper purposes.

We pointed out the complaint had been given to the *New York Post* three days before it was served on my clients. In two articles prompted by Trump's representative, the paper quoted Trump as telling the *Post*, "I don't like being pushed around and now they're beginning to learn it," and, classic Trump, "The rich have a very low threshold for pain."

My sanctions brief to the district court argued:

> The real reason for this frivolous action against defendants is not difficult to discern. [Trump's] goal could

not have been to win *this* case. Instead, [Trump] hoped
to stop defendants from so effectively representing
their clients . . . By attacking defendants' ardent advocacy . . . as "racketeering activity," [Trump] hoped to
force them to restrain their efforts...

The clincher, I believe, was the final paragraphs of our
brief and moving affidavit:

> Defendants believe the record is already replete
> with evidence of [Trump's] improper purpose, and
> that no more is needed to levy sanctions against
> [Trump] and his counsel. If this court is not so per-
> suaded, defendants seek permission to fill out the
> record and demonstrate the full of extent of [Trump's]
> malicious intent....
>
> If, and only if the court deems it necessary to the
> decision of this motion, we ask the court's leave . . .
> to conduct a brief deposition of Donald Trump on
> issues relevant to this motion . . . .

We never did get to take Mr. Trump's deposition.
Fischbein and his partners had big smiles on their faces,
and Rick had a new framed memento for his office wall.
Trump had paid, and Fischbein framed a copy of the check
and hung it on his office wall.

Hmm . . . is there a lesson here that informs our national
political discussions? Will the weight of the office temper
President Trump's approach to conflict, or will he play
hardball with the Iranians, or the Chinese, or the Russians?
WWPTD? (New bumper-sticker-speak for "What Will
President Trump Do?") What if, like my clients, the adversary refuses to buckle in the face of bully tactics, and not
only holds its ground, but fights back?

And for fun, another "what-if" – what if President Trump's bright son-in-law and key advisor, Jared Kushner, who in 2005, spent the time between his second and third years at Harvard Law School working as a Paul, Weiss summer associate, had been on the scene thirty years earlier? My bet? Trump wouldn't have sued the Fischbein firm in the first place.

Hubert Humphrey for President

I don't know how many other lawyers out there have repre- sented two Vice Presidents of the United States of America. Hey, stuff comes in, and you work the problem. My first Veep representation was Spiro Agnew's predecessor. Hubert Humphrey, however, faced no criminal charges. He was just seeking a promotion.

✦

It is often said that World War II was our last "good" war. That may be arguable, but for sure, there is virtual universal agreement that Vietnam is an outstanding icon for a "bad" one. After he was elected in 1964, President Lyndon Johnson announced his determination to bring that war to an end by winning it.

There were 16,000 U.S. troops in Vietnam when Johnson became President in 1963, and 500,000 by the end of March, 1968. The President's efforts had been an obvious failure. The war was going badly, and the U.S. citizenry was bitterly divided. The divisions were so serious that the sitting President was challenged by members of his own party for the Democratic nomination for the coming election contest in November, 1968. In December, 1967, Minnesota Senator Eugene McCarthy opened an impressive primary campaign, running on an anti-war platform. In mid-March, 1968, JFK's younger brother Robert F. Kennedy threw his hat in the ring and challenged McCarthy for the leadership of the anti-war faction.

With two anti-war adversaries from his own party snapping at his heels, on March 31, 1968, Johnson virtually conceded his win-the-war strategy had failed, and announced he would not seek re-election. His speech threw Democratic Party national politics into disarray. The following month, with the primary season all but over, Vice President Hubert Humphrey declared his candidacy, and it became a three-way race for the nomination, until the unimaginable happened: in June, Bobby Kennedy was assassinated! The two surviving candidates, anti-war McCarthy, and sitting Vice President Humphrey, battled it out in Chicago two months later.

The contest was bitter, both inside the convention hall and out. Humphrey won the nomination, but the combined lawlessness of the demonstrators and Mayor Daley's police was to become an issue in the Humphrey/Nixon contest in November.

In New York State, the Democratic Party, by virtue of past performance, was entitled to a line on the ballot, and it had put up a slate of 43 citizens who committed themselves, if elected in November, to cast their ballots for Humphrey when the Electoral College met in December. A second group had qualified, by petition, to get a line on the New York ballot under the label of the newly formed "Coalition

Party," and their would-be electors had pledged to vote for Eugene McCarthy.

The week after he lost the Democratic Convention contest, McCarthy issued a formal statement declining "any and all nominations I may receive." Accordingly, the New York Secretary of State printed ballot cards for the voting machines without a line for the McCarthy electors. A Coalition Party electoral candidate sued. He lost in the trial court and appealed.

In a stunning blow to the Humphrey camp, the Appellate Division reversed. It held that under New York's Election Law, candidates for public office are qualified if they accept their nomination, and the Coalition Party candidates for the post of elector had accepted their nomination as delegates. It was the electors who were the candidates in November, not the person for whom they said they would vote in December. The court directed the Secretary of State to put a line on the ballot under the Coalition Party label, reading, "Presidential Electors for Eugene J. McCarthy for President."

This was a potential calamity for the Humphrey forces. New York's 43 electors were a material part of the 270-vote majority needed for election. New York, like most others, was an all-or-nothing state: the candidate with the greatest number of popular votes wins all the electors. If the McCarthy supporters could get on the ballot and split the Democratic vote, the state could go to Richard Nixon. Time was short. The appellate court decision came down on October 7th, four weeks before Election Day, and in the interim the state election officials had to print and install the necessary ballot cards in some 14,000 lever-action mechanical voting machines with all the local candidates in proper order.

Up to that point, the court contest had been between a McCarthy elector named Robert M. Ginsberg, and the N.Y.

Secretary of State, Mr. John P. Lomenzo. Hubert Humphrey retained Paul, Weiss partner Eddie Costikyan, and John Dickey from Sullivan & Cromwell, to seek Court of Appeals permission for Humphrey to intervene in the litigation and prosecute an appeal from the Appellate Division's decision. Eddie invited me to help. I loved the drama. The adverse appellate decision came down on October 7th, 1968. The Court of Appeals granted our motion to intervene and set a crash schedule. We were required to file our brief on October 15th, were heard in the Court of Appeals on October 16th, and that Court decided the matter on October 17th.

Oral Argument

The New York Court of Appeals courtroom in Albany is a classic. Beautiful paneled walls, impressive dark woods, cork floors, high ceilings, even the seats are comfortable. Costikyan, Dickey, and London departed New York City before dawn on the 16th to drive up to Albany. We arrived hours before the court opened for business.

Well before the 10 a.m. call of the calendar, the courtroom was packed. Spectators stood along the back and side walls. Word had gotten out that Vice President Humphrey had chosen Paul, Weiss's new partner Arthur Goldberg to argue in a case that could decide the national election. Goldberg, who had a distinguished career as Secretary of Labor, Justice of the United States Supreme Court, and United States Ambassador to the United Nations, had joined the firm just months earlier. Though Eddie and I and Dickey had written the brief and fashioned the theory of the appeal, we were going to be observers to this historic argument.

Goldberg had been in Washington D.C. on the day before the argument, and instead of coming to New York that evening, he accepted a Humphrey supporter's offer of a ride on a small jet from D.C. to Albany on the morning of the court appearance. But whatever his other qualifications, Mr. Justice Goldberg was not a Rifkind-trained lawyer and thus did the unthinkable. He violated the absolute first rule for litigators: **Be in court when your case starts.** A few minutes before 10 a.m., the three of us were sitting in the front row (our case was first on the calendar) and saving a seat for Goldberg, when a clerk came over and handed us a note. Goldberg's pilot had radioed in a message that they had encountered fog and our champion would be an hour late! This was Goldberg's first court appearance as a Paul, Weiss partner, indeed his first court appearance since he left the Supreme Court bench, and he didn't get to the church on time. Not a good career start.

Eddie and I talked it over. He was totally relaxed and said, "Okay, Marty, you handle the calendar call." When Chief Judge Fuld called our case, I went to the lectern, explained the delay and asked the court to move our case to the bottom of the calendar. Motion granted. I returned to my seat and with a chuckle, whispered to Eddie, "Hey, we're on a roll. I have already won the first motion of the day, so if Goldberg doesn't show, I'll take the argument, okay?" Eddie laughed, and said, "London, in your dreams, I got this one!" And we sat and waited and listened to the other arguments. I was impressed by Costikyan's *sangfroid*. I would have been frantically scribbling my back-up argument. This was a case that could decide the Presidency! But Eddie just sat back and seemed to enjoy the arguments.

Mr. Justice Goldberg arrived about half way through the calendar. I can still see the picture. He was wearing a light gray silky suit that looked as if he had slept in it. The wrinkles had wrinkles. As did his brow. When our case was called, he approached the lectern, pulled out of his breast pocket a 4"x 6" gummed-at-the-top notepad upon which he had written his argument with a felt tip pen. He clearly was uncomfortable being in the well and not on the bench and proceeded to *read* what was written on the wrinkled pages. As if that weren't bad enough, he committed the unpardonable sin of reading the same page twice. I wanted to hide under my chair.

The next day, October 17th, the Court rendered a unanimous decision that I suspect had been prepared in advance. The court concluded:

> In the present case, Senator McCarthy unequivocally and formally notified the Secretary of State that, far from giving consent, he was "declining any and all nominations which I may receive for the office of candidate for the President and/or Vice President of the United States" . . . Having chosen a candidate who is unwilling to have his name thus used, the proposed electors . . . are disqualified.

Our efforts were in vain. Humphrey carried New York State, but Mr. Nixon and his running mate, who would later become my client, campaigned across the land under a "Law and Order" banner, and won the general election by 2 million popular votes and 101 electoral votes.

So now hanging on my office wall are "thank-you" endorsed photographs of two former Vice Presidents of the United States. No Presidents – yet.

To Martin London — with best wishes
Hubert H Humphrey

THE VICE PRESIDENT

WASHINGTON

October 24, 1968

Dear Mr. London:

Ambassador Goldberg and Ed Costikyan have informed me of the very fine work you did on my
behalf in connection with the litigation in the matter of the New York State ballot. I can't tell you
how much I appreciate what you did.

Please accept my heartfelt thanks.

Sincerely,

Hubert H. Humphrey

Martin London, Esquire
Paul, Weiss, Goldberg, Rifkind,
    Wharton and Garrison
575 Madison Avenue
New York, New York 10022

Part IV:

JUST PLAIN
HARD WORK
AND LEARNING
NEW STUFF

"The Lady in the Flowered Dress"

S *ooner or later, most cases come out right, and justice is done. Many judges I know are wont to say juries get it right 90% of the time. I don't believe that, but happily the system has mechanisms to repair some jury errors.*

In 1991, Armstrong World Industries, Inc., incurred a staggering $240 million adverse jury verdict in the federal district court in Newark. This, despite the fact that it was represented by a distinguished Washington, D.C. law firm while the plaintiff was represented by a solo practitioner. Our assignment was to change that result in a retrial that lasted four months. We had no magic bullet, no Constitutional principle overlooked the first time around. What we had going for us, was us.

✦

When I was a child, all the floors in our apartment were covered by something called "linoleum." So was everyone else's on the block. The product came in large rolls, was cut to size, and glued down. The manufacture and sale of that floor covering was a very large business, and in 1984, Armstrong World Industries was a dominant supplier in the U.S. market. It sold to wholesalers, who, in turn, distributed it to local hardware and paint stores, lumber yards, and other retailers.

In 1983, Mr. Elliot Fineman, via his corporation The Industry Network Systems, Inc. (TINS), approached flooring product wholesalers, many of whom sold Armstrong's products, with a unique idea: he offered to sell them a monthly video magazine subscription that they could "tag" with their own message and, in turn, resell to their retailers. He urged that his video magazine would increase the wholesalers' sales to retailers, and the latters' sales to consumers. But TINS and Armstrong tangled over the sale of the program to wholesalers who carried Armstrong products, and TINS accused Armstrong of illegally interfering with its prospective customers. In December, 1983, the parties settled their dispute. But TINS later claimed Armstrong breached the settlement agreement, and sued in the New Jersey federal district court for: i) breach of the settlement agreement, ii) interfering with the TINS' business prospects, and iii) violating the antitrust laws.

That case was tried in 1991 before District Judge John Bissell and a jury, sitting in Newark, New Jersey. Plaintiff was represented by solo practitioner Steven M. Kramer, who had an office in New York City, and Armstrong was represented by the distinguished Covington firm of Washington, D.C. Each side employed New Jersey counsel as well. Plaintiff retained the firm of Crummy, Del Deo, and Armstrong used the firm of Stryker, Tams, with its partner Edith Payne as the Stryker lawyer working on the case.

The jury found for TINS on all counts and rendered the $240 million verdict.

The Covington firm petitioned Judge Bissell to grant a new trial on several grounds, one of which was that the misconduct of plaintiff's lawyer, Steven Kramer, poisoned the record. With a $240 million verdict at stake, TINS upped the legal star power of its team, and recruited the Honorable John Gibbons, the distinguished former Chief Judge of the Third Circuit Court of Appeals, and Professor Laurence Tribe of the Harvard Law School, to resist Armstrong's demand for a "do over." But even the brilliance and distinction of Messrs. Gibbons and Tribe could not overcome the facts; Judge Bissell granted Armstrong's motion, and threw out the jury verdict. He ruled there was a reasonable probability the jury's verdict was influenced by the improper conduct of plaintiff's trial lawyer, who, he noted, had earlier been sanctioned by other courts in the Third Circuit. The district judge found:

> Mr. Kramer, during the course of his closing arguments in particular, repeatedly testified to his own truthfulness and trustworthiness, . . . supplied "facts" not in the record about what he knew, didn't know, found out, etc., . . . expressed his opinion, on countless occasions, that Armstrong concealed information and lied during the course of the trial. . . .
> Perhaps most troubling to this Court is the unadorned disparaging attack on defense counsel. . . . [Kramer] continued to refer to defense counsel as liars . . . and in a particularly egregious example of misconduct, . . . inferred that one defense attorney either counselled a witness to lie (as was suggested by the language he used) or engaged in sexual misconduct with a witness (as was suggested by his tone and the innuendo inherent in his statements.)

The judge quoted from Kramer's summation:

> Look, when [defense witness Alan Abrahamson] got up here on the witness stand after spending 22 hours with Edith Payne holed up in a conference room, God knows what he was doing for 22 hours for three hours of testimony.

and

> That's perjury. He's admitting it. I cannot believe my ears. I really cannot. This is the same Alan Abrahamson, yeah, Ms. Payne's in the room. She's in the second row. There, flowered dress. She spent 22 hours in a conference room with Alan Abrahamson.

and

> I know what they did. You know what they did. I don't have to tell you what they did during those 22 hours.

Judge Bissell found:

> At the very least, the obviously intentional double entendre inherent in these crude statements was calculated to amuse the jury by personal embarrassment of defendant's co-counsel. . . .
>
> Thus, the essence of Mr. Kramer's closing concerning defense counsel was that counsel had lied to the jury, had suborned perjury from witnesses (flavoring these comments with the titillating remarks regarding Ms. Payne), and had done so for money.

(Some years after the end of this litigation, lawyer Edith Payne, "the lady in the flowered dress," went on to have a distinguished career as a trial and appellate judge on the New Jersey Superior Court. Lawyer Steven Kramer, on the other hand, was disbarred. The New York court cited 38 instances in which Kramer had been criticized or sanctioned by courts.) The

Gibbons/Tribe legal team ably prosecuted an appeal from Judge Bissell's decision, but the Third Circuit, noting Mr. Kramer's "particularly offensive summation," unanimously opined it was "clearly convinced" that Judge Bissell's decision was correct.

The first trial result having been erased, the battle was to be fought anew. For the rematch, the legal roster was entirely different: TINS retained two powerful plaintiff's law firms: Milberg, Weiss, and the Cotchett, Pitre law firms from California. Armstrong retained me and my partners, the late Cameron Clark, and first-year partner Jeh Johnson. The second time around it was a different ball game.

We faced several issues that I have never encountered before, or since. Picture this, please: during the first trial, one of the Armstrong lawyers (not "the lady in the flowered dress") prepared an important witness in a restaurant. While they discussed the planned testimony, the lawyer allegedly made derisive remarks about the racial composition of the jury. At some point, the Armstrong lawyer heard what sounded like the clicking of computer keys, turned around, and saw plaintiff's lawyer Steven Kramer sitting in the booth behind him, tapping away on his laptop, apparently getting down every word. The Armstrong lawyer was outraged, and demanded Kramer trash his notes. Kramer refused. The next day, before the jury was in the box, Armstrong's counsel reported the facts to Judge Bissell, and asked him to bar any use of the overheard conversation between lawyer and witness. Bissell denied the application, saying, in substance, "Look, if you're foolish enough to prepare your witness in a public restaurant where anybody could overhear the conversation, I'm not going to make any blanket rulings. When the witness is cross examined, and you have an objection to a specific question, I'll rule on it at that time." Armstrong's counsel couldn't risk having the plaintiff reveal the alleged comments to the jury, and decided not to call the witness.

We wanted this witness' testimony. *We* had not said anything to the witness about that jury's racial composition, the witness's testimony was about events in 1984, and prior counsel's restaurant remarks in 1991 were totally irrelevant to this trial before this 1994 jury. Moreover, the judge had earlier ruled the jury was not to learn there was a prior trial.

Jeh applied to the judge for a ruling barring any use of Armstrong's former lawyer's alleged statements about the 1991 jury. The judge ruled he would listen to the witness' planned testimony outside the presence of the jury to determine whether counsel's earlier remarks were in any way relevant to the substance of what the witness had to say. We did that, the judge barred use of the prior lawyer's alleged racial slurs, the witness testified, no problem.

Cameron had to deal with two other unique witness issues. In another "first," one of TINS' witnesses – a minority shareholder – was a woman of such girth, she literally could not leave her home because she was too large to get through the doorway, and there was no effective way to transport her to the courtroom! Plaintiff had medical testimony and photographs to back up that claim. The judge ruled her testimony was to be taken in her home, and the video could be played to the jury. I was happy that cross-examination chore was Cameron's, not mine. Another of Cameron's crosses was of an elderly gentleman who was an expert witness for TINS. The retiree literally did not know what he was talking about, and Cameron skillfully demonstrated as much without insulting the very senior citizen. Impressive.

I had one personal hiccup. The trial started in April and ended in August. At some point, I had switched from wearing my winter suits to my lighter weight summer ones. I was cross-examining a witness when I absent-mindedly stuck my right hand into my jacket pocket and felt a plastic bag. I had failed to have the suit cleaned in the fall. The plastic bag was there because I had one in every piece of clothing I owned so that I would be prepared when our beloved Labrador Retriever "Maggie" took a dump on the New York City streets. But Maggie had suffered an untimely end from cancer weeks before the trial, and the plastic bag brought back a rush of memories so powerful I was overwhelmed. I literally could not go on. When I faltered, I asked for a recess. Perhaps he saw the distress on my face; Judge Bissell never asked why. He just banged his gavel and gave me some time to compose myself.

The Summations

In the four-month trial, we examined scores of witnesses, and offered in evidence hundreds of exhibits. The key elements of the lengthy trial are cogently revealed in the summations. Following New Jersey practice, defendant went first, and then was not heard from again.

I focused on two major themes.

The first attack was directed at the TINS claim that it was Armstrong's wrongful interference that caused a key wholesaler to decide not to buy TINS' video magazine, which in turn precipitated a cascade of failures that led to TINS' collapse. We had two arguments in opposition:

a) Armstrong did not interfere with the wholesaler's consideration of the TINS magazine, and, even if it had,

b) the video magazine project failed because of the poor quality of the magazines. TINS had produced a high-quality promotional video that it used very effectively to sell subscriptions to the wholesalers, but, we argued, the evidence showed the monthly magazines failed to live up to the promise of the promotional video. Some customers even refused to pay for the magazines. To emphasize those facts, I argued that TINS, by employing the higher quality promotional video as its sales tool, had effectively sold the wholesalers "a pig in a poke." But before I put that idiom to work, I tasked our stalwart team of Maria Keane and Bob Kravitz to dig out its derivation. As much as I liked the phrase, I loved the derivation more: "poke" is from the French word "poche," meaning a sack. When a naive customer went to market to buy a small pig for his family's meal, a dishonest merchant would show him the desirable piglet, but surreptitiously put a cat instead of the pig in the sack. When the rube got home with his "pig in a poke" and untied the sack, "the cat was out of the bag." Two idioms for the price of one. I thought the jury loved the explanation. I came back to the "pig in a poke" metaphor over and over again, (and was happy to see plaintiff's lawyer repeatedly remind the jury of the analogy in his summation.)

I also did a number with one of Fineman's high-pressure sales techniques, which was to tell small dealers the videos were expressly designed for small dealers, and tell large dealers the videos were expressly designed for large dealers. I analogized this to the clothing salesman who pulls the suit jacket tight or loose, depending on the customer's concerns. I did a physical stunt with my suit jacket. I loved it and the jury laughed. I thought they got the message.

At the end of that trial day, when we were back in the office we rented across the street from the courthouse, Jack Jordin, the Armstrong Vice President who sat at our table during the trial, made his daily telephone report to Armstrong headquarters. He told them he loved my summation. He called it "Shakespearean." Cameron overheard him and doubled us all over when he cracked, "Shakespeare? More like Borscht Belt!"

My second major summation theme was that even if the jury concluded that Armstrong *had* interfered with TINS' efforts to sell its video magazine, *TINS was not entitled to any damages because there was no compensable injury. No matter what Armstrong did or did not do, TINS was a failed enterprise from the start, had no prospects of financial success, and TINS' effort to prove otherwise was not credible.*

The burden of proving plaintiff's damage case rested primarily on the shoulders of Mr. Elliot Fineman, the founder, principal owner, and CEO of TINS, and the company's salesman extraordinaire. Over our objection, the judge had ruled he was qualified as an expert and this allowed him not only to give his version of the facts, but testify to his opinions as well. He testified for days. In addition to giving his version of conversations with Armstrong's executives and wholesalers, he also testified about TINS' sales projections, its likelihood of success, meeting plan targets, and the financial consequences of Armstrong's alleged interference with what he described as a promising business. Fineman's major theme was that his **business plan** projected a 30-million-dollar annual net income, and though TINS had never before made a profit, his plan would have succeeded but for Armstrong's wrongful conduct.

In short, the TINS business plan was the foundation stone of its damage claim, and Elliot Fineman was not only the architect of the plan, but he was the chief executive officer charged with its execution. His testimony was the key evidence establishing TINS' damage claim construct.

Crafting the cross-examination of Fineman was a major enterprise. There was no doubt from day one as to what my major attack would be. As I told the jury in my summation:

> His Honor will instruct you that if you conclude that a witness in this case has testified falsely under oath, you are free to disbelieve not only the testimony you believe to be false, but you can choose to disbelieve every word that witness has said. . . .
>
> I respectfully suggest to you that is what you should do with the witness Elliot Fineman. You should reject every syllable he has uttered from that chair, every syllable, because he has dishonored his oath so completely, so thoroughly, that he is a totally unreliable person.

In that summation, I pointed to more than twenty instances where we thought his testimony was contradicted, either by his own admission, or by other evidence. I thought the mass of contradictions in Fineman's testimony was overwhelming, but in two areas in particular, his testimony on cross was most dramatic. It is every cross-examiner's dream to hear a witness say the equivalent of, "Yeah, I testified falsely under oath." We came very close to that in this case.

First, in supplemental discovery before the second trial, we found a letter Fineman had written to a bank **in December, 1983**, seeking to borrow money for TINS. **The date is important because Fineman claimed that Armstrong had interfered with and damaged TINS during that calendar year.** The progression of his testimony on that subject is best illustrated by excerpts from my summation as I walked the jury through the evidence:

> [Fineman] was on the witness stand, and we were talking about his business, . . . and I asked him if he ever sought to borrow money from a bank and he said "Yes."
>
> *And I asked him, "**when you communicated with the bank, did you tell them the truth?**" He said "Yes."*

I said, "the whole truth as if you were under oath, – the same kind of truth you tell here, – as if you were under oath?" He said "Yes, sir."

So he wrote a letter to the bank, . . . a letter dated December 27, 1983, and it's exhibit 635. [Document placed on the screen]

It's an important letter because in the letter he made what I submit was a rather extraordinary confession. Certainly extraordinary in the context of this courtroom in which he is seeking to recover millions of dollars of damages for the TINS corporation.

[The letter] says for the previous year [1983], he said ***first year planning called for TINS to show a substantial loss.*** *He planned in advance to show a substantial loss, and that it* ***was his intention that TINS show the maximum possible loss for the first fiscal year*** *. . . It was his intention that TINS show the maximum possible loss to be able to start showing positive results in 1984, and maximize [Fineman's] tax write-off . . .*

Wow. A home run! How could Fineman claim *Armstrong* had caused TINS' losses in 1983 when he confessed he intentionally arranged for the company to lose as much money as possible so that he could benefit from a tax write-off on his personal income tax return? And the evidence confirmed he *did* use the loss to write off a huge gain he had from an unrelated stock transaction that year. *So the weakness of his company was really attributable to Fineman's personal income tax planning.* What a confession! But the witness sought to avoid the consequences of his planned-tax-loss-confession by making another confession. As I explained to the jury:

When I showed Mr. Fineman that letter, he did something that is very unusual for somebody who sees a written letter that has his signature. **He said that statement [that the loss was planned] in that letter is false.** That is what he said from the witness chair!

So after swearing he told the bank the truth, *"the whole truth as if you were under oath, the same kind of truth you tell here,"* **Fineman then testified his letter to the bank contained a knowingly false statement.** He applied for a bank loan, admitted to the bank that his company lost money, but sought to induce the bank to make the loan by *falsely* explaining away the loss as just part of his "plan." I pursued the subject by asking Mr. Fineman about his knowledge of the federal statute that made it a crime to defraud a bank into making a loan. There was a considerable dispute at sidebar as to what I could say, both on cross and in summation. The judge had ruled I could argue that Fineman committed a federal crime, but I could not refer to the statutory prison sentence for bank fraud, or refer to him as a "criminal." I did not understand the logic of the ruling, but I could live with it.

Back to my summation. [Fineman] conceded under oath that he knew it was a crime to knowingly write a false statement in connection with an application for credit from a bank.

[Reading from transcript]:

Question: Are you aware, sir, that it is a crime to make a false statement to a bank in connection with an application for credit?
Answer: I certainly am, Mr. London.

A cross-examiner's holiday. Plaintiff's chief witness testified on cross that i) his statements to the bank were true – every bit as true as his statements under oath at this trial, and ii) his statements to the bank were false, he knew they were false, and he knew that it was a federal crime to make false statements to a national bank!

But the witness was not at a loss for an explanation. It was a twist on "The devil made me do it" defense. He testified *a bank officer, a Mr. Haggerty, told him to lie on the application!*

Would anybody believe that? Anybody?

And Haggerty actually took the stand, *called by TINS' lawyer yet, who was eager to rebut the notion that TINS was nothing but a tax shelter.*

Continuing from my summation describing my cross-examination of Haggerty:

> And Haggerty was asked: "Mr. Haggerty, did you tell [Fineman] to write this statement?" Haggerty is the Vice-President of a bank in New York. I don't know how in the world one could expect Haggerty to say, "Sure, I told him to write the false statement to the bank, so it would sit in the file of the Office of the Controller of Currency."
>
> Haggerty said "No way. I did not."

[Reading from cross of Haggerty]:

> Question: When you received this document, did you know that Mr. Fineman knowingly made false statements? Answer: Did I know? No.
>
> Question: Did you instruct him to make false statements? Answer: No.
>
> Question: Did you counsel him to make false statements? Answer: No.
>
> Question: Did you suggest that he make false statements? Answer: No.

And as if it were not clear enough, I read to the jury snips of contrasting testimony from the two witnesses:

> *Fineman*: **Question: And Mr. Haggerty told you to write that inaccurate statement and you did it? Answer: That is correct.**

> *Haggerty*: **Question: Did you tell him to do it? Answer: No.**

Fineman was cooked no matter which version the jury accepted. If he were telling the truth when he testified that, at Haggerty's instruction, his letter to the bank contained false statements, then it follows that: i) Fineman testified falsely when he first assured the jury he had told the truth to the bank, and ii) Fineman knowingly committed a federal crime to get a bank loan.

If Haggerty were telling the truth, then: i) Fineman testified falsely when he assured the jury he had told the truth to the bank, ii) Fineman knowingly committed a federal crime to get a bank loan, and iii) Fineman testified falsely when he testified Haggerty told him to do it.

In either case, I argued, the jury should reject all of Fineman's testimony, and if they did that, there was no basis to award TINS one nickel.

Second: Aside from the credibility question, I had another arrow in my "no-damage" quiver; there was a failure of proof. In my summation, I took what looked like a risk (but wasn't) and issued a challenge to my adversary counsel whose summation was to follow mine. Because TINS had never made a profit and its entire damage claim was based on *projections* contained in its **"business plan,"** we urged **there never was a *forward-looking* business plan:** all the TINS testimony looked backward, not forward. In effect, their witnesses would look at a chart that showed past performance and say, in effect, "See, that's just what we planned, exactly as we intended, we met our target, our business plan is on the money." But, we argued, those were just "trick charts" prepared for trial, always looking backwards.

TINS lost money in 1983, and **Fineman testified that after a December 15, 1983 settlement talk with Armstrong, *he had a business plan – the basis of his damage claim.***

I told the jury we had counted **157** mentions by plaintiff of **TINS' "business plan"** in its case in chief, **20** mentions in its opening statement alone. Where was that business plan? I challenged TINS counsel, in his summation that would follow mine, to show that business plan to the jury. **No plan, no recovery.** I suggested to the jury that when TINS' lawyer got up to address them, they should send him a silent message, a thought-wave request: "Mr. Pitre, please show us the business plan!"

To harden the attack, I took a whiteboard, and did my version of a drawing of the courtroom projector both sides had often used during the long trial, and told the jury:

> When I was in high school, I took a memory course. . . . They taught us if you want to remember things, use an association device. So I am going to ask you to do something. I want you to associate the projector with the letter "B." [Pointing to my drawing]. It looks like a "B", doesn't it? "B" for business plan. And every time, **since it's the guts of the case**, every time Frank Pitre goes over to this machine and wants to show you a document, I want you to think, "Is this it? Now am I going to see the business plan? Why is he showing another document?... Show me the business plan!" . . . **Every time he walks near that machine. Look at it. "B". "B" for business plan. No business plan, no loss. No loss, no case.**

Pitre had been dealt an impossible hand. **There *was* no business plan in evidence.** Nevertheless, when his turn came, he stepped forward and said "Mr. London has challenged me and I accept his challenge." He then proceeded to talk about "the Holy Bible," God, Watergate, and even read a passage from Galatians. But he never showed the jury a business plan. That was hardly a surprise to us. I would never have issued the challenge had the Keane-Kravitz team not assured me the record contained no such document.

Pitre's efforts to defend against the attacks on Fineman's credibility only made matters worse for him, I thought. While I was not allowed to use the word "criminal" in reference to Fineman, Pitre did so twice, saying "He gets attacked on the witness stand as if he were a criminal." Thanks, Frank, couldn't have said it better myself. He said, "I have never seen a man so picked apart in my life." Me too, actually – with perhaps one exception.

The New Jersey practice of having the defendant sum up first means he cannot rebut anything plaintiff's counsel says, but, by going first, defendant's counsel is able to frame issues, talk about his chief points, and put the plaintiff on the defensive. I am not sure what I would have done were I standing in Frank Pitre's shoes. There was no way to escape those facts.

The Verdict

After four months of trial, it took the jury little more than a day to reach a verdict. The judge had given them a four-page verdict form approved by counsel. The key questions and the jury's answers were:

> 2. A. Has TINS proven its claim that Armstrong breached the Settlement Agreement of January 12, 1984?
> Answer: Yes.
>
> B. If your answer to Question 2. A. is "Yes," has TINS proven that it sustained injury proximately caused

by such a breach of contract by Armstrong such that TINS is entitled to an award of either compensatory or nominal money damages?

Answer: No.

4. A. Has TINS proven its claim that Armstrong wrongfully interfered with TINS' contractual or prospective business relationship with [Armstrong wholesaler] Stern & Company?

Answer: Yes.

B. If your answer to Question 4.A. is "Yes," has TINS proven that it sustained injury proximately caused by such wrongful interference by Armstrong such that TINS is entitled to an award of either compensatory or nominal money damages?

Answer: No.

5. Has TINS proven its claim that Armstrong committed a violation of the federal antitrust laws by engaging in a conspiracy in restraint of trade in the relevant product market?

Answer: No.

I turned to Cameron and Jeh, and whispered, "Did we just win?" My partners smiled and said "Yes."

The transcript then reads:

THE COURT: Counsel, is there anything further before I excuse the jurors? Mr. Roddy, Mr. Pitre?

MR. RODDY: No, sir, your Honor. Thank you.

THE COURT: Mr. London?

MR. LONDON: No, sir.

(The jury is excused.)

Plaintiff later moved to set the verdict aside on the ground it was internally inconsistent because though the jurors found Armstrong had wrongfully interfered with TINS and breached the settlement agreement, they nevertheless awarded no damages. Judge Bissell denied the motion on a number of independent grounds, two of which were: i) any inconsistency was waived by plaintiff's failure to raise the issue before the jury had been discharged, so if there were a reparable problem, they could have tried to fix it, and ii) he ruled:

> The jury could have reached a decision that TINS was fatally flawed economically. . . . The jury was free to reject Mr. Fineman's testimony about TINS' financial viability. There was the letter to the bank at the end of 1983, . . . and Mr. Fineman's testimony about that which the jury was free to find was totally incredible.

TINS appealed the verdict to the Third Circuit, which issued a one word ruling eight days after oral argument: "Affirmed."

Several years later, while interviewing prospective associates for the Paul, Weiss litigation department, I encountered a young woman who was finishing up a judicial clerkship. She had asked our recruitment coordinator to arrange for me to be one of her interviewers. When I asked her why, she said her boss was Judge Bissell and he told her:

> If what you want to do is to try cases, go to Paul, Weiss. Those people really know how to do it.

How nice is that?

"Mr. Five Percent," aka "Mr. Copper"

One of the most difficult cases I ever handled contained elements that stressed every component of a lawyer's craft: complicated facts, uncertain international legal principles, onerous physical demands, management of a large group of colleagues and staff, and a language barrier to boot. The plus side: I made friends with former enemies.

✦

"London-san, why is our President in a tree?"

In June, 1996, I was in Tokyo, trying my best to answer that question.

Mr. Masatoshi Inada was a member of the legal department of the 400-year-old Sumitomo Corporation, headquartered in Tokyo. The corporation had become a diversified trading company, and a principal supplier of copper to the world markets. In that connection, it traded on the London

Metal Exchange where it bought and sold warrants (essentially receipts for physical copper held in registered warehouses), futures, options, and other trading devices to hedge its positions in order to protect against price swings. It tried to keep its copper book long and short positions in balance; its copper profits were from the sale of physical copper to customers, and its LME trading activities were exclusively in support of that activity. Or so Sumitomo's management believed.

The historical culture of the major Japanese corporations had a lot to do with the problem Sumitomo encountered. The company is, by nature, extremely paternalistic toward its employees, offering housing to the young recruits, care for their professional development, and Sumitomo expected them to spend their lifetimes working at the company. That loyalty was reciprocal; there was a bilateral trust that is absent in U.S. companies.

As a result, while U.S. banks and financial institutions had extensive rules and safeguards designed to prevent employees from deceiving the company (and we know even those rules and restrictions often fail), their Japanese counterparts had fewer such systems in place. And the same was true for the Japanese independent accounting firms. The extensive confirmation and double-check systems employed by the major accounting firms in the United States were not standard operating procedure in Japan, even when the same Big Six accounting firm was doing the audit.

In December 1995, when the LME raised questions about the size of Sumitomo's copper positions, the United States Commodities and Futures Trading Commission asked to depose a representative of the company's copper trading department, and my partner Toby Myerson, who had brought the Sumitomo client to the firm, asked me to step in and help. Toby spoke fluent Japanese, and while I had not one word of that language, almost all Sumitomo executives and managers had spent time in the United States as they were promoted up the corporate ladder, and had fair English skills. It was a second language for them, but basic communication in English was still reasonably effective.

The manager of Sumitomo's copper trading department was Mr. Yasuo Hamanaka, a 50-year-old Tokyo resident, who seemed totally cooperative when we interviewed him in our office in advance of his CFTC on-the-record inquiry, though Toby Myerson and our partner Richard Rosen had earlier caught him in some contradictions and told me they had some concerns about him. The Commission lawyers came up from D.C. to do the deposition in a New York City hotel conference room. Hamanaka was an extremely heavy smoker and refused to testify in a government building where smoking was banned. We rented two hotel rooms, a non-smoking deposition room, and an adjacent room to which our witness could repair every half hour for his nicotine fix.

Our team had thoroughly prepared our witness, thought we knew what the questions would likely be, and what the answers were. But in the course of what I hoped would be a run-of-the mill morning, CFTC counsel revealed the existence of documents we had never seen before despite our extensive preparation – Powers of Attorney apparently signed by Sumitomo officials, authorizing the opening of trading accounts at three investment banks. The reason I had not seen the documents before was they were neither in our client's files, nor had they been revealed in our interviews of the witness. They bore Hamanaka's signature, and the apparent signature of his superiors. I hate even small surprises in a deposition, and this one was anything but small. I broke off the deposition in the middle of a question,

telephoned my clients in Tokyo, Hamanaka flew back
to Japan to talk to his management, and in New York we
worked on learning about the accounts opened via those
documents. We soon learned the higher management signatures on those documents were Hamanaka forgeries, but
had no idea of the scope of what we would soon learn was
the largest employee rogue trading deception in history.

Weeks later, I received a call from Mr. Sakuo Namba,
the General Manager of Sumitomo's Legal Department. He
was the closest analogue to an American company's inside
General Counsel. I had met him before, both in New York
and in Tokyo, and knew him to be an intelligent and charming guy. Our telephone conversation was brief: "London-
san, I am arriving in New York City tomorrow. May I pay you
a visit in your office?" The next afternoon we sat together in
my office and he told me a hair-raising story.

The short version is this: the company had just learned
that Hamanaka had, for years, been running a secret, off-
the-books unauthorized trading operation. He used his fax
machine at home to buy and sell in Sumitomo's name, and
hid the confirms that came in to Sumitomo's copper trading
department. That was not as straightforward as it sounds.
The dozens of traders and clerks in the copper group sat in
one large room, desks facing each other. At the head of the
room, at a desk perpendicular to theirs, sat Mr. Hamanaka,
looking out over his bailiwick. At the far end of the room
was the department's fax machine. Hamanaka later told me
a particularly difficult part of the scheme was to sit there,
hearing and seeing the machine receive a document, and
not rush over to pick it up. He had to bide his time, then
casually walk over and take the page out of the machine. If
you are going to be a world-class crook, you need nerves of
steel, and Mr. Hamanaka qualified.

Hamanaka was losing money in his trades and was carrying huge positions. We later learned he was known on the London Metal Exchange as "Mr. Copper" and also as "Mr. Five Percent." In the United States, a "Five Percenter" connotes graft, i.e., taking a five percent kickback on government contracts, etc., but in this case, it meant that the market believed Hamanaka owned five percent of the world's supply of copper. Actually, through the use of warrants, forwards, calls, and a whole variety of trading devices and deceptions, he controlled a lot more than that. It was the squeeze of all squeezes, the price of copper was at record highs, and if the scheme had not been scuttled, the LME would have been shattered by the chaos, and the shorts would have been slaughtered.

In the end, he got tripped up by a minute detail. While Hamanaka could manage the deception by controlling all the mail and faxes that came into his metals department, he had no control over Sumitomo's Treasury Department, located on another floor. And that is what did him in. To keep the balls in the air, Hamanaka kept doubling down by, among other things, selling options, which in turn, earned him fees. He directed his trading partners to send those fees to an unauthorized account he had opened at UBS. But when UBS sent its year-end statement of the account to Sumitomo's Treasury department, the clerk who received it was befuddled. The statement showed a five million USD balance, but she had no record of that account and called UBS, whose account executive told her, "I'll get right back to you." He then called Hamanaka, who urged him to tell her to "forget about it." But the Sumitomo Treasury clerk had five million dollars she couldn't account for and "forget about it" was not on her list of options. She pressed for an answer. The UBS guy called Hamanaka back and told him the bank had no choice but to tell her the account was under Hamanaka's control. Ominously, Hamanaka did not come to work the next day, but the following day he came in and confessed all. That's when Mr. Namba flew to New York and was in my office the same day he landed at JFK. He told me the facts (all of which we later fully reported to government investigators in the United States and the United Kingdom), and said, "London-san, I have been instructed to come right back to Tokyo tomorrow, and to bring you with me." I said, "Namba-san, now? This is a crushing week for me, how about late next week?" I can still see him sitting there, big smile, shaking his head side to side, "Now, London-san, now. The big guys want you there NOW."

My partner Bruce Birenboim and I were Tokyo bound with Namba-san the next day.

The Japan Airlines flight to Tokyo is 14 hours. It is brutal. I have made that trip dozens of times and have never figured out how to do it gracefully. As Bruce put it, you go on and on, it seems like the longest flight ever, and then you look at the digital clock on the front bulkhead that informs you there are seven more hours of flying time to Tokyo! The amenities offered in the JAL first class section are impressive, though we never got around to taking full advantage of them. They literally offer you a set of pajama-sweats, and if you board wearing suit and tie, you can change, they will hang up your business clothes for you, and you can sleep or lounge in your JAL pajamas and get dressed again as you approach your destination. I have seen Japanese businessmen do that all the time.

The plane lands at Tokyo's Narita Airport at about 2 p.m. local time, on the day *after* you left New York. I could not ever wrap my brain around that apparently 36-hour voyage. It was our practice to wear casual clothes – jeans, sneakers, sweatshirts – on the plane because the trip was not over when the plane landed. After the fourteen-hour flight and up to an hour of customs and immigration delays, we still faced a two-hour cab ride to downtown Tokyo. Our normal practice was to then have an early dinner at the hotel and go immediately to bed. It was the only shot at being somewhat bright and shiny the next morning.

Namba-san had arranged a car to carry us from Narita to downtown Tokyo. I asked him to drop us off at the Imperial Hotel, our regular hang, but he casually said, "London-san, I want to stop off at the company first so my young guys can give you some documents you might want to look at tonight to be prepared for tomorrow's meetings." I politely declined. I was tired, my eyes felt like they were full of sand, I needed a shower and a shave, I was dressed like a slob, and I was not about to go into the headquarters building for a meeting with anybody, even "the young guys." The documents could wait for the morning. But Namba would not relent, and after several rounds, I surrendered. Hey, ya gotta let the client win the small stuff.

I knew we were in trouble the moment we got off the elevator on the high floor of the Sumitomo Building. On several earlier visits, we had worked on a lower floor where we exited the elevator onto a vinyl tile floor entryway that led directly into the trading room. This time, our sneakers trod upon a polished wood floor covered by a rug that looked to be of museum quality, and there was a receptionist who could have been last year's Miss Japan. Namba-san escorted us down a plush corridor to a pair of paneled wood doors, opened them, and with a proud smile, invited us to sit at a broad conference table, where he introduced us to the gentlemen facing us: the President of the Corporation, Mr. Kenji Miyahara; the Chairman of the Board of Directors, Mr. Tomiichi Akiyama; and the Board's Executive Committee.

They had convened for the express purpose of greeting us, and had been patiently awaiting our arrival! I had never met any of these gentlemen.

President Miyahara welcomed us, apologized for imposing on us immediately after our long trip, and then said, "Mr. London, what is your plan? What should we do now?"

While we had not expected such a high-level meeting on the day of our arrival, we had anticipated the question, conferred the night before and on the plane, and agreed on a recommended program. We had even typed out an outline on a laptop, and printed it on a portable printer we had brought onto the plane. We distributed our printed recommendation and explained it.

I noted that our plan might not be in accord with the usual Japanese practice in these matters, but the world was changing fast. Daiwa Bank had recently lost $1.1 billion because of a rogue trader. The bank had tried to cover up the scandal, was convicted, fined, and barred from doing business in the United States.

President Miyahara thanked us, and said his group would discuss the matter and get back to us in the morning.

After the next day's client meeting, we began a program of full cooperation with all the government agencies, keeping them current with our exhaustive investigation of all the facts, the trades, the outside co-conspirators, etc. Our inquiry was an enormous task. At its height, Paul, Weiss personnel occupied two full floors of a downtown Tokyo office building. We were, for a time, by far the largest law firm in Asia. For our internal discovery program, we employed more than one hundred paralegals, accountants, translators, and security personnel, in addition to utilizing the invaluable services of the litigation and corporate departments of the Paul, Weiss offices in New York, Tokyo, Hong

Kong, London, and Washington, D.C. We examined millions of documents, interviewed scores of witnesses, and by the end, understood every detail of how Hamanaka had run his super-complicated scheme.

On that first post-confession trip to Tokyo, my team and I spent six full days in a room with Hamanaka. He was courteous and cooperative. After the first day, I created a hand-written no-smoking sign that I taped to the wall. I feared a rebellion, but my eyes were killing me from the cigarette smoke in the poorly ventilated conference room. On day two, Hamanaka walked in, looked at the sign, smiled, and put away his cigarettes. (Whether I had effected a lifetime cold-turkey cure, I dunno.) He made a full confession to us and to the Japanese police as well. I was in Tokyo for two weeks, and then flew directly to London, and then directly to D.C., where our mission was to bring the authorities up to date on what we knew so far.

In London, in addition to meeting with the Serious Fraud Office and with officials of the LME, I was also tasked with the burden of dealing with the "B" accounts, opened via the forged powers of attorney. Two were relatively easy because they had small positions, but one of the accounts had a huge forward position that had to be liquidated skillfully, lest it crash the market and do extensive damage to many firms, including, of course, Sumitomo. This was obviously way beyond Paul, Weiss's brief, and I was instructed to see if I could hire Goldman Sachs for that job. First, I had to locate the right Goldman partner for this assignment, and got a recommendation from a GS associate I knew in London. I was functioning on Tokyo time, and the position of the hands on the analog clocks in the city of London was irrelevant to me. I needed help, and I needed it instantly. I called a partner of J. Aron & Co., a Goldman subsidiary, at home late Saturday night, London time, told him who I was and what I needed from him. He listened, and said he would get back to me. By 8 a.m. Sunday, his colleagues in New York had made the necessary contacts with Sumitomo management in Tokyo, the appropriate contracts had been signed, and the J. Aron guy and the Paul, Weiss team were having breakfast in our hotel conference room where we spent the rest of what was Father's Day in the U.S. By 3 p.m., he had eight Goldman analysts from New York on a plane to London. Two of them, he boasted, had been interrupted playing soccer in Central Park that morning. I later commented to Bruce that if I could exercise that kind of power, I could rule the world. On second thought, maybe that's how Goldman Sachs does it?

At the height of the inquiry, I made ten trips to Tokyo in one 12-month period, and frequently flew from there to London, or Washington, D.C. Class action litigations in the United States were handled by Bruce and me, though Bruce did much of the heavy lifting. We discovered that two U.S. banks were implicated in trading with Hamanaka while plotting with him to keep his superiors in the dark. We pursued, and won significant compensation for their participation in the scheme.

Managing this enormous task from halfway across the globe was extraordinarily difficult. We had been handling this problem for a while with New York lawyers taking weeks-long tours of duty in Tokyo.

An incident I remember well: one of the Tokyo tours was taken by Jeh Johnson, then a young partner in the New York office. (Jeh was later appointed Counsel to the Secretary of Defense, and then served as Secretary of the U.S. Department of Homeland Security in the Obama Administration before he returned to Paul, Weiss in January, 2017.) On one of the

"Paul, Weiss" floors rented by the client for our operations was an area that contained our work product – copies of key documents we had translated and analyzed, Paul, Weiss memos, analyses, and client communications. At 2 a.m., New York time, I received a call from Jeh. I laughed when I answered the phone and said, "Well, I KNOW this is important, what's up?" He told me he had just been informed that a detachment from the Japanese Prosecutors Office was *en route* to our operations center with instructions to seize *all our documents*. Do I have any suggestions? Jeh and I hatched a plan. When the cops arrived, Jeh greeted them, showed them the corporation's documents, and told them they could have whatever they wanted, but we'd like to copy the stuff before they took anything away. They agreed. But as to the work product section, Jeh told them they could not look at those documents because that section of the floor was basically a Paul, Weiss law office, and those documents were privileged under United States law. To appreciate the chutzpah of Johnson's declaration, one must understand that there was no such thing as attorney-client privilege or work-product protection in Japan. I am not sure whether or not these guys knew that, but Jeh proclaimed it with such calm and authority, they agreed to stay out of that area, and the problem was solved.

The subject of privilege brings to mind another remarkable event. At some point during the investigations by the governments of Japan, the U.S. and the U.K., and while the class actions were being litigated in the United States, a group of Japanese shareholders commenced a derivative action in a Japanese court. Nominally acting for the benefit of the corporation, they were suing Sumitomo's executives for alleged mismanagement relating to the Hamanaka rogue trading. There were no derivative shareholder litigation provisions in Japan's legal code, but the courts there are heavily influenced by U.S. practice, and permitted the suit to proceed. The corporate executives were represented by a Japanese law firm and the matter was not in our portfolio until the plaintiffs served a document demand that called for all Paul, Weiss client communications and other work-product documents. The company's local lawyers called for help, and I flew to Tokyo, and the next day took the bullet train to Osaka, where the court was sitting.

This was a unique court experience. A three-judge panel was considering the question of whether to require compliance with the plaintiffs' document demand. I was called as a witness at a hearing addressing that question. Sitting in the witness box facing the judges (all of whom spoke excellent English), I was asked to explain the United States rules respecting the privileges and protections attaching to lawyer-client communications and lawyers' work product. I basically gave a law school lecture, tracing the origins and the reasons for the privileges. I stressed that these privileges really protected the client, and that revealing the documents pursuant to Japanese court order would likely strip them of their privileged status in the U.S and elsewhere, where the claims were being pursued not against the executives, but against the corporation. In short, the release of the documents would likely harm the very company the plaintiffs sought to benefit.

There was no cross-examination. After a brief recess, the court quashed the subpoena. Whether that ruling grafted an enduring attorney-client privilege or work-product protection rule onto the Japanese legal system, I do not know, but it certainly accomplished that for the purpose of this case.

But I struggled with Paul, Weiss's internal management problem. Cycling people in and out of Tokyo for two to ten

week shifts was inefficient and stressful. I needed a full-time
Paul, Weiss manager in Tokyo, but that would require someone to give up his or her legal practice entirely for what could
be a year or more. I ultimately resolved the issue with a dar-
ing move. We had a seventh-year litigation associate, Roberta
Kaplan, with whom I had worked on other matters. She
was bright, had an engaging personality, and was a problem
solver. At that time, Robbie was on a leave of absence from
the firm, serving as a law clerk to Judith Kaye, Chief Judge of
New York's Court of Appeals, the state's highest court. I knew
she had about six months to go on her two-year commitment,
but I took a shot and called her anyway. Would she come and
live in Tokyo for as long as it took, and run the Paul, Weiss
Sumitomo law firm? I explained the risks. While her lack of
knowledge about the details of the matter could be cured by a
crash course of study, there remained the problem of her gender. Though the U.S. had for some decades been moving ever
so slowly towards gender equality in the business world, there
was no such movement in Japan, and Sumitomo, like all other
Japanese corporations, lacked any women in its leadership
ranks. Would my Japanese clients respect Robbie? Would they
take her advice? Would they even seek it? Knowing the clients,
and knowing Robbie, I was willing to bet the answers to those
questions would, in a short time, be an unqualified "Yes."

Robbie checked with Judge Kaye, who told her, "If
Marty London wants you to go to Tokyo, you go to Tokyo!"
And she did. Things were fraught for a while, but the clients were smart people, recognized talent and intelligence
when they saw it, and came to honor "Robbie-san's" advice
as highly as mine or Bruce's. (Fifteen years later, Robbie,
by then an accomplished Paul, Weiss partner, became
nationally famous by winning the DOMA case in the
United States Supreme Court – the case that established

the equality of same sex marriage respecting all federal benefits. That case, in turn, led to the Supreme Court decision two years later establishing same sex marriage as a federal Constitutional right.)

Kaplan had only one flaw. The kid from Shaker Heights, Ohio, never did accommodate herself to eating raw fish. I loved the stuff, but Robbie could not bring herself even to give it a try. And she was not the only one on our team who was so handicapped. I recall one evening when the clients took Bruce and me to a traditional Japanese restaurant where we sat on pillows at low tables and were served foods that were absolutely unrecognizable. I struggled to stifle open laughter when I watched Birenboim try to fake it by dipping his chopsticks into his small dessert dish and just push the contents around. He later told me, "Marty, I swear, whatever it was, it was alive and it was moving!"

Tokyo was dramatically affected by the Paul, Weiss invasion. We taught em lots of things beyond American law. In New York, the firm regularly had a Christmas party, and I decreed our Tokyo chapter would do likewise. I sent one of our Japanese-speaking associates, Yuki Hirose, out to make the arrangements. Christmas is big in Japan, and it was difficult to find a party facility at the last minute, but she did it. She made arrangements at a hotel for the space, food and drink, but had trouble arranging for music and a wooden dance floor. The hotel management had no ability to supply either. How come? The catering manager said they don't dance at company Christmas parties in Japan. Yuki said, "Well, what do they do?" and he said, "They make speeches." Yuki told him "Well, not at this party!" and she went out and found a dance band and a company that would lay a dance floor in the hotel's carpeted party room. We invited the entire Sumitomo legal department. They danced the night away with their U.S. colleagues. The mood was set when boss Namba-san arrived wearing a pair of reindeer antlers. I don't know how Sumitomo corporate Christmas parties could ever go back to speeches-only events.

Now back to the opening line of this chapter. As I said, our Tokyo clients all spoke English to a degree, but none had learned it as a first language, and there is only so much one can absorb from tutors, textbooks, and limited exposure to English speakers. My time there made me appreciate how much of our – or at least my – speech is studded with American idioms that make no sense if translated literally.

Inada-san, a hard-working and totally serious member of the client's legal department, came to me one day and sought my approval of a press release the public relations department wanted to put out under President Miyahara's signature. I deleted a line I was uncertain we could substantiate, and said, "Inada-san, please strike this sentence. We don't want to put President Miyahara out on a limb." Inada agreed and took the amended statement back to the PR people. The next day he said to me, "London-san, please help me with my English. What does it mean to say we don't want to put President Miyahara out on a limb?" I explained the analogy: sitting on the end of a tree limb was a precarious spot because the limb was thin there, it might sway, or break, or even be sawed off. It is a risky place to be. He thanked me profusely, but the following day asked, "London-san, thank you for your help with my English, but please, why is President Miyahara sitting in a tree?"

During the years I worked with my friends from Sumitomo, I collected a long list of these American idioms that totally confused my Japanese colleagues. If one reads them literally, it is easy to see how mystified they were. The clients occasionally blushed when I said that on a particular issue, "we just have to take our licking," or, "on this issue we need to bare our breast," or "make a clean breast of it," or "let's not go off half-cocked," or "he wrote a cover-your-ass memo". More often they would just be totally confused. Once, when I told Inada-san, "If we do that, his nose will be out of joint," he responded, "London-san, please, how does his nose come out of his elbow?"

Here are just a few of the scores of idioms that confused my clients. A literal translation reveals their consternation:

There's more than one way to skin a cat;
We gotta bite the bullet;
We can't stonewall on this issue;
His goose is cooked;
He's barking up the wrong tree.

There is one idiom they understood immediately, and laughed and laughed when, referring to a U.K. official, I said, "Fellas, let's not get into a pissing contest with that guy."

It took ten years to bring the matter to a close. In the end, we were able to settle the major government cases with the Serious Fraud Office of Britain's Financial Service Agency, the United States Commodities and Futures Trading Commission, and with the private plaintiffs. With the trading losses, the entire episode cost the company 2.6 Billion USD, and the company rebounded in good shape. Hamanaka was sentenced to eight years in a Japanese prison, and the company incurred no other regulatory consequences.

In all, the Paul, Weiss team endured two earthquakes, too much sake, some difficult away-from-home family strains, but made friends, helped a client, and maybe even helped U.S.-Japan relations.

I retired from the firm at the age of 71 in 2005. Early in that year, I received a call from Mr. Namba: "London-san,

Sumitomo Corporation wants to honor you by giving you a retirement gift. Please come to Tokyo with Mrs. London, and we will take you on a tour of Japanese mountain inns. They are very beautiful and few foreigners have ever visited them. It will be a great treat. Will you come?"

We accepted, and Mr. and Mrs. Namba accompanied Mr. and Mrs. London on a fantastic tour of places I never knew existed. The Nambas were gracious hosts and good company. Each inn we visited was distinct, had its own character, and Namba-san had kindly made advance arrangements at each place we visited to have a room with a western bed so Pinks and I didn't have to sleep on tatami mats. The inns also had another common characteristic: in public areas, guests always wore traditional Japanese dress – a kimono. We still laugh about the first inn, where, immediately upon our arrival, a young lady outfitted me with a kimono that barely came to my knees. The manager was greatly embarrassed, took the kimono away, and came back with a suitable-length garb that they actually sewed while I waited. The Japanese bath was also a unique experience – one first goes into a shower room and scrubs. You are given a little wooden stool and hard bristle brush and soap, and you scrub until the skin glows and is sensitive to the touch. Only then do you proceed to the "bath," which is really a large communal hot tub.

The trip was a wonderful experience for both couples. I still get letters and Christmas cards from some of my Tokyo buds, and see a smattering of hits from Japan on my blog page.

Sumitomo weathered a serious storm and survived in good shape.

Sometimes doing the right thing really works.

Saipan

Successful litigators go where the cases are, and some of us find ourselves in cities all over the world. I had appeared before judges, arbitration tribunals, and administrative bodies in 20 U.S. cities that I can recall, and outside the U.S. in Rotterdam, Osaka, and London. And I have lectured in Beijing and Hong Kong.

But the most unusual locale was my appearance in a United States federal district court on the island of Saipan in the Northern Mariana Islands.

✦

To reach Saipan, one flies to Tokyo, spends the night at the airport hotel, and flies to Saipan the next day. I appreciated the floor mats outside the elevator banks in the Narita Hotel: "Good Morning. Today is Wednesday." Very helpful when your brain is telling you that when you went to sleep last night it was Monday.

Similar to each state in the U.S., Saipan has two court systems, a local court and a federal court. The United States District Court for the Northern Mariana Islands was created by an international contract that provides for the appointment of a U.S. federal judge for the district, appointed by the President of the United States to a ten-year term. The appointment is subject to U.S. Senate confirmation. The District Court follows the U.S. Federal Rules of Civil and Criminal Procedure, and appeals are taken to the Ninth Circuit sitting in California.

Saipan is an historic battle site of World War II. It had been occupied by the Japanese after WW I as a trusteeship awarded by the League of Nations. The invasion by U.S. forces in 1944 was part of the costly WW II island-hopping campaign that ultimately led to Japan's surrender in August, 1945. Saipan was tactically important because its neighboring island, Tinian, had a topography amenable to the construction of runways that could accommodate B-29 bombers within striking distance of the Japan home islands. The planes that dropped the atomic bombs on Hiroshima and Nagasaki were based on Tinian.

The purpose of my visit to Saipan was to argue a summary judgment motion my client's local lawyers had made in a civil case pending in the federal district court there. The contract dispute was in the federal court on account of its diversity jurisdiction. I read the documents and the briefs and was thoroughly prepared. Summary judgment motions are generally an uphill climb, but I thought I had a decent shot at winning this one. I confess to feeling a bit of, "Hey, I am a hot shot New York lawyer who has parachuted into this case, and I'll show you locals how it is done."

The courthouse was sure different from any others in which I had appeared. In this one-story building, the lawyers wore open collared short-sleeve shirts. A row of black cotton jackets hung on wall pegs in the anteroom, and counsel donned them upon entering the courtroom and returned them to the pegs upon departure.

When my case was called, I made my argument, and was comfortable I had hit it out of the park. The American judge was attentive and when I was finished, I sat back as my much younger adversary, who had flown down from Guam, approached the lectern, unrolled some charts and graphs that he hung on easels he had brought with him, and proceeded to clean my clock. He basically shredded my argument. When he was finished, even I would have decided the motion in his favor. The judge reserved decision but there was no doubt in my mind which way he was going to decide. After hanging up our borrowed jackets, the Guam lawyer and I talked over a pleasant lunch at an outdoor cafe, we each made some phone calls, and the case was settled.

A year later, Bruce Birenboim and I returned to Saipan on another matter, this time to meet with the United States Attorney for Guam, who had jurisdiction over the Northern Mariana District as well. When we got to Tokyo, we learned that a typhoon had ravaged Saipan the day before, and it was uncertain whether we would be able to get there on schedule. The next morning, the airline assured us the typhoon had passed, the sun was shining on the island, and the Saipan airport had returned to full operation. We flew, and discovered some stuff the airline did not tell us. Much of the island, *including our hotel*, remained without electricity. No lights (except battery powered flashlights and emergency lanterns in the stairwells), no air conditioning, and worse, no water! The weather was stifling. Bruce and I rehearsed our negotiating strategy while walking barefoot, suit trousers rolled up, at the shoreline.

Our meeting with the U.S Attorney in his stifling office the following morning went well and we disposed of the matter. It's remarkable how the lack of air conditioning tends to shorten argumentative speeches and hasten resolution of differences. We caught a late plane back to Narita, and I had never been so happy to return to the hot showers of my home away from home, the Imperial Hotel in Tokyo.

Antitrust Arcana

In the HARD WORK category, an antitrust case I tried for nine months in Greensboro, North Carolina, is at the top of my "brutality" list. Every aspect of that case was awful. The subject matter was arcane, the evidence confusing, the jury was in over its head and unteachable, the adversaries were thoroughly unpleasant, and the physical strain was extreme. (It took two hospital visits for me to complete the trial). My recollection of this case is so painful, I would not have been able to write about it if the result had been different.

✦

For the nine months between July 5, 1989 and March 1, 1990, I lived in the Sheraton Hotel in downtown Greensboro, North Carolina. Along with a large team of Paul, Weiss lawyers, paralegals, and secretaries, and two local lawyers, I was defending Brown & Williamson in a multi-million-dollar antitrust suit brought by its competitor cigarette company,

Liggett & Myers. The trial, which commenced after five grating years of discovery and pre-trial motions, was before federal Judge Frank Bullock of the Middle District of North Carolina and a jury of nine.

From day one, I thought Liggett's antitrust complaint was a "fabricated-by-paid-expert" claim unsupported by the facts, brought in an unsuccessful effort to frighten off a competitor. In 1980, Liggett, the weakest of the six major cigarette companies, jumped on the "generic" bandwagon that seemed to be doing so well for toilet paper, canned peas, and dog food. It packaged unbranded cigarettes in plain white packages with black lettering. Four years later B&W announced it too would start selling black and white generics, but before it sold the first stick, Liggett sued with a mishmash of unfair competition claims that were all later rejected. But a later-added "trademark infringement" claim and an antitrust "predatory pricing" claim ultimately went to the jury.

The trademark claim was simple enough: Liggett's package had black letters on a white surface, that read "20 Cigarettes" as did ours. The package top had a small, barely noticeable black and gold seal with a leaf on it. Ours did too. That was it. It seemed laughable to me, but it got to the jury anyway.

Liggett's "predatory pricing" antitrust claim was far more complicated. To succeed, the plaintiff needed to prove *two things*:

> i) the defendant sold its goods at **predatory prices**, i.e., **prices it set *below its cost*,** for the purpose of driving its competitor out of business,

and

> ii) after its competitor had been vanquished, the defendant used its newly-acquired **monopoly market power** to **recoup** the losses it suffered during the

predation (below cost) period. It does that by jacking up the price of its product, charging **supracompetitive prices** – *prices that were higher than they would have been if there were genuine competition.* Obviously, it can get away with selling its wares at those jacked-up prices only if it has "**monopoly power**," sometimes called "**market power**."

If either prerequisite fails of proof, either i) the *predatory pricing* phase, or ii) the *supracompetitive price-recoupment* phase is not proven, the plaintiff loses.

The architect of Liggett's antitrust claim was economist William Burnett, who developed an unorthodox hypothesis. Burnett fashioned this theory:

1. B&W sold its generic cigarettes below its cost of manufacture,

2. Liggett could not afford to absorb the losses it would incur by matching those prices, consequently it would be forced to raise its price for its generics, and B&W would lead the price of generics upward,

3. The generics price increases would narrow the price gap between generic cigarettes and branded cigarettes,

4. Reducing that price gap made it likely B&W would sell more branded cigarettes,

5. Selling more branded cigarettes would allow B&W eventually to recoup its earlier below-cost losses by earning excessive profits, *because its branded cigarettes sold at supracompetitive prices,*

6. B&W would be able price its cigarettes at supracompetitive levels normally obtainable only by

a monopolist, because B&W enjoyed, in effect, a **monopolist's market power** by reason of its *membership in **the six-company (which included Liggett!) cigarette-manufacturer oligopoly that employed tacit collusion to fix cigarette prices at those supracompetitive levels.***

7. Therefore B&W, via its predatory pricing of generic cigarettes, harmed consumers' welfare and injured competition, and Liggett was injured thereby.

If your head is spinning as you read that, welcome to the club.

Before trial, we moved for summary judgment. We argued that, aside from its legal impairments, Burnett's theory didn't work because its key factual underpinning, *that tacit collusion by all six tobacco companies produced supracompetitive prices,* was baloney. It was false. As a matter of fact, there was neither tacit collusion nor supracompetitive prices in the industry, and we had indisputable proof. Liggett's executives gave pretrial testimony explicitly saying **there was no tacit collusion, the cigarette industry was not a collusive oligopoly, and the companies do not reap excessive profits via supracompetitive prices**. Wow, game over, right? No tacit collusion, no supracompetitive prices, no antitrust violation. Easy.

How did we get Liggett's executives to make that confession? And why didn't it end the case right then and there?

Shortly before the trial began, our partner Arthur Liman had been retained by Michael Milken in a major criminal case. Marty Flumenbaum, my young partner who was a valued member of our trial team (and a former Assistant United States Attorney), was asked by Arthur if he could join the Milken team. Marty asked me to let him do it. That would mean I had to go to trial without him, but I had Andy Peck (now a federal Magistrate Judge) and a strong team, and I said, "Okay, but I am swamped with trial prep. We now have Burnett's expert report, and the judge has given us another crack at the Liggett executives. I need you to take their depositions before you depart. That's your exit visa." He agreed.

I had scheduled several days for the depositions of the Liggett President and the Vice President in charge of sales, but did not intrude upon or inquire of Flumenbaum about what his deposition plan was. I was upset when he came back in mid-afternoon of the first day and told me he was finished with both witnesses. "What happened?" I asked, "Did they fail to show, walk out, refuse to answer, what?" "None of the above," he said with an ear-to-ear smile. "They told the truth, and I did what you taught me – when you get what you want, stop, and go home. I got what I wanted, so I stopped and here I am." I saw the transcript the next day and saw our opportunity to win this case without a trial.

In the deposition, Flumenbaum asked the Liggett executives if the prices they set for their branded cigarettes were identical to B&W's prices. They said, "Yes." He then asked them if *their* prices were the result of industry-wide *tacit collusion* and they said "No." When he asked if *their* profits on branded cigarettes were *excessive or supracompetitive*, they said, "No." In effect, Liggett's executives said Burnett's theory was all wet.

We put all that in our motion papers for summary judgment and asked the judge to throw the case out. But Liggett's lawyers, recognizing their clients had just given away the game, threw a "Hail Mary" pass by drafting affidavits in which their clients swore they were "only businessmen and not economists," and were confused by Flumenbaum's questions because they did not really understand words like "competitive," and "collusion!" The trial judge, to his later regret, denied our motion and let the case go to trial.

So began nine months of torture.

The Trial

It took several days to pick the jury. We ended up with some unemployed homemakers, some retirees, and some low-level job holders. No one had an education beyond high school. (At one point, in a robing room conference, I implored the judge to accept the offer (from both sides!) to discharge the jury and decide the case himself. I said people with no more than a high school education could not grasp and apply the complicated legal, economic and accounting principles involved. With a smile, he said he suspected that some of those jurors even "fudged a bit about having a high school diploma"). But he declined to take the case away from the jury.

The impaneled jurors were enthusiastic about sitting on this case. My sense was that they were not sacrificing income by being on this jury, and, to the contrary, their attendance fees were a welcome addition to family income. It was an outing for them. Extraordinarily punctual, never missing a day (we had court during Hurricane Hugo and all showed up, on time), they appeared to be alert, except for juror number four, who had a job as a night janitor at the local public school, and caught up on his sleep in the afternoon sessions. I guess both sides figured no harm would come from that.

The level of juror devotion to this apparently endless trial was marked by their sociability. This was a paid picnic. Some examples:

On a Friday in month five, a female juror asked Judge Bullock if she could have the following Monday and Tuesday off because her husband was having open heart surgery, but she didn't want to give up her seat on the jury. Bullock obliged, saying, accurately enough, that the lawyers looked tired and he was sure they wouldn't mind a four-day weekend, and we would resume on Wednesday. When court resumed the following week, the judge asked the juror how her husband was. She replied the surgery had been delayed, and it was "today." The good judge immediately offered to suspend the trial for another day. Her response brought the house down:

> "No thank you, Your Honor, I've just spent the last four days with my husband. I can't take any more. It's not like *I'm* performing the surgery!"

At another point, the jurors who had to drive the farthest from home to the courthouse (some lived almost 100 miles away), asked the judge if he could arrange to put them up in a local hotel. He agreed. A week later, the other jurors, even those living reasonably close to the courthouse, asked the judge for similar treatment. They were now pals and wanted to be together! The good judge granted that request too. If he gave a "do not discuss this case" instruction, I don't remember it. Not that it would have made any difference if he did or did not. This was a tight-knit group.

On Friday in Week 20, as the jury filed in at 9:30 a.m., the judge, counsel, and spectators started to titter, then laugh, then roar. The jurors had broad grins. As more of them filed into the room it became clear they had cooked up their own little conspiracy. All the jurors were packaged in generic dress: black pants and white shirts. The women even wore white shoes, and the men wore black shoes with white socks. The clerk informed me that juror number eight was also wearing a necklace with a gold leaf – another one of the package design elements at issue in the case.

Unfortunately, no degree of internal sociability could improve the jurors' comprehension of the issues. The best example of the complexity of the proof served up to them was an element of Liggett's claim that B&W's generics were sold at "below cost." I keep one artifact from the trial, a 4"x6" colored Styrofoam block that sits on my bookcase to this day. It bears the number "10." Its purpose? We had denied plaintiff's fundamental allegation that B&W sold its generics below cost. The proofs on both sides were of staggering volume and intricacy, and the Velcro-backed Styrofoam block was part of a trial demonstration of a technical aspect of the profit/loss issue.

Our goal was to show that B&W's decision to make generics was a profitable one, i.e., the company's bottom line results were enhanced by manufacturing and selling generics. We asserted that income tax savings generated by expanding into generics should be considered when judging the profitability of the generics program.

So in that section of our proofs, we focused on two elements of cost: i) the value of the raw materials used to make the company's products, and ii) taxes. Those two aspects are very much related. Assigning a higher accounting cost-value to the leaf inventory consumed in the manufacture of all B&W products after commencement of the generics program resulted in lower accounting profits and therefore lower actual income taxes on all products. This was because all cigarettes, branded and generic, were manufactured using tobacco leaf inventory stored in the company's warehouses. That inventory had been purchased over the years and each year's tranche was at a different cost number, in accordance with market variations. There are accounting conventions to determine inventory cost and the one adopted by many companies, including B&W, was LIFO, i.e.,"Last In, First Out." This means that, *for accounting purposes,* the cost of leaf most recently used, (first out) for both branded and generic cig- arettes, was the amount of money paid for the *most re- cent,* "last in," leaf purchases, even though the physical tobacco leaf *actually used* was purchased years earlier, when the price was lower. Bottom line, we asserted that by adding the generic volume, B&W was required to buy more leaf, which cost more than the old leaf. Using the "last in" higher leaf prices in computing profits *for both branded and unbranded* cigarettes (even though manufac- tured from lower cost older leaf), produced less account- ing profit, and therefore less income tax.

In other words, our goal was to show the jury that by go- ing into the generics business and therefore being required to buy new leaf for that production, the company avoided, *for income tax purposes,* applying the lower-cost LIFO book values of its older tranches of tobacco inventory that would have resulted in greater *taxable accounting profit on all cig- arettes. The result was that* B&W saved on taxes by avoiding decrementing the older inventory leaf tranches that had low- er book values. This "LIFO Decrement Avoidance" saved mil- lions in taxes, and therefore the manufacture and sale of ge- nerics was profitable to the company. Those savings, when applied to the decision to make generics, reduced B&W's variable cost of making generic cigarettes, and therefore its sale price was not lower than its variable cost. Got that?

How do I teach the arcane notion of LIFO Decrement Avoidance to 10th grade students? Probably hopeless, but there is no surrendering in this game. We designed and built a big board with rows and columns of velcroed spaces, and fashioned velcroed colored blocks with inventory val- ues printed on the front, and demonstrated that by avoiding descending into the ranks of the lower-cost rows on the board, we reduced accounting profits and therefore income tax liability. We did that through my direct examination of a witness, with two team members adding and removing Styrofoam blocks in a carefully rehearsed ballet coordinated with the testimony. I gotta say myself, it was brilliantly conceived and executed. Unfortunately, I saw no evidence, at any time, that the jury got this. I'm not even sure the judge got it. One of our young lawyers, who had been working on other aspects of the case for months, actually came up to me after the direct testimony and said he now understood the concept for the first time. So what!

What was it like living in that hotel and that courtroom for nine months? The Greensboro Sheraton was three blocks from the courthouse and two blocks from our office, which consisted of adjacent storefronts on the main street, each store having an upstairs loft, which was our file room, and a basement where people worked. We had between 20 and 25 people from New York who spent time there, about ten of whom were full timers. Andy Peck was our rock – everybody, including the judge, relied on Andy to keep score of what was in evidence, what was not, and he was the leader of our Trademark team (which, he has good-naturedly reminded me more than once, was the team that WON at the jury level.) Paul, Weiss' Dan Leffell and Julie Domonkos got on so well they were later married and now have two kids. And the Winston-Salem team consisting of the late Norwood Robinson and his son Mike (now a North Carolina judge) added depth on the trademark issue.

As a diversion, I sent memos back to the firm from time to time. My *Greensboro Diary* consisted of nineteen entries, some of which describe the less painful aspects of our life in North Carolina:

TO: The Paul, Weiss Daily Bulletin
FROM: The Greensboro Gang
July 24, 1989

If nothing else, our team is well-fed. Working with Aubrey Holder, the caterer, has developed a trans-regional menu for us which has included, on different occasions, barbecued pork, barbecued chicken, barbecued beef, barbecued yellow stickies, and barbecued barbecue. They do try though. Saturday lunch is a local version of lox and bagels with cream cheese, and last Friday night's dinner was brisket of beef with noodle pudding. (As good as our North Carolina communications equipment is, it just cannot bring itself to transmit the words *lukshin kugel*).

Our worst problem here is a mysterious water leak in the basement part of our offices where Jennifer Conovitz and Jean Collins work. In one section, the carpeting squishes when you walk on it. Farther to the rear, the water is a little deeper. So far I've caught two small blues on the outgoing tide, but no stripers. This is really a wonderful opportunity for me. North Carolina has no minimum-size limit for basement-caught striped bass. The landlord is working to find the source of the water, but meanwhile Jennifer and Jean are getting a little moldy. If conditions do not improve, we may have to permit them to be exposed to some sunlight each day. I fear our case will suffer irreparable injury.

Dictating this is more fun than analyzing market graphs, but the latter pays better. See y'all when the leaves fall.

[I was only off by half a year!]

August 13:

There are times when diversions become necessary to the maintenance of equilibrium. I can remember one semester of law school when I read Perry Mason novels while cramming for finals. These diary notes on life in Greensboro are my escape from cramming.

We work an outrageous schedule on trial days, and we work on Saturdays and Sundays too. This past weekend the Emperor [c'est moi] decreed "No work" on Friday and Saturday night. A result of that relaxation order is this report . . .

Friday night we went to dinner at Greene's Oyster Bar, a popular local establishment recommended by our maintenance man, Bill Sykes. Bill comes into our office every day at 6:00 p.m., collects the trash, vacuums the carpets, instructs us regarding local history and culture, and provides us with fresh garden tomatoes. Also, he is making an audio tape for Julie Domonkos so she can have her personal copy of a dramatic reading of General Lee's Ninth General Order.

The Oyster Bar was exactly what we hoped it would be – large, plain, noisy, and very crowded. As one might expect, the specialty of the house is fresh Chesapeake Bay oysters and draft beer sold by the pitcher. The sound system plays loud country music and the patrons vary from meticulously coiffed ladies to young people in jeans holding infants. Everybody (but the infants) smokes cigarettes. The men are *real* men: they do not take their hats off when they eat.

September 18:

On September 7th, counsel were discussing the

schedule with Judge Bullock and the issue of the Jewish holidays came up. We wanted to go home, and Bullock obliged by suspending the trial for the week, saying, "I think that's best. I'll use that time for sentencing for all Baptists, Presbyterians, Methodists, Episcopalians, Catholics, whatever."

October 5:
We have an office pet . . . Collins adopted a stray black kitten with a white dot on its forehead. On the third day in its new home, the kitten disappeared. She was discovered a day later when Collins looked for a file in her bottom desk drawer. Oh, yeah, the cat has fleas.

And, later in that Diary entry:

The witness now testifying is Liggett's economist William Burnett. He has been on the stand for two days on direct. ... The following is a true account of an elevator conversation between two Liggett paralegals: First para: "How much longer will Bill still be on the stand?" Second Para: "They're estimating two more days on direct – and three weeks on cross."

December 5:
Paul, Weiss Greensboro will hold its First Annual Christmas Party on Monday, December 11, at 6:30 p.m. (No trial on Tuesday). The locale is the Paisely Pineapple, 600 South Elm Street. If any New Yorkers are in town, come on by. Yes, the dress is black tie.

By the way, this was the occasion of my first taste of alligator. They were right: it tastes like fishy chicken. Not bad! The whole team did indeed import their tuxedos and gowns.

We had canned music, and were rowdy. When the restaurant threw us out at 11 p.m., we repaired to the hotel bar and were rowdy there, too. Some of our team caught the flu at the bar and did not come to the office Tuesday morning.

So much for the pleasant stuff. Back to reality. The pressure imposed by this trial was incessant and wearing. We had been sentenced to the judicial equivalent of the gulag. Preparing for twenty-five witnesses, many of whom would be testifying for days about complex economic theory, accounting issues, and disputed facts, was an excruciating grind. We had to examine some three thousand exhibits, letting some in, fighting over others, arguing about the admissibility of deposition transcripts (the judge insisted that counsel work that out amongst ourselves – a miserable chore, given Liggett's ornery New York lawyers), while constantly researching and briefing key evidence points. The physical strain was such that mid-trial I had to go to the emergency room in Greensboro Hospital for serious neck problems. The doctor who attended to me was surely too young to be able to legally buy a beer, and after I received his diagnosis ("Natural aging process. You are getting old, Mr. London."), I asked Mike Robinson to get me an appointment with a real doctor at the hospital in Winston-Salem. He did, and I got a prescription for some pills and exercises that helped.

It was hard on everybody. Our secretarial staff from New York worked shifts, often starting at 6 a.m., and finishing at 2 a.m. On trial days, paralegals worked around the clock right along with the lawyers.

Judge Bullock was tireless. The trial day began at 9:30 a.m. on the dot. Luncheon recess was at noon sharp, (the judge had to go home to walk his dog) and lasted one hour, not a minute longer. We never recessed before 5:00. When we got back to the office at 5:15, it was, for us, the start of the second half of the day. The only break was a 6 p.m. catered dinner in our basement "conference" room. No alcohol, because we worked late. Except for rare occasions, Saturday and Sunday were full-time work days. It's a good thing the Paul, Weiss team was a harmonious group or we all would have been institutionalized.

The trial droned on and on. We started in July, and the judge told the jury they would be done by October. He missed by only six months.

Remember HAL, the classic renegade computer in the motion picture, *2001, A Space Odyssey*, who spoke the memorable lines to his creator, "Dave, I know you are planning to disconnect me, and I cannot allow that!"? This trial too, had taken on a self-determined existence. Because we were occupying the Grand Jury Room for our exhibits and copying equipment, a suffering Assistant U.S. Attorney asked me how much longer the trial would last. I replied, "I don't know, you'll have to ask it."

I did get back to New York City about once a month, and Pinks came down for the summations. On her visit, she was stunned by the tension, the pressure, the deprivation. She said it was truly like visiting people in prison.

After nine months of trial, the case went to the jury. They deliberated. And deliberated. And deliberated. While they did that, I went nuts. My last missive from Greensboro revealed the extreme degree of my dementia.

February 22, 1990:
Flies. Dead flies. I am reminded of them when I look at the large calendar board on my office wall, and see all the too-early picks in the Paul-Weiss-Greensboro-Jury-Verdict-Date-Lottery Calendar. Dead flies. The

longest dead is the entry in the box marked February 14. Aubrey Holder was excessively optimistic. Ever enter a house that's been unoccupied for several months and notice, on the window and sliding glass door sills, dead flies? Where did they come from? Why did they die? Boredom? Tension?

Deliberations didn't even begin until the afternoon of the 15th. Nobody guessed the 15th, but Gnat Smith and many others bit the dust when Friday the 16th ended with nine obviously tired jurors quitting for the weekend.

And again on Tuesday, February 20th, when the Judge inquired of the jurors at 5 p.m. if they were near a verdict and would like to stay a little longer, they responded as one, "No, we've had enough. Home, home, we wanna go home!" On Wednesday, the 21st, the jurors i) asked for and received 500 pages of trial transcript; (ii) asked for and received the Court's permission to take an afternoon walk to get some sun; and (iii) quit for the day at 5:05 p.m., again showing obvious signs of fatigue.

We're all tired. The jury has been out for a week, and our eyes tire from the strain of reading those obscure patterns in the sludge at the bottom of our coffee cups. (Tea, you know, comes in bags now, and is absolutely worthless for the purposes of conjuration and prognostication.)

What to do to relieve the tension? Early morning jogging and 6 p.m. exercise at the gym. Yeah, that's the ticket. Yeah. We'll call Stacy and get some paralegals down here to do that for us. Yeah.

Sam Silverman used to say that in some cases a final judgment is a victory. Right, a final judgment here is a victory. That is my mantra: Five repetitions before each meal, and ten before bed. (Notice I said bed, not sleep.) So how come I don't believe it? Because, Sam, it just ain't true. A final judgment is a victory only if you win. That is not a pretty truth, but Dan Quayle is Vice President of the United States, there ain't no Easter Bunny, and we shall all be very depressed if the jury makes a mistake here.

On a brighter note, the weather is sublime. The dogwoods are in full bloom. Really. Of course, they will probably be killed by next week's ice storm. Remember Dan Quayle and the Easter Bunny.

My colleagues call. There's a 2 p.m. showing of "To Kill a Mockingbird" in the basement.

I know how that one comes out.

See y'all soon, heah?

After ten days of deliberation, the nine jurors reported out a verdict that illustrated their confusion. Sensibly enough, they threw out the trademark claim, but then stunned us by giving Liggett a 150-million-dollar antitrust verdict. There simply was no way they could understand the complexity of the economic theory, or the relevance of the testimony regarding cost and price, predation, supracompetitive pricing, etc. It is an absurd flaw in the law that posits these questions to be answered by high school students. As an indication of their confusion, they actually deducted the amount of plaintiff's damages claim on the trademark issue from the calculated amount of plaintiff's damages claim on the antitrust issue!

It was a crushing setback for us, but it meant we could now force a *court* to address the issues we had been pushing since day one. Before trial, the Liggett executives had

successfully weaseled out of their deposition testimony
by submitting affidavits asserting their illiteracy. But we
didn't have the opportunity to cross-examine the "Hail
Mary" affidavits. At trial, though, we nailed 'em. On the
stand, the Liggett executives wheedled and whined, but
they were pinned butterflies, and I wouldn't let them
escape from their deposition confessions. By the end of
the cross, they had basically told me – and the judge and
jury – the same thing they told Flumenbaum: **they and
their competitors did not engage in tacit collusion, the
industry was not an oligopoly, and did not earn supracompetitive profits.**

We moved to set aside the antitrust portion of the verdict. Judge Bullock granted our motion, writing:

> The only record evidence supporting [Burnett's]
> theory was Burnett's opinion testimony which was
> contradicted by witnesses from the Liggett boardroom.
> *Liggett's most senior executives, including the president
> of the company, K.V. Dye, unequivocally testified at trial
> that there **was no tacit collusion on branded cigarette
> pricing decisions, that the cigarette industry has
> never been a collusive oligopoly, and that the industry
> does not reap excessive profits.***
>
> Liggett seeks to explain this obvious problem
> by arguing that the decision-makers at Liggett are
> not economists and do not understand economic
> terms such as oligopoly, tacit collusion, and
> monopoly profits. This argument was considered
> at the summary judgment stage since these exec-
> utives gave basically the same testimony at their
> depositions. The court allowed the case to go to
> trial in part because the Liggett executives were

not economists and in part because of affidavits from the Liggett executives stating that they were confused by the questions asked by B&W lawyers and did not mean to contradict the testimony of Burnett. *However, at trial, despite having consulted extensively with Burnett and having had adequate time to familiarize themselves with concepts such as tacit collusion, oligopoly, and monopoly profits, these Liggett executives again contradicted Burnett's theory. . . .* **Burnett's expert opinion testimony on these issues cannot be considered substantial evidence . . . in light of unequivocal and contradictory trial testimony from the senior executives at Liggett who made the pricing decisions**. [Emphasis mine.]

After he threw out the verdict in a post-trial opinion that tracked our brief precisely, Judge Bullock, in a robing room conference, said with an embarrassed smile, "Well, Mr. London, I guess I should have paid more attention to your pre-trial papers." And to his post-trial opinion, Bullock added this apologetic footnote:

An ever-expanding court docket does not always provide an atmosphere conducive to pre-trial analysis of complex economic and legal issues.

I'll drink to that.

Liggett appealed and hired one of the country's leading antitrust experts, Philip Areeda, to argue its case to the Fourth Circuit Court of Appeals. Ernie Pepples, the B&W General Counsel who had retained me in 1984, had since retired, and to put it as politely as I can, his successor and I had so many disagreements during the stressful nine-month trial, that by the time Judge Bullock dismissed the case in 1990, Pepples' successor and I were barely speaking. As was his prerogative, he went elsewhere for appellate counsel. Of course, I was eager for him to select somebody who would preserve what we had worked so hard to accomplish, but I was not consulted. He chose the distinguished former Fifth Circuit Court Judge, and former U.S. Attorney General, Griffin Bell.

Unfortunately, the gentlemanly Judge Bell was clearly not up to the task. This was a complicated, fact-intensive case, the nine-month trial record was enormous, and it was apparent to all in the Fourth Circuit courtroom that he had not done his homework. He *read* his argument from a script his team had prepared for him. Most embarrassing, when a member of the three-judge appellate court asked him a question, he looked down, turned a few pages in the loose leaf binder from which he had been reading, then looked up and said, "Your Honor, I'm sorry, that is not in my book." Ouch.

I guess, in the end, one could not say that choice was a mistake, because the Fourth Circuit affirmed the post-trial judgment we had won in the district court, though the appellate decision was based on a legal theory different from the one we had successfully argued to Judge Bullock.

When the Supreme Court granted *certiorari*, B&W's general counsel retained Robert Bork. Once again, I was not consulted about B&W's choice of counsel, and Mr. Bork never consulted me about his planned approach. My only meeting with His Arrogancy was a chance encounter in a Supreme Court corridor shortly before the argument. I introduced myself as the trial lawyer who made the record and who wrote the brief that led to the decision he was defending. As I wrote to my colleagues on the day after the argument,

He was not uncivil, but he clearly showed disdain for the likes of a lowly trial lawyer. I gather from others that he is a man who thinks so highly of himself it's almost impossible for him to focus on somebody else, and therefore I am inclined not to take it personally, but given the fact that I made the record on which he was relying, he had every opportunity to be a mensch, but it was not in his nature.

Bork was well prepared and I thought he did an okay job, though Ken Elzinga, the brilliant economist from the University of Virginia who, from the witness stand, had patiently explained why Burnett's theory was full of holes, thought Bork earned no better than a B-, C+. After the argument, I commented to my colleagues that Bork was looking up to a bench from which he believed he should be looking down, and that his demeanor reminded me of the story of a Brooklyn Democratic politician named Goldfarb, who, after years of political loyalty, finally got a sought-after party nomination to a seat on the bench. Given the local political climate, his election was such a sure thing that in the interim between the nomination and election day, his secretary answered his law-office phone, "Good morning, office of Judge Herman Goldfarb." But the unthinkable happened, a Republican won the seat, and the secretary thereafter answered the phone with "Good morning, office of Former-Judge Herman Goldfarb."

Bork addressed the Court as if he were lecturing his intellectual inferiors. Happily, like me, they did not take it personally.

The argument was an old home week gathering of sorts. All the Liggett lawyers were there. We did not pal around. I did not like them during the trial, and nothing since had changed my mind. I got a kick out of the presence of one Clarence Eads, a North Carolina cigarette distributor who became the butt of

everyone's (on our side, anyway) jokes when, in apparent confusion, he testified for Liggett and said the *lowering of generic
prices hurt his generic sales!* But he had a great southern accent,
and I guess the Liggett team had calculated that the jury would
relate to him. Hmm, maybe they were right.

The nicest comment of the day came from Bynum
Hunter, the lawyer for Grand Met, Liggett's parent. I quote
from my March 31, 1993 report to the firm:

> [Hunter] was gracious and said, in a voice that was
> more than loud enough for [B&W's General Counsel]
> to overhear, "They've made a big mistake, Marty,
> you're the guy who should be arguing this. What's
> the matter with them?"
> I smiled and said, "Thank you."

The Supreme Court, after a lot of palaver, affirmed
by a vote of 6-3. It bypassed the Fourth Circuit opinion,
and instead adopted the argument we had made to
Judge Bullock. The Supremes quoted extensively from
Bullock's post-trial opinion. After all these years, it came
down to Marty Flumenbaum's deposition of the Liggett
executives, and their inability at trial to escape from the
admissions he had wrung out of them. Flumenbaum can
practice law for a long time before one of his depositions
is again cited by the Supreme Court of the United States
as the basis of its decision.

Glad we won, and glad I don't have to do that again. In
the end, it was an extraordinary demonstration of what lawyers can accomplish if they're reasonably smart and very
tough. I barely squeaked through on both counts.

Part V:

A LITIGATION
POTPOURRI

A Rose is a Rose is a Rose –
But Not Always

Oral advocacy is an art. Most lawyers are plodders.
Few are Masters.
Anon

✦

In 1964, the non-profit *United Housing Foundation* conceived of an enormous project to ameliorate the shortage of housing for middle income residents of New York City. The size of the proposal was staggering. The Foundation would borrow 250 million dollars at below-market interest rates and build a "city" on a square mile of former swampland in the southeast Bronx. New York State granted the construction loan under the auspices of its Mitchell-Lama program, which encouraged affordable housing.

The project would consist of 35 apartment houses, plus townhouses, stores, garages, ballfields, firehouses, schools – a community of 45,000 residents that, if it were an independent political entity, would be the tenth largest city in New York State. Co-op City remains the largest cooperative housing development in the United States, and perhaps the world.

Applicants for an apartment in Co-op City were required to meet specified minimum and maximum income levels that had been established to accommodate New York's civil servants and others in similar earnings brackets. Residents were required to buy shares of the common stock of the cooperative corporation that owned the entire site. As in other co-ops, residential leases were inextricably tied to shareholder status. Beneficiaries of the state's largess had to submit to a number of important restrictions: while the co-op shares could be inherited by a spouse, they could not be sold on the open market unless the tenant/shareholder first offered his shares back to the cooperative corporation, which would return his purchase price. If the corporation elected to refuse the shares, they could be sold only to someone who met the same income qualifications, and the shares could not be sold for more than the original purchase price.

Co-op City was a great bargain for those tenants who qualified. A 1967 applicant for a three-room apartment could purchase stock in the cooperative corporation for $1,350, and was predicted to incur a monthly "rent" bill (i.e., co-op maintenance charges) of $69. But inflation was brutal and by 1974, the "rent" for that apartment almost doubled to $119 – still a great bargain compared to New York City market rents.

While the initial offering circular contained a number of warnings about the possibility of increased costs, in 1975, a small group of tenants retained the famous trial lawyer Louis Nizer to bring a federal class action against the officers and directors of the co-op and the United

Housing Foundation. Plaintiffs claimed the offering circular violated the antifraud provisions of the federal securities laws by inducing them to purchase their shares of common stock in the cooperative corporation by failing to reveal the likelihood of construction-cost increases that would be passed on to the tenants in the form of increased monthly maintenance charges. To defend against the claim, Co-op City's Board of Directors came to Rifkind, who recruited young partner London, who conscripted young associate George Felleman.

George and I reviewed the pleading, the facts, and the law, and came up with two defenses.

One: The facts were on our side. We thought the offering circular fully disclosed the possibility that inflation would drive up costs, and there was no merit to the allegation that our clients had misled prospective tenants. For sure, there was some language in the circular that could be troublesome if taken out of context, but a fair reading of the entire document would likely convince a judge to dismiss the complaint on the merits. If not, we thought we had a strong jury case – but that, of course, was a last resort.

Two: We campaigned to persuade Rifkind that our first attack should be on the subject-matter jurisdiction of the federal court. The anti-fraud statutes relied upon by the plaintiffs applied to transactions involving:

> [A]ny . . . stock, . . . investment contract . . . or in general, any instrument commonly known as a "security" . . .

The two of us sat opposite this intellectual giant of the bench and trial bar, and tried to persuade him that a share of "stock" in this non-profit cooperative corporation was not a share of "stock" covered by the statute, though there was no specific language in the statute saying that.

(In fact, a few months later, a judge sitting in the same district court held that shares in a regular "for profit" New York City residential co-op were indeed "stock" under the federal anti-fraud statute.)

It was a tough sell. Rifkind kept saying, "But fellas, the statute says 'stock,' which is what our clients sold to the plaintiffs – a share of 'stock,' right? Where does the statute say Co-op City 'stock' is not 'stock'?"

It took several meetings before we wore him down. I am not sure he was ever really persuaded we were right, but he finally said, "Okay, you two smart guys are really convinced it's worth a shot, so let's do it," and we moved to dismiss on the "this-stock-is-not-a-stock" jurisdictional defense. I have always wondered whether it was his doubts about our theory, or his confidence in me, that led Rifkind to say, "Okay, Martin, it's your idea, so you argue the motion."

My opponent was Nizer's partner George Berger, who mustered a solid presentation. But not good enough. District Judge Lawrence W. Pierce issued a 22-page opinion dismissing the complaint for lack of federal jurisdiction. With no direct precedent, he held:

1. The Co-op City share of "stock" is not a share of "stock" covered by the Securities Acts. Ours was a real estate transaction, not a securities transaction, and the non-profit co-op stock had none of the attributes of a share of stock intended to be covered by the laws designed to regulate the securities markets, and

   Plaintiffs' argument that the co-op stock nevertheless fit under the statute's definition because it was an "investment contract" was flawed. Co-op City stock was not an "investment contract," because it lacked any possibility of *earning a profit*, which, by definition, was an essential element of that financial instrument. Plaintiffs' assertion that elements such as below-market rents, tax deductions for part of the maintenance fee, or the income from the basement washing machines were "profit," do not fit within the ordinary meaning of that word.

Plaintiffs appealed Judge Pierce's ruling, and the big guns were moved up to the front line. The Second Circuit courtroom was packed to hear the main event: Louis Nizer v. Simon Rifkind. Historic. Well, not as it turned out. Rifkind was brilliant, but his adversary had very serious vision problems, and was ill-prepared. Nose to the lectern, he read his argument from a thick book of pages upon which someone had hand-printed words in inch-high letters. In terms of courtroom skills, it wasn't a fair contest.

But that had little or nothing to do with the result. The appellate court voted 3-0 to reverse. It held:

> 1. A "stock" is a "stock" is a "stock."

And, belt and suspenders,

> A share of Co-op City stock was also an "investment contract" because it had elements of "profit" via the below-market rents, the tax deductions, and incidental income from the washing machines.

The Supreme Court agreed to review the Circuit Court reversal. It would be a Rifkind-Nizer rematch. Felleman and I wrote the briefs and worked with Rifkind for hours preparing him for oral argument. We went over every legal precedent, the strengths and weaknesses of every argument pro and con, the questions that might be asked, etc. We were merciless with our septuagenarian leader.

This was Rifkind's ballpark, his métier. He was ready. More, he was downright eager.

As we sat at the appellants' table in the well of the Supreme Court, George and I were astonished when Rifkind began with an argument we had never heard before:

> Mr. Chief Justice, and may it please the Court: Words can have many meanings. One can have an oak tree, a coat tree, or a whiffletree. Obviously three different things, so we need to know more about each of them, what purpose they serve, before we can decide how to deal with them.

George and I looked at each other as if a Martian had just set down in front of the bench. *Whiffletree?*

Rifkind then went on to make his carefully prepared argument showing how Co-op City "stock" differed from the "stock" intended to be covered by the Securities Acts.

Sadly, either no one on the other side of the case had the courage to tell Mr. Nizer the truth, or if they did, he had refused to listen. The frail lawyer rendered up yet another embarrassing performance.

I could barely wait until the argument was over, and as the three of us walked down the courthouse steps, I said, "Okay, Judge, give! A *whiffletree*? What's that?"

He grinned. He was like a six-year old who had just swiped a candy cane from the Christmas tree while nobody was looking. He explained:

> Well, I knew that Justice White grew up in a very small town in Colorado, and he would know what I was talking about. A whiffletree is a wooden bar,

parallel to the front of a wagon drawn by a team of horses. The left and right team's harnesses are attached to the respective ends of the bar and an iron ring on the back side of the bar is attached to a stem affixed to the wagon. The center of that stem provides the forward pull. When one side of the team pulls a little harder or faster, the wooden bar pivots and evens out the pull on the stem.

What, Martin, you didn't know that?

Well, maybe they had these things in the Lithuanian shtetl where Rifkind spent his first 10 years, but I recalled no whiffletrees on Carroll Street in Brooklyn.

I had never seen Rifkind so "high." He knew he had nailed it. And he was right. Two months later, the Court, by a vote of 6-3, rejected the Second Circuit analysis and adopted, almost word for word, the opinion of District Judge Pierce. The case was over.

The word "whiffletree" was neither in the Supreme Court's opinion, nor in the dissent, *written by Mr. Justice White.*

Beware of Relatives
on the Jury

The perceived wisdom in legal circles is that jury selection is an art, and only trial lawyers really know how to do it. Maybe so, but that's not to say that all of us know what we're doin'.

◆

In 2003, District Judge Robert Sweet dismissed a case against McDonald's, in which a group of teenagers claimed Mickey D's hamburgers and fries were the cause of their obesity. The common sense judge dismissed the plaintiffs' claims, holding, "it's not the place of the law to protect them against their own excesses."

Sweet later helped the parties settle a multi-billion dollar securities case involving a failed industrial corporation and a bank I represented. Once again, his common sense was key.

I concluded that Sweet occupied the "Common Sense" seat in the Southern District of New York when I realized that he had succeeded to the chambers of the Honorable Inzer Wyatt who had given up his active duty status on the Southern District bench in 1977. Inzer Wyatt was common sense personified. I am not objective about that, and here's why. In my first year as a partner at Paul, Weiss, a major international construction firm retained me to try their criminal case. The company had been indicted for perjury in connection with its application to the United States Agency for International Development, for funding a dam project in India.

In filling out the sworn-to USAID form, my client had answered "No" to a rhetorically contorted question aimed at discovering whether illicit commissions or kickbacks had been paid to win the contract. The government contended that a fee my client had paid to a New Delhi firm required a "Yes" answer to the question.

During jury selection, Judge Wyatt started out the *voir dire* by asking if anyone on the panel knew either of the lawyers. A nicely dressed woman of a certain age, a Vassar graduate, raised her hand. She told the judge she didn't know me, but she was a cousin of my partner Lloyd Garrison whom she saw at infrequent family gatherings. That was both a surprise and a disappointment to me. Given the nature of my planned defense, I wanted educated jurors and was sorry to lose her. Wyatt asked her if she could nevertheless decide the case on the merits, and she said "Yes," but I was certain the government would use one of its peremptory challenges to strike her. I certainly would have in their place. But at the end of the day, she was still in the box, and was going to serve on our jury. Why did the government keep her? I could not imagine, and have never found out.

The government's principal witness was a federal law enforcement agent who explained to the jury what USAID did, how that helped developing countries, which, in turn advanced United States foreign policy interests, blah, blah, blah. He put my client's sworn questionnaire in evidence, offered up uncontroverted proof of my client's undisclosed payment to a New Delhi firm, and sat back in his witness chair content he had driven the final nail in my client's coffin.

On cross, I asked him a series of hypothetical questions about how *he* would answer the form's "kickback" inter-rogatory: would he answer "yes," or "no," if my client had made a payment to a local architect, to a local engineer, to a local employment agency, to a local vendor of heavy equip-ment, a secretarial service, etc. Planted among the string of hypotheticals was the important one, the one to which my client *had* paid money, a local firm that was involved in providing planning services. To that question, the by-now confused agent said "I'm not sure." Bingo. At the end of the government's case, Judge Wyatt granted our motion for a judgment of acquittal. His common sense approach was revealed when, in a post-trial robing room conference with counsel, he asked the AUSA, "How could a jury convict this company for swearing to the wrong answer to the govern-ment questionnaire if the government itself doesn't know the right answer?"

Unlike New Jersey, the New York courts have no rule that bars talking to jurors after the trial is over, and after meeting with the judge, I hustled out to the corridor to see what we could learn. Elevator service in the old courthouse was vir-tually non-functional, and there were still jurors waiting for the next car. I approached Lloyd Garrison's cousin. I hoped she would be frank and I was eager to learn how I had done with the jury.

I introduced myself, and we chatted pleasantly for a minute or two. Then I asked her, "If you had to vote at the end of the government's case, what would you have done?" Her response took me down a peg. She said, "Well, it was all too complicated. I did not understand what you were getting at with that federal agent, and if I had to vote when the judge discharged the jury, I guess I would have simply gone along with whatever the jury foreman said."

The foreman was a New York City bus driver. I have no idea what he thought about the case, but I know for sure he did not have a degree from Vassar.

Shalom and the
Second Amendment

In 2008, the "Scalia Court" decision in Heller vs. The
District of Columbia, *drastically changed a 130-year-old
understanding of what the Second Amendment meant. The
Court significantly limited the government's ability to restrict
the right to own and carry guns. While I have strong opinions about that subject, the issue was, for me, largely an aca-
demic matter. Up to the beginning of my legal career, my
only close association with guns was in the army. I had never
personally confronted a dangerous or threatening situation
involving a gun. But try enough cases and sooner or later . . .*

✦

In 1965, when I was a mid-level associate, Paul, Weiss
was called upon to represent the Broadway musical genius
Jerry Herman. Before his colossal musical hits, *Hello Dolly*,
Mame, and *La Cage Aux Folles*, Herman had written the

music and lyrics of an off-Broadway show called *Shalom*, a positive ode to life in the new Israeli democracy. When the show was produced on the Broadway stage, the title was changed to *Milk and Honey*. It ran for two years and earned five Tony nominations. The lead number in the show was the upbeat song *Shalom*, the Hebrew greeting that can mean hello, goodbye, peace, etc.

But onto this parade, some rain did fall. An automobile mechanic from Colorado claimed he had written a song with the same title years before Herman did, and sued for copyright infringement.

I knew nothing about music, but in another case I had learned quite a bit about copyright infringement, and Martin Kleinbard asked me to work on the matter with him. Some basic principles: to make out a successful claim, a copyright infringement plaintiff must prove that the defendant, consciously or unconsciously, *actually copied* the work. Similarity is not enough. If two people happened upon the same series of notes or words independently of one another, there is no infringement. Because the plaintiff must prove *copying*, he must prove the defendant had direct or indirect access to the original piece because you cannot *copy* something you never saw or heard. Without access, there could be no copying, and therefore, no liability.

The auto mechanic had indeed written a song entitled *Shalom* that preceded Herman's. There was no claim the music was similar, only the lyrics. Titles are not copyrightable, and Martin Kleinbard and I thought the lyrics were only vaguely similar. Plaintiff's song was a sad dirge, while Herman's was a joyous celebration. We were confident we could win a dismissal on the similarity question, though the law is sharply tilted toward jury determination of that issue. But before we made our motion based on similarity,

I was sent to Denver to take plaintiff's deposition on the access question. If there were no access, there could be no question of our right to get the complaint thrown out.

I borrowed a lawyer's office there, arranged for a stenographer, and was seated at the conference table reviewing my notes when the plaintiff and his lawyer walked in. I was dressed in my New York City lawyer uniform: dark suit, white shirt, and silk tie. The plaintiff's lawyer was dressed in his Denver lawyer uniform: whipcord trousers, sport jacket, western shirt, and string tie. The plaintiff wore his John Wayne ensemble: cowboy boots, jeans, western shirt open at the collar, and the biggest revolver I had ever seen. The gun screamed "Look at me," nestled in its bright tan leather holster, hanging from a tooled gun belt. To me, at least, it seemed to reach from his hip to his knee.

If these guys thought that bringing that six-shooter into the deposition room would alter my approach to the inquiry, they were absolutely correct. This was not my first deposition, and I knew that things sometimes get a bit testy. I try to be polite, but my job was not to make nice-nice, and my questions sometimes piss off the witness. There was no way I was going to depose a man bearing a gun. Not a chance. In the politest terms I could muster, on the record, I told the plaintiff's lawyer I was not about to interrogate his client while he was armed. That was not negotiable. The lawyer responded that his client had a right, under Colorado law, to wear an open-carry pistol. I said I didn't know anything about Colorado's laws or customs, but one thing I did know was that there was no way I would proceed with this deposition, whether the weapon was possessed legally or otherwise, open or closed carry, whatever. I suggested we mosey on down to the federal courthouse and take the deposition there. If his client had a hankering to keep his shooter, he could take the matter up with the federal marshals.

That was the winning argument. He relented. The deposition was delayed while the plaintiff went home, hung up his cannon, and returned after lunch, unarmed, whereupon he told his story.

He had a pet cat that lived outdoors, and on cold nights, it sometimes crawled up onto the still-warm engine block of his truck and slept there. The plaintiff's pickup was a standard model: under the hood was the engine, just forward of which was the fan that pulled in cooling air across the fins of the radiator behind the grill. One morning, Tabby was sleeping soundly on his preferred perch atop the engine block when plaintiff started up his truck, the fan whirred, and, sigh, decapitated the kitty. The mechanic was heartbroken, and was moved to say goodbye to his pal by writing a song entitled *Shalom*.

Was the song ever published? No. Did plaintiff have any evidence Herman had ever seen or heard the lyrics? No. The best plaintiff could do was to allege his song was played once, on a low-wattage radio station in the mountains north of Denver, at a time Herman was working in Manhattan. Did plaintiff have any evidence Jerry was in the vicinity at that time? No. Or that someone, anyone, had heard it and told him about it? No. Jerry Herman wasn't there, had never heard, or heard of, plaintiff's ode to his dead cat. End of case.

I haven't taken a deposition in Colorado since.

My Fair Lady: Performance Interruptus

A nother trip to The Great White Way poses these questions: When George Bernard Shaw premiered his play Pygmalion for the first time in 1913, could he possibly have anticipated the success of a Broadway musical version of it a half-century later? Or the six years of litigation that followed the untimely close of that show?

✦

The 1956 production of *My Fair Lady* permanently imprinted on the minds of all who saw the Broadway musical or the subsequent film, the delightful story of Eliza Doolittle and Professor Henry Higgins. Paul, Weiss client Herman Levin produced the Tony Award-winning Broadway show starring Julie Andrews and Rex Harrison. Nobody who has heard the Lerner and Loewe score and libretto will ever forget Professor Higgins' lament, "Why

Can't a Woman Be More Like a Man?" and Eliza's retort, "Just You Wait, Henry Higgins, Just You Wait!" Reviewers called Levin's production the "best musical of the century" and predicted it "would run forever."

But it didn't run forever. When ticket sales slowed in the sixth year of the run, the owner of the Mark Hellinger Theatre, real estate entrepreneur Stanley Stahl, effectively throttled the show by announcing he had advised his box office personnel to refuse to sell tickets for performances after February 24, 1962. He cancelled the theatre agreement, and entered into a new lease of the Hellinger to Richard Rodgers' *No Strings*.

Levin immediately sued for a judgment establishing his right to keep the show in the Hellinger and requiring Stahl's box office to continue to sell tickets. Levin's lawyer was Paul, Weiss associate Arthur Frommer, whom I later succeeded at the firm. The court put the case on a fast track, but trial judge Owen McGivern ruled for the theatre on the contract issues at the heart of the dispute, and on February 13,1962, concluded:

> The defendants [theatre owners] were entitled to terminate the lease of the parties. The complaint is dismissed and the plaintiff is directed to vacate the premises involved herein on or before February 22, 1962.

That pretty much ended the show's run. It managed to play for six weeks at The Broadhurst Theatre, then moved again to a third theatre for some months, but the momentum was lost, advance ticket sales had been crippled, confusion reigned, and the show closed in September of that year. An autopsy report on the cause of the show's demise could fairly read: *Performance Interruptus*.

But the closing of the show did not ring down the final curtain on the legal dispute. Levin appealed the lower court decision, and the Appellate Division reversed. That court ruled that it was the theatre owner who breached the contract by instructing his box office personnel to stop selling tickets, and Stahl's cancellation of the lease "does not appear to have been in good faith." The court concluded:

> [E]ven though the Liza Company vacated the theatre, in compliance with the judgment . . . there remains undetermined the rights of the parties with respect to alleged damages.

The Court of Appeals unanimously affirmed that decision.

Those decisions led to a new round of litigation. When the matter went back to the trial court, a different trial judge ruled Levin was not entitled to any damages because the law does not award damages resulting from obedience to a court order, even if the order were later reversed.

Sigh, back to the Appellate Division, and a unanimous five-judge panel (including Owen McGivern, the original trial judge who ruled against Levin!) reversed again, holding it wasn't McGivern's erroneous decision that caused the Liza Company's injury but,

> [T]he damages . . . were caused by the prior breaches of this defendant and were not the consequence of the entry of the judgment. The cessation of the advance sales of tickets, which occurred long prior to the entry of judgment . . . caused damage to the plaintiff. . . . The defendant's breaches made removal an economic necessity.

Next step, a trial on the question of the amount of our client's damages. The roster of plaintiff's trial team: Simon H. Rifkind and his young associate, Martin London.

There were to be four witnesses at this non-jury trial to fix the amount of the damage award: principals Levin and Stahl, and each side's accountant. Rifkind and I split the chores: pre-trial, I was to do the depositions and prepare our witnesses. At trial, I would examine both sides' accountants, and Rifkind was to do the direct of Levin and the cross of Stahl.

Preparation for the trial was a substantial effort. There were many elements to our client's injury: loss of ticket sales, moving expenses, missed performances, contract differences with the successor theatres, increased advertising costs, etc. I took the depositions of Stahl and his accountant, and defended the depositions of our two witnesses. I worked with our accountant and the client to calculate the costs, prepared the schedules, gathered the trial exhibits, prepared direct examinations for Levin and his accountant, and prepared my cross of Stahl's accountant. Rifkind was to prepare his own cross of Stahl.

At trial, we were the plaintiff and went first. We got off to a good start. Rifkind's direct of our client Herman Levin was silky smooth and there was not much on which they could cross him. I led our accountant through the numbers, backed them up with bills, checks, and other financial records, and basically, our adversary did not lay a glove on him.

The defendant opened his case with his accountant. I knew everything he was going to say because I had deposed him. I had spent a zillion hours preparing his cross, and I was pleased with the result. That left the final witness, Mr. Stanley Stahl. This was Rifkind's cross, and when Stahl took the stand, I finally relaxed. I had no more courtroom duties. I switched off my brain and sat back to watch the show.

But about a quarter of the way through Stahl's direct, I felt a jolt in my left rib cage. Rifkind had the sharpest elbows in town, and having sat next to him in court before, I not only knew that jab, but I knew how long it would take for the black and blue mark to fade. But it wasn't the physical injury that concerned me. I feared the worst and was right. When I Iooked at my boss with raised eyebrows. he said, oh so casually, "Y'know, Martin, I'm feeling a bit tired. Why don't you take this one?"

Holy cow! I have a love/hate relationship with cross-examination. To be done effectively, it takes meticulous preparation that can be extensive and exhausting. That part is not fun. It's often torture. Then, in court, knowing precisely how I am going to deconstruct the witness, totally confident of where I am going, center stage, in charge, adrenaline pumping, I am flying. I love that part.

But now my boss, indeed, the boss of bosses, wanted me to jump in and cross a witness for whom I had not prepared one question, with not one note to guide me. In fact, I hadn't even really listened to the first part of his direct; I had been on vacation. But it's not like I had a choice in the matter. Hey, I am in court. I am a lawyer, on trial, so I gotta behave like a trial lawyer, right? Suck it up, London.

The good news, as Rifkind well knew, was I had taken Stahl's deposition. There was a section of it I remembered with clarity. I dug it out of my bag. I was asking the witness about his decision to tell his box office people to sell no tickets for performances after February 24th. Stahl, like so many businessmen being deposed, was cranky. He was annoyed at the court rulings holding him liable and questioning his good faith, and he was annoyed at this young kid badgering him with questions about his business decisions. In the deposition, I pressed: Did there come a time when he learned to which theatre the show was moving? "Yes." Did he post a written notice outside his box office informing patrons where the show was going? "No." Did he send such a note to people who mailed in for tickets? "No." Did he instruct his box office personnel to give that information to callers? "No." I took a no-lose flyer, and the Q & A were to this effect, "In fact, sir, you really didn't give a damn whether any of those customers ever got to buy tickets to My Fair Lady, correct?" and he snapped back, "Correct."

It doesn't get much better than that, and I used it as the centerpiece of a brief but biting trial cross. The witness was just as angry with me at trial as he had been at his deposition, but the point was a powerful one and the trial judge awarded us $102,641.30.

Back up the appellate ladder we climbed. At the top rung, in response to a brief written by London and an argument by Rifkind, a unanimous Court of Appeals wrote:

Judgment affirmed, with costs, no opinion.

Ahh, "Wouldn't it be loverly?" Yes, Eliza, it would, and it was.

Seasickness, Aeronautics, and Mr. Rockefeller

Donald Trump was not the only wealthy "celebrity" adversary I encountered. A suit against the Rockefeller family taught me a lot about the physics of airplane flight and airport construction. It was my only sojourn into the world of personal injury litigation, and proved to me that this «specialty,» like every other category of litigation, can be mastered by study and hard work. The case also taught me, early in my career, elemental differences in class among the super-rich.

✦

In the late '60s, the Rockefeller family's resort arm built a beautiful hotel on the island of Virgin Gorda in the British Virgin Islands. The guests were accommodated in charming little cottages fashioned to look like grass-roofed huts, each of which was but a short walk to a white sand beach bordering Little Dix Bay, which provided the resort's name. The hotel's dining room was an open-sided pavilion, and the starched white tablecloths, immaculately costumed efficient dining room personnel, and excellent food, all combined to provide a fine dining experience for the hotel's well-to-do patrons.

But in its first year of operation, the hotel's managers confronted a problem that threatened to bring about the demise of the venture: to get to the hotel, guests were required to fly to neighboring Beef Island and then take a ferry across a rough channel to Virgin Gorda. Hotel guests arrived bearing a facial pallor matching the color of the shallow sea that covered the reefs and sandbars surrounding the tropical island – puke green.

The Rockefellers desperately needed an alternative transportation scheme. They needed a flat piece of land on this volcanic island upon which to lay down an airplane landing strip. They were marginally successful and acquired some reasonably appropriate acreage bounded on the west by a big hill. They could level and pave the scrub plain, but no way could they dispose of the hill, and had no choice but to construct their airstrip to the east of it. The prevailing easterly winds exacerbated their aeronautical problem. In normal airplane landing descents, the aircraft gradually reduces airspeed, which in turn results in a gradual loss of lift, which in turn results in a gradual loss of altitude, *all the while maintaining virtually level flight* until the wheels touch down. One of the many skills involved in landing an airplane is synchronizing the level-flight loss of altitude with the need to touch down close enough to the beginning of the runway so as to permit the aircraft enough run-off room to stop or at least slow down before turning off the active strip.

Because of the hill, a level approach and descent was not possible on the new Gorda strip. To make matters worse, the easterly wind deflected up off the hill and provided unwanted lift to overhead light aircraft. As a result, incoming planes were required to effectively power dive downhill, then, at the bottom of the hill, flare out to restore level flight and still touch down no farther than one third of the way down the strip. If the pilot misjudged the approach and touched down too far down the runway, he was required immediately to reapply full power, lift off, and go around again. That maneuver is not so rare on aircraft carriers and those Caribbean airstrips located windward of a hill.

To promote the opening of their new airstrip, the management of the Little Dix Bay resort announced a "Fly-in". They invited local pilots from all over the Caribbean to land at the new strip and be treated to a sumptuous lunch at the hotel. To make the occasion more festive, hotel employees installed a row of gaily-colored pennants mounted on 25' metal flagpoles at the eastern end of the strip. Great idea for a parade, not so much for an airport runway.

Amateur pilots flying single engine planes and landing at this unfamiliar location had problems fighting the hill's updrafts. Many had to go around again, some more than once. One in particular (flying in with his wife and two of their three children), flew over from San Juan, struggled with the wind on the approach, touched down too far down the strip, and applied full power to go around again. He successfully lifted off, but a wing tip caught one of the poles, the plane pivoted and crashed into the rocks at the end of the strip. Both parents were killed. The children in back miraculously were spared serious injury.

The executor of the deceased parents' estates was Howard Seitz, a Paul, Weiss Trusts and Estates partner, and he asked litigation partner Martin Kleinbard to look into the question of whether there was liability and possible recompense for the children.

Kleinbard was a beloved and brilliant litigator, but he was the kind of guy who had trouble recognizing one end of a screwdriver from the other. Enter Martin London, boy lawyer, boy mechanic, a fifth-year associate, who took the laboring oar. I proceeded to read every treatise I could find on airplane crash cases. I read every court decision, law review article, and bathroom wall scribbling on the subject. Most were not very helpful. After all, there was not much doubt about liability, I did not need to deal with class actions or enlisting other victims, I was not worried about the size of the defendant's insurance policy, and no international compact limited the amount of damage recovery. I made the first major step toward success when I discovered the Rockefeller resort ownership pattern for new hotels: for arcane tax reasons, the properties were owned individually until they became profitable. The owner of the *Little Dix Bay* resort that planted the poles was Mr. Laurance Rockefeller himself. We sued Mr. R for an appropriate telephone book number, in New York Supreme Court, the jurisdiction of his residence.

The Kleinbards and the Londons booked an investigatory stay at the hotel. Subsequent to the crash, the authorities regulated access to the strip to twin-engine planes, a regulation that effectively barred amateur pilots, and the flagpoles were gone. No, we did not think it necessary to identify the purpose of our visit, but it was helpful to see the scene of the tragedy. The visit was especially rewarding, when, on the way home, I spent several days digging around in San Juan. I found newspaper files containing photos, and visited a local TV station that had 8mm movies of the crash. Some of the images were gruesome. I also found and interviewed eyewitnesses, including other pilots. All were eager to help.

At some point in the legal proceedings, it was time to take the deposition of the defendant. This experience was unusual in two respects.

First, I was prepared for a lot of 'tude. Many CEOs and prominent businessmen strongly resent the deposition process. They come into the room all puffed up, secure in the company of their top-flight, impeccably dressed lawyers. The executives often convey a baked-in arrogance, a "Why are you bothering an important person like me with this stuff?" attitude. And add to the mix, in this instance the lawyer asking the questions was what my father would call a "piker," a guy who did not earn in a year what the witness probably earned while sitting there. To my surprise, this witness was attentive, courteous, and entirely professional. In fact, he was particularly interested in aviation, having been an early investor in Eastern Airlines. He listened, answered my questions directly and, so far as I could see, frankly.

Second, normally, the questioner tries to elicit the other side's version of the facts, pin him down about what he saw, what he said, what he heard, what he knew, so he cannot change his story at trial. Additionally, the goal is to gather all the evidence there is, good and bad. That's why it's called "discovery," the opportunity to discover the adversary's evidence and legal theory.

Mr. Rockefeller was hardly a hands-on hotel manager. He had not been there on the day of the crash, was not involved in the planning of the day's festivities, and knew nothing about the poles until after the crash. I, on the other hand, knew a lot about the facts, and spent much of the time in the deposition teaching Mr. Rockefeller the details of what his employees had done, and the consequences to my clients. I asked a lot of "Did you know" questions. I showed him photos of the crash scene, the poles, the crumpled plane with the decedents hanging upside down in their seatbelts, the injured children being taken away on stretchers, etc. One of the film clips appeared to show some movement by the mother while she was hanging suspended by her seatbelt, a grisly but important fact in getting compensation for pain and suffering prior to death.

While I was sure he had been prepared by his competent counsel, I sensed he was ultimately staggered by what I taught him that day.

Adopting a suggestion plucked from one of the books I had read, after the deposition, I prepared and submitted to Mr. Rockefeller's lawyers a "Settlement Brochure." In it I put crash pictures and film strips, and pictures of the family before the crash, from the birth of the three children up to the fatal day. I included the children's report cards, camp letters the kids had written to their parents, stuff like that. I supplied textual and documentary support for my estimates of what the deceased parents reasonably could have been expected to earn in their lifetimes. That scrapbook made *me* teary, and I was the one who put it together!

Not long after the deposition and the submission of the settlement brochure, Mr. Rockefeller's lawyers called with an offer that made my head spin for its generosity. After some brief negotiations, the case was settled for a sum that Messrs. Seitz, Kleinbard, and London considered more than fair.

I have not been back to Virgin Gorda. Instead, my wife and I regularly visit St. Barths, which, ironically enough, has an almost identical flight approach over a hill at the western end of a short east-west landing strip. The roller coaster dive approach to the bottom of the hill is certainly attention-gathering. But the commercial planes that carry us are piloted by professionals who are specially certified to land there. And there are no poles at the end of the strip, no rocks, just white sand and gentle St. Jean Bay. When an occasional plane overruns the end of the strip, the beachgoers have been known to applaud the relieved passengers as they step down onto the white sand, or in one case, into the shin deep warm water. Hey, no harm, no foul.

Come on down!

Man's Best Friend:
My Canine Practice

*C*lients sometimes ask their lawyers to solve the most unexpected problems. Every now and then, a case comes along that does not require grinding hours of legal research, brief writing, or fact investigation: just common sense and reliance on personal experience. Those cases, when they turn out right, are fun. The final two matters reported here involve dogs. I confess my attraction to these engagements derives in large measure from my love of the beasts. The odd result: dogs were good for business and advanced my career.

◆

When I was a young Paul, Weiss partner, an important partner of a significant investment bank client of the firm came to me with a litigation problem that seemed trivial. His estranged wife had rented a house in the Berkshires for the summer. At the end of her stay, the owner asserted that the living room carpet was "ruined" because her small dog peed on it. Our client had not seen the claimed damage, but knew the dog and thought him capable of that, and more. He agreed to pay for having the rug professionally cleaned.

The owner rejected the offer. Apparently, this rug was hand woven by a sect of blind widows located somewhere in the Himalayas, and was made from scarce inner-ear hair of pregnant Yaks ... or something like that. Anyway, it could not be cleaned, it had to be replaced, and the cost of that would run to five figures.

Enter the lawyers. I sent the owner a letter, re-offering the cleaning option, suggesting that was the limit of my client's generosity. I assured him my client did not want to litigate this issue, but was prepared to do so if necessary. The naive hope that my letter would resolve the disagreement was shattered when I received a reply from the owner's lawyer, a distinguished former federal judge, now heading the litigation section of a major New York City firm. The letter was a powerful indictment of the dog's urinary propensities. He insisted we replace the carpet, or else.

My client was outraged. He instructed me to communicate a withdrawal of his offer to clean the carpet, and to prepare for litigation. Ah, just what I wanted, a dog-pee case. I was in for it. I did some checking and learned the cottage owner was wealthy, and reputed to be an aggressive litigation-oriented pain in the ass. Bottom line: this case was not about a peeing dog; it was about a bull elephant who wanted to demonstrate the size of his testicles.

As it happened, I knew my adversary counsel; Pinks and I had had drinks and dinner with him and his charming wife at a Federal Bar Council shindig in the Caribbean a few years earlier. As a result, out of the presence of our clients, we were able to discuss the momentous issues of the dispute without bombast. He was reasonable, I was reasonable, we persuaded our clients to agree on a responsible rug cleaner who was prepared to say he specialized in cleaning rare Yak-hair carpets, the blind Himalayan women were spared the burden of weaving a replacement masterpiece, and the pregnant Yaks were left in peace.

Not only did I add to my store of knowledge about dealing with bull elephants, I impressed an important Paul, Weiss client, who thereafter asked me to handle more substantial matters, not the least of which was the negotiation of his separation agreement. You can be sure the wife got the dog.

The Case of the Singing Weimaraners

The misadventures of the peeing rat-dog was not my first canine legal experience. When I was a young Paul, Weiss associate, I had a Weimaraner who "sang." If I vocalized, she mimicked me by whimpering, howling, crying, whatever sounds a dog can make that track human pitch. She had long silky ears, stunning blue eyes, she was sleek, gentle, and I loved her with all my heart, as did my children.

One morning, a litigation partner popped his head into my office and said, "Hey, Marty, you free to come with me to a new-client meeting in half an hour? The guy is a big time real estate developer who has a litigation problem. Big pow wow." That means lots of lawyers. One of my clients referred to these kinds of meetings as "Elephant Fucks." When I asked him to explain, he said, "These meetings have three things in common with Elephant Fucks: i) they take place at a very high level, ii) there is a lot of trumpeting, braying, and foot stamping, and iii) nothing happens thereafter for a very long time." I loved Elephant Fucks, and said "Sure." Actually, I would have said "Sure" even if I didn't love Elephant Fucks. Ya don't have fun in this business by saying "No."

The distinguished elderly client insisted on a lunch meeting – in his penthouse. Glad my mother taught me to wear a clean shirt every day.

The luncheon group was large. Present were the client, his son, his CEO, his in-house lawyer, his outside real estate lawyer, that lawyer's young partner, the real estate partner from my firm who brought in the client, the Paul, Weiss litigation partner, me, and some others. There were perhaps a dozen people sitting facing each other at the long table in the client's dining room. One thing I recall with dead certainty. I was the lowest guy on the totem pole, and while the client was at the head of the table surrounded by legal poobahs, I was at the other end – in the cheapest of the cheap seats.

Before the butler brought out the first course, I heard click-clack sounds that were familiar to me. If I didn't know better, I would swear that a large dog was approaching the table from behind me, and the sounds were his toenails on the polished wood floors. I turned around, and saw the Weimaraner approach the table. The dog was drop-dead gorgeous – he could have been a littermate of *my* Weimaraner, Blue II. Svelte body, beautiful short silky grey coat, graceful hanging ears, an intelligent pointed face, highlighted by the pup's gorgeous blue eyes. A perfectly irresistible animal. If I could have stolen him, I would have considered it. The pooch walked down the length of the table, leaving a trail of water dripping from his muzzle, sat down at his master's side, and stared up at him. The millionaire real estate mogul took the beautiful starched linen napkin off his lap, and used it to dry his pet's snout. The other guests looked on, appalled. I chuckled. It is exactly what I would have done.

The client apologized to the group and explained that he puts out water bowls, but His Highness prefers to drink out of the toilet bowl. The rest of the table struggled unsuccessfully to mask their revulsion, while I struggled to cope with Rule One in the *Young Associates' Handbook for Conduct at Client Meetings*: "Do not speak unless you are asked a direct question."

But I could not help myself. It was like talking about your child. I ignored the high-ranking legal stars and addressed the client at the other end of the table. "Amazing," I volunteered, "I have a Weimaraner who is a double for yours. And she too loves to drink out of the toilet. Indeed, if we leave the toilet lid down, she whines until we lift it for her."

Here we are in the Situation Room, and the Generals and Admirals are silently fuming at the Corporal sitting at the far end of the table, who, unbidden, dares speak directly to the Commander in Chief. And about dogs, yet!

Too bad for them. The client is intrigued. He explains that he, too, has tried the close-the-toilet-lid maneuver and been whimpered into submission by his blue-eyed dumb-child. From that point on, the prospective client and I might as well have been the only people in the room. After some more dog stories, he boasted that his dog sings! He demonstrated: He crooned, and the dog lifted his nose to the ceiling, opened his mouth, and crooned. The client howled and the dog howled. The client whimpered, and the dog imitated him. The rest of the meeting attendees struggled to hide their eye-rolling mockery of this performance. But I was astonished by this parallel, and told the client my dog does the same thing! When he gave me a skeptical look, I howled and then heard the toenail clicks as His Highness approached. He sat down at *my* side, fixed me with those blues, pointed his face at the ceiling, and howled. I crooned and the dog crooned. The client cheered.

The other lawyers at the table were by now visibly furious, and were gnashing their teeth, clanking their silverware, shuffling their feet under the table. No business was getting done and what's worse, the lowest guy on the totem pole was monopolizing this very important client.

We ultimately did get down to business and the problem was later solved. I do not remember the details. But what I do remember is that some time later the client got into a more serious problem, and called *me*, by then a first-year partner at the firm. I helped him. A few years later, his son had a business problem and *he* called me. That too worked out well.

I am not sure, but I thought the litigation partner who took me to the first meeting may have been a bit out of sorts because the clients called me and not him. But hey, he did not have a Weimaraner. He didn't even have a dog. Served him right. Ah, another stepping stone in my career at the bar.

Do I owe some of my success to my darling Blue II? Maybe, maybe not. I loved that pup, even though she had a screw loose. Do we not love our "challenged" children? I lived in the suburbs and she took it as her duty to protect our house from all invaders, and I mean *all*. My kids complained that friends couldn't come to play without making an appointment and getting an "it's ok" personal introduction to her. She always honored those arrangements. But when a man came to deliver a new refrigerator, we took no chances, and put Blue II on a leash, securely tied it to a hook screwed into the paneled wall in the den, and reassured her. She sat and anxiously tracked the uniformed stranger wheeling the big box into *her* house, and after twenty seconds of whimpering anxiety, she charged the invader. The leash was secure around her neck, the hook held in the wall, but her lunge was so determined she ripped the wooden paneling off the wall, hook and all. I appreciated the loyalty, but . . .

Fortunately, one of the kids caught her before she took a chunk out of the delivery man's behind.

Later, while playing football with the kids on the front lawn, she met an untimely end defending her team from a passing motorcycle. She will always remain in my pantheon of greats.

Part VI:
PERSONAL

Out of Brooklyn, and a Big Assist from Mario Puzo

My mother's parents and my father were part of the great 1890-1910 wave of East European immigration. They were included among those whom fourth-generation German-Jewish immigrant Emma Lazarus unflatteringly described as the "wretched refuse of your teeming shore." Those words had not yet been installed on the base of the Statue of Liberty when my ancestors passed it on their way to Ellis Island, but even if they had, nobody in my family would have been offended because they understood only Yiddish, along with a smattering of Russian and Polish.

I never got to talk about the immigrant experience with my mother's parents, but my father remembered much of his history and it tracked a familiar pattern. One of eleven children, his two older brothers came first to earn passage for the rest of the family. Dad arrived with his parents and eight siblings, none of whom spoke a word of English. He had no idea of his birthdate, and he was placed in a Lower East Side public school with kids approximately his size. There is a prevailing assumption he was about ten years old. He learned to speak English because he had to. My mother, younger than my father, was born in this country to parents who, like him, came from somewhere in Europe that was Poland for a while, then Russia, then somewhere in-between.

It is unclear whether my father ever finished high school. In his late teens, he rented a pushcart and sold nuts he bought wholesale at the docks. Later, he bought an interest in a garage in East Harlem, and married my mother, whose sole jobs thereafter were to raise their three children, keep the family checkbook, and occasionally work in Dad's store. She died of breast cancer at the age of 44.

In the late '20s, the family moved to an apartment above a hardware store Dad bought in Glen Cove, New York. My older brother Philip and I were born in that town. Near the end of his life, Dad confessed to me (with a smile) that he had supplemented the store's hammer-and-nail revenue with the profits from an occasional gallon tin of grain alcohol he delivered to the great estates on the North Shore of Long Island. After the repeal of Prohibition, he got one of the first liquor licenses, and the family moved to Brooklyn where he established *London Wines and Liquors* on Utica Avenue, four blocks from the two-family attached house he eventually purchased. The store was a family enterprise. While my father was the principal operator, his sister's son worked there as a clerk when he was discharged from the army after the war, my mother helped out behind the counter during the Christmas and Passover rush, as did my brother when he was home from college, and I moved cases of wine and liquor in the basement where I had to remain hidden because I was under age.

In the early 1940's, kids my age were obsessed with World War II. We collected cardboard for paper drives and brought it to school where we also bought 25-cent "savings stamps" to aid the war effort. We pasted the stamps in a special book, and when the book was full, you reached $18.75, and traded it in for a $25 War Bond. At home, we collected every ounce of scrap metal we could get our hands on. There was a six-foot-high scrap pile at the curb two doors down from our house, and as soon as it was picked up by a Sanitation Department truck, we started it over again. We followed the battle maps in the newspapers, cried when FDR died, and thrilled to the street celebrations on VE Day, and then VJ Day. It was beyond imagination that 50 years later I would be making trips to Tokyo, representing a major Japanese corporation that likely had contributed to that country's war effort.

Daily life was simple. Public school (PS 221 on Empire Boulevard through grade six, then PS 167 on Eastern Parkway for grades 7 and 8.) As young-uns we played marbles at the curb, traded and flipped baseball cards, played Ringalevio and Hide and Seek. In our teens, we lied about our age to get into the burlesque theatre in Union City, New Jersey, went to Coney Island where we smoked cigarettes, and to the roller skating rink on Empire Boulevard where we tried to pick up girls. Our most constant activity was stickball, punch ball, and two-hand touch football in the street. We ran from the cops when a patrol car came by and broke up our game. (It never occurred to us to ask why they did that. Hey, they were the cops, they were the law – no questions asked.)

We were law-abiding kids, except for an occasional comic book heist. The petit larceny ended when, while walking to Dad's liquor store, my big brother and I stole two 10-cent mechanical pencils from Woolworth's Five and Dime store on Utica Avenue. They were irresistible. You twisted the barrel and got answers to the multiplication tables up to 12! Technology! We got out of Woolworths safely, but were not cut out for larceny. The brilliant plan was to tell Dad we "found" the pair of shiny new devices at the curb outside the store. He terrified us with tales of child-criminals locked in Woolworth's basement. Returning the stolen merchandise was the only way to avoid imprisonment. We confessed and took a plea deal: Dad took the stolen merchandise, said he would "take care of this" for us, but we were banned from ever going into that store again. I fully complied with the terms of my probation. What luck we were not caught and put in that basement! It turned out I was to be a lucky person for the rest of my life.

When my brother Philip graduated from Brooklyn's Tilden High School in 1947, he could not get into college. I am not talking about the college of his choice; he could not get into college, period. The schools were flooded with returning G.I.s and simply could not expand fast enough. There were not enough classrooms, teachers, books, or living accommodations. My parents searched the country relentlessly, and Phil was finally admitted to a small community college in Defiance, Ohio; a few years later he was able to transfer to the State University of Iowa, where he got his degree. Mom and Dad were determined that son number two not have the same problems; they sought advice from I-don't-know-whom, and I ended up in the Horace Mann School for Boys, in Riverdale, whence, they were assured, I was certain to be admitted to a college. The subway ride from the Utica Avenue station in Brooklyn to the 242nd Street station in the Bronx was one hour and twenty minutes. In the morning, I read the paper and slept; coming home in the evening, I just slept (exactly the routine I followed 15 years later when I lived in Westchester County and traveled to and from my office in New York City on the New York Central Railroad.)

My sister Richela, the youngest of the three London kids, went to public schools in Brooklyn, and later in Queens, when the family moved there three years before our mother died.

I was a fish out of water at Horace Mann. I was a kid from Brooklyn who got dropped into a claque of boys who grew up in "The City," i.e., Manhattan. They wore clothes I didn't have and couldn't afford, carried expensive leather briefcases when I was using a faux-leather plastic sample case my father got from a shoe salesman. Most shocking, my classmates actually took girls on dates and paid for their dinner! I could count on one hand the times I had ever eaten in a restaurant, and could not fathom the notion of paying for somebody else's dinner. On top of all that, by attending Horace Mann, I lost my "hood." I became somewhat estranged from my Carroll Street crowd, who went to public high school, didn't need to spend three hours a day on the subway, and were free to play when I had to study on weekday nights. No more hanging out with the girls on Eastern Parkway. My life was ruined. Well, sort of.

Horace Mann did have one saving grace for me: football. This was the real deal. No two-hand touch on the street. This was blocking and tackling on real grass, with designed plays, coaches, painful workouts, smelly locker rooms, all the good stuff. At 6'2" and 170 pounds I was big enough for the game, but slow. In truth, I was not very good, but still loved it. For the first three years, I was on the Junior Varsity. But even on Horace Mann's football field, I was not quite "equal." Horace Mann did not supply football equipment to members of the JV team. The only thing the school gave me was the loan of an HM jersey for game day. My pads, pants, and helmet were all second-hand stuff purchased from an equipment shop off the HM locker room. Only the cleats were new, from Davega. On the field, my black *leather* helmet was outstanding. I was the only kid who lacked one of the newer plastic ones. No matter, the game was fun, and in my junior year, I even got to play a couple of minutes for the varsity team in the last game of the season. I eagerly looked forward to my senior year when, I was assured, I would be a full-time member of the varsity squad, and have my own maroon plastic helmet with that attractive white stripe running fore and aft.

The Horace Mann Varsity was hardly what one might call a "good" football team. Aside from one or two "ringers" (fourth year transfers who were bigger, stronger, faster than everyone else), the level of play was hardly up to the standards of the varsity coach, Chuck Avedesian. To this day I have a clear memory of him: short, wide, deep "Brooklyn" accent, Coach Avedesian had been an offensive lineman for the New York Giants! A professional football player was a rare jewel in that school league. He was a memorable figure in all respects.

My most vivid recollection of Coach Avedesian was an off-the-field incident. Football at Horace Mann was not high-priority stuff, and the administration required coaches to do double duty as teachers. In an egregious example of poor position posting, the school administration assigned Avedesian to teach Biology to a class of 15-year-old boys. The course had a sex education segment, which would have been a challenge even to the most sophisticated educator. Chuck didn't stand a chance.

One day, while explaining the human reproductive process, the coach employed the talents that came naturally to him. He was a physical guy, and used his physicality in the classroom. If he saw you talking to your buddy or dozing in class, he would launch in your direction an eraser, a piece of chalk, a book, anything at hand. When describing sexual intercourse, he went beyond just using words or pictures to describe the deed. He opened the door at the front of the classroom, stood there, and said, "OK, guys, see, I am the penis and this corridor is the vagina." We stared open-mouthed as he then rushed out the door, ran some 10-15 yards down to the end of the corridor, and shouted back to us at the top of his lungs, "See, fellas, I'm way up the vagina now!"

Pandemonium. Boys laughed so hard some fell off their chairs. Hoots, hollers, desk poundings. Books and papers flew off desks. Total chaos. When Avedesian returned to the classroom, it took him minutes to restore order. Nobody could suppress the memory of that demonstration. Hey, I still replay it today. In time, the guys did settle down, but smiles and muffled giggles popped up here and there for the rest of the hour. One kid, whom I shall call Sheldon, just couldn't keep it in. After the class had quieted, and Chuck was lecturing on a less stimulating subject, Sheldon started giggling, then just burst out laughing. He couldn't stop. Some switch in his brain got stuck and he was out of control. Coach was furious. Again, he was a man of action, not so good with words. Saying nothing, he calmly walked to the classroom door, pinned it open, walked over to Sheldon, grabbed the back of his shirt collar with his left hand, the back of his belt with his right, lifted him up out of his seat, carried the helpless teenager to the doorway, pitched him out like a sack of garbage, and slammed the door shut. The classroom erupted again. Sheldon suffered only minor bruises. He went on to become a prominent rabbi.

My HM football career was influenced by my father's homeowner-tech approach. He was an early adopter and in the summer of 1950, he had our house's heating system converted from coal to oil. The coal company had been only too happy to run its truck up to the back of the house, drop a chute through an opened cellar window, and let slide a load of anthracite down into the basement coal bin. I recall actually enjoying watching the process. But this was not Zappos; the coal company did not accept returns. You bought it, you owned it, and upon the conversion to oil, we found ourselves with a half bin of unwanted coal. Dad had an extraction scheme, and I was the operative part of it. Every day he brought home a few empty cartons from the store, and my assigned duty was to fill them with coal and carry them up the basement steps and out to the curb for garbage pickup. Good training for the coming football season, right? Well, no. The result was the first in a lifetime series of herniated discs. Not only was I in pain for months, I could not play football in the fall. I was despondent. This was my senior year, and I had been excited at the prospect of playing my interior line position on the varsity.

But my injury turned out literally to be a life-saver: in my senior year, the Horace Mann football season was cut short when four boys on the team, three of whom would have been playing right next to me on the line, contracted polio, the contagious viral disease that terrified all parents of that era. One boy died, and two of the three survivors incurred life-long disabilities. My coal-shoveling injury was the lucky break that kept me out of the disease cluster.

Horace Mann delivered on the original premise, and I was accepted by Cornell, where I did well and was admitted into a program that allowed me to earn my undergrad and law school degrees in six years instead of seven. I did the last two years of law school at NYU because I could no longer afford to live away from home, even though at Cornell I had delivered newspapers, waited on tables, and washed dishes for my board. While my law school classmates were working as "summer interns" at major law firms, I was making much more money at a Long Island beach club doing double duty as a cabana boy during the day and busboy in the dining room at night. I slept in an empty cabana, used the shower there, and drove back to Queens on my day off to do my laundry. It was a good life. Youth will be served.

"London, you are fucked."

That incisive diagnosis from an expert marked the next step on the path to my career at Paul, Weiss.

When I graduated from law school in 1957, my draft card read "1-A." WW II was still a vivid memory, the cold war was intensifying, and it would be another 20 years before Congress abandoned the draft. Like every other reasonably healthy guy with zero political clout, my career planning involved consideration of my military service obligations.

I had three options: i) enlist in the service of my choice – a three-year commitment, ii) submit to the draft – two years in the Army, or iii) enlist in the National Guard or Army Reserve – six months active duty, then five and half years in the active reserve, which meant drills one night a week and a two-week summer camp each year.

Eager to begin my legal career, I chose the last option, and enlisted in an Army National Guard 120mm anti-aircraft gun unit, located in Flushing Meadows, Queens, now the site of the Mets home turf, Citi Field. One week after the July bar exam, I was in Fort Dix, N.J. starting an eight-week course of basic infantry training. Upon "graduation" from that segment of my military career, I was shipped to Fort Bliss, Texas where I did four months of advanced 120mm anti-aircraft gun training. I actually learned how to operate that monster weapon, which fired a fifty-pound fused projectile that was inserted in the breech just ahead of an equally heavy powder bag. But two weeks before the end of my tour at Fort Bliss, a detachment of Army engineers arrived, and took our guns away. The army had decided those WW II weapons were not useful in tracking modern jet aircraft, and the guns were to be melted down. Hey, somebody had to be the last person to be trained on every piece of obsolete equipment, why not me?

Once I got back from Fort Bliss, I found that, naturally enough, the National Guard 120mm gun company in Queens was gone. I was offered the option to transfer to a Nike anti-aircraft missile battery on the eastern end of Long Island, 70 miles away. Way too far to drive back and forth every Wednesday night, so I said "No, thanks." I put the problem behind me, and got on with my life and career. But I was not yet a good enough lawyer to read the fine print.

Two years later, I was a married man with a year-old son, and was developing my litigation skills at a small general practice law firm when out of the blue arrived a piece of government-franked mail that obliterated my complacency. It was from the President of the United States, the text started with the word "Greeting," and ordered me to report ten days hence to the United States Army Induction Center on Whitehall Street in New York City, with three days' worth of clean socks and underwear. I was being drafted into the army for two more years of military service. WTF?

I visited my draft board immediately. "A mistake," I explained, "I am in the Army Reserves. I never quit the reserves. My Army National Guard unit quit me!" But buried in the regulations is a clause providing that draft exemption is afforded only to those in the *active* reserves, whereas I, no longer affiliated with an *active* reserve unit, was in the *inactive* reserves, and it made no difference to my draft board how or why I got there.

I was out of ideas. My ticking clock was down to five days when a colleague at work suggested I visit the Army Reserve Center on 42d Street and speak to one of the two guys who administered the several units headquartered in that building. I bolted from the office, took a cab across town, entered the drab brick building on the north side of the West Side, between 10th and 11th Avenues, ran up to the second floor where, in a large open space at the front of the building were two desks, one empty, the other occupied by a short, heavy set guy who clearly had not shaved in days. He was wearing a wrinkled, short-sleeved, white-on-white shirt, with black smudges around the breast pocket. He spoke with a distinctly New York accent, and was chewing on a dead cigar butt. He was one of the two administrators of the several reserve units that met there.

Using my best legal skills, I described my problem succinctly and plaintively, and showed him my induction notice with its approaching deadline. He listened, looked at the document, and rendered his professional diagnosis:

"London," he said, "you are fucked."

He nevertheless volunteered to do what he could, and immediately got on the phone to a First Army Headquarters clerk at Fort Jay on Governor's Island. During his 20-minute conversation, he was twice bumped up the ladder until he was speaking to someone whose first name was "General." Remarkably, though, my advocate never dropped his commanding tone. Toward the end of the conversation, I heard him say, "Look, General, I know the units are full, but this is a good guy with a new baby who is being screwed by the system. Ya gotta open a slot for me!"

My advocate listened, grunted, and hung up the phone. While I sweated, he reached into a desk drawer, extracted a form that he rolled into the carriage of his typewriter, filled out the boxes, pulled it out of the machine, signed it, peeled off the carbons, and handed the original and one copy to me:

> Ok, Private London, your ass is saved. Take this to your draft board and they will cancel your induction. You are now an active member of the United States Army Reserve Graves Registration company that meets in this building. This is one of my units. Now go, I am busy.

I expressed undying gratitude, did what he told me to do, the draft board did what he said they would do, my induction was cancelled, and I went back to him the next day bearing a box of the best cigars I could find. When we chatted over the following weeks, my savior told me he was studying writing in graduate school at Columbia University, and he hoped someday to write a novel.

His name was Mario Puzo.

Yup, *that* Mario Puzo. Years later, after *The Godfather*, Puzo wrote a book called *Fools Die*, in which the main character was a corrupt Army Reserve administrator who went to jail for taking bribes. "Not me!" he told me after the book came out. From time to time, I would run into Mario on my way to work, and we would chat. I would encounter him hanging out in front of the Regency Hotel on Park Ave, smoking cigars. I guess they wouldn't let him smoke them in the hotel lobby. He wore a leather jacket that looked like it had been borrowed from a homeless person. Oh, yeah, he still needed a shave, and he was still a nice guy.

A short time after I became a member of the Graves Registration company, there was another army reorganization, and my unit was dissolved – again. This time I was not left out in the cold, and was placed, without consultation, in the 411th Quartermaster Company (Petroleum Depot), which also met in that building. I knew as much about petroleum depots as I knew about graves registration, but I always showed up on time, and my new company commander, Captain Lawrence Forella, was only too happy to have somebody in his organization who not only could compose a comprehensible report, but type it as well. I was a real military asset, an "Orderly Room Commando." Hey, like being a lawyer, it's indoors and sitting down. The new unit was not controlled by my savior Mario Puzo, but by the other administrator in the building, whom I shall call Sal Adamo. I knew who he was, would say hello to him from time to time, but had little to do with him.

For three years after completing my six-month tour of active duty, I worked long hours, six-day weeks, at the same small law firm in Manhattan. My life at the firm was a mixed bag. I could handle the hard work, and I was learning fast at the feet of two excellent litigation "junior partners," but a senior partner for whom I worked was a thoroughly unpleasant person. "Mr. Big" was a stiff, disconnected personality. He insisted on being called by his last name, and I remained "Mr. London" even though I saw him almost every day for three years in that small environment. He referred often to his alma mater, but he never called it "the Harvard Law School," just "The Law School," an annoying, arrogant affectation. One of two anecdotes that best describe my boss: one day, he and I were due in court on a mortgage foreclosure inquest for our lender-client. The debtor had defaulted, and this was a simple one-sided judicial inquiry to confirm the amount remaining unpaid, which was unchallenged. The other side would not show up. I had done all the prep, assembled all the necessary documents, packed them in marked folders in triplicate in the bag we would take to court the next day. The entire court proceeding would take 30 minutes or less.

On the day of the hearing, I arrived two hours before we were due at the courthouse – a 25-minute cab ride away. But when I walked in the office, I found a pacing, angry boss. "You're late! Mr. London. Have you no sense of responsibility?" "But," I said, "Mr. Big, sir, there's plenty of time, we are 100% ready, there is no need to be nervous." His response revealed remarkable self-awareness. "Nervous? Nervous? Mr. London, one day long ago, in my first job as a lawyer, my boss told me I had to go to court. I got nervous then and I have been nervous ever since." Well, he got that right.

In November 1960, I voted for John F. Kennedy, and with the aid of my vote, he defeated Richard M. Nixon. It was impossible to foresee the transformative effect that election would have on my personal and professional life.

Within months after Kennedy's inauguration, the Cold War intensified. The Russian-sponsored East German government built a wall to separate East Berlin from West Berlin. The President (perhaps with the advice of his advisor Ted Sorensen, who was later to become my law partner at Paul, Weiss) responded with saber rattling; he mobilized "strategic" reserve units, including the 411th Quartermaster Company (Petroleum Depot). How the military could have possibly considered the 411th "strategic" was beyond my imagination, but the important thing was I was back in the military soup pot and this time my buddy Mario Puzo couldn't help.

The call-up presented, among other things, a personal financial challenge of major proportions. At Mr. Big's law firm, I was earning an annual salary of $7,500, could reasonably expect a $2,500 bonus at the end of the year, and was just getting by on that $10,000 annual income. My family had just moved to Queens, to a bargain apartment I loathed. My salary as a sergeant on active duty (yup, two promotions) would be $1,080 a year, plus a housing allotment of $90 a month. That's a 75% pay cut! On the other hand, my return to active duty had several legal plusses: under the provisions of New York's "Soldiers' and Sailor's Civil Relief Act," I was entitled to terminate my lease of that awful apartment, and I was guaranteed the right to get my job back when I was mustered out. The first was a very good thing, the second, not so much. I was not eager to return to Mr. Big's firm.

As the day for reporting to active duty approached, I learned from many of my army buddies (almost all of whom had families by then) that their employers had assured them they would not suffer financially; they would be kept on the books and receive a stipend equal to the difference between their army pay and their civilian salary. Nice. So I was hopeful when I saw Mr. Big come down the corridor to approach *my* office. That was a first. In three years, all our encounters were on *his* turf. He came into my small room, closed the door, sat down opposite me, and said,

> Mr. London, we need to talk. You will be leaving us soon. You have been a loyal employee, and you are leaving to serve our country. This firm has an obligation to you. I know your military service will be a financial hardship for you and your family, and I

want you to know we are here for you: *if you need to borrow some money, call me.*

My mother raised a good boy. I choked back the response that came to mind. I said, "Thank you, sir," and he got up and left so quickly you'da thunk he'd been sitting on a hot stove.

For the first week of active duty, the 411th met daily at the 42nd street reserve center. It was there that we experienced a big surprise; before the call-up, we had some 150 men in the company, but on day one of active duty, over 200 guys showed up. Whence these "Dead Souls"? Was this a reverse of Gogol's novel, in which a large number of names on the voting rolls were dead people? I had no idea what was going on, but followed standard army practice; I kept my head down and my mouth shut. I couldn't figure this out, and didn't need to. This was somebody else's goof, not mine.

Next stop, Fort Lee, Virginia. On a weekend reconnaissance trip, I had rented a small garden apartment in Hopewell, Virginia, a ten-minute drive to the base. The rent was $90 a month, and given my housing allowance, access to the low-cost base commissary, free family dental and medical, etc., we almost got along on my military pay. What little savings I had would see me through, as long as my tour of duty did not last for more than a year. After that last conversation with Mr. Big, I would have eaten the bark off the Virginia pine trees before I borrowed money from him.

Once ensconced in Fort Lee, I discovered that nobody else in the unit knew any more than I did about how to run a petroleum depot, and my knowledge was limited to watching the service station attendant put gas in my car. The 411th watched training films, did other military stuff like Marching, firing rifles, and finally got to practice at the Fort Lee Tank Farm. This facility was exactly what it sounds like: A dozen or so large petroleum tanks, all interconnected via a network of pipes, valves, pumps, and gauges. The tanks contained a volume of "practice" oil, and the training involved moving stuff from one tank to another. Sounds simple enough, but it's not. Timing the manual valve openings and closings, monitoring the pressure gauges, engaging the big diesel-driven pumps, calculating tank volumes, rate of transfer flows, etc., required training and experience – qualities totally absent in our group.

Despite our "strategic" designation, the company's on-site training at the tank farm proved to be short-lived. When our guys successfully pumped 2,000 barrels of petroleum into a 5,000 barrel tank that already had an initial volume of 4,000 barrels of product, the South Carolinian Commandant of the facility had enough. The Major stormed into his office and returned wearing his army-issued web belt from which hung his .45 caliber semi-automatic pistol. He actually drew the weapon, pointed it at our Company Commander, and in his best southern accent, got right to the point:

> Captain, get your fucking people off my facility. Right fucking now. If I ever again see one of you fucking New York sons of bitches within spitting distance of my tank farm, I will shoot his fucking balls off. I swear to God I will.

Our leadership was persuaded.

I heard every detail of that incident over and over again when the guys returned to the company area. While I was sorry I didn't see and hear that scene first hand, I shortly thereafter did get to be a percipient witness to an even more dramatic event: the solution of the *Dead Souls* mystery.

One morning, as the company "fell in," i.e., we lined up in four ranks on the drill field in front of the barracks, the usual

ceremony began: the First Sergeant, in front of the forma-
tion, faced the troops, ordered the squad leaders to report,
and each of them responded with the standard, "All present or accounted for, Sergeant!" The First Sergeant then
did a snappy about-face and made that same report to the
Company Commander. Before the Company Commander
could respond, lightning struck. An angry soldier in the
rear rank, a person whom I had not seen prior to the
active duty recall and who obviously did not appreciate
this interruption of his career as a budding New York real
estate tycoon, shouted out at a volume all could hear,
"Fuck you, Captain. I paid $500 to stay out of the fucking
army and I am sure you got part of that. Now here I am
in the fucking army. I am done with this shit!" Hands in
his pockets, he broke ranks, and sauntered back to the
barracks, muttering something about taking a nap. Yikes!
I expected a squad of Military Police immediately to
descend from a Black Hawk helicopter and take this guy
straight to Leavenworth. But nothing happened. Two hundred men stood there holding their breaths and finally the
captain spoke. "There will be a meeting of the entire company in the Day Room immediately after dismissal at the
end of the day. This is not an official meeting, *but everybody will attend.*"

And everybody did. Smoking was allowed in the Day
Room (in the '60s, smoking was allowed everywhere) and
the air became thick as the room heated up. It was a scene
out of a gritty black-and-white Humphrey Bogart movie.
The Captain spoke first:

> Listen up, goddammit. I am an honest guy. I have
> been an honest guy all my life and I'm not going to
> take this insult. I have never, I repeat never, taken
> a nickel from anybody. Never. I want to get to the

bottom of this. If someone paid money to get into this unit, I want to know about it. I want to know everything, dammit. I wanna see a show of hands from anybody who says he paid to get into this unit.

Emotional stuff. I knew this guy and believed every word he said. So did the troops. Hands were tentatively raised, first to ear-height, and then as the guys looked around and saw other hands going up, a small forest started to grow around the room. In thirty seconds, there were dozens of people reaching for the ceiling.

I could not be silent, and asked the Captain if I could speak. He and I were buds – we worked together in the orderly room the greater part of every day, I knew he respected me, and he said "Sure, London, go ahead." And I did:

> Listen guys. You may know that I am a lawyer in civilian life. Here, I am not a lawyer, just a soldier like you. I do not have a license to practice law in Virginia, and I am not giving you legal advice. Nobody here is my client. Personally, I think confession may sometimes be a good thing. It clears the air. But I also think it is probable that accepting a bribe in connection with getting into a military unit may be a federal felony, and quite possibly, so is paying one. So if I had something to confess in that regard, I'd consider speaking to a lawyer first.

The arms went down as if flattened by a tornado.

The Army's Criminal Investigation Division was in the company area the next morning, and were soon thereafter replaced by the FBI. Every one of the 200 plus soldiers in the company, including me, was individually interviewed by the suits. One morning about a month later, I answered the phone in the company Orderly Room with the required military greeting, "411th Petroleum Depot, Sergeant London speaking, Sir." The caller identified himself as Lieutenant Somebody-or-other, and asked if I were indeed Sergeant Martin London. When I assured him I was, he ordered me to report to the Commanding General's office immediately. Uh, oh, Commanding General's office! In the army, that's God-level! Glad my boots were shined. When I reported, a snotty clerk directed me to a typical army conference room: painted stud walls, furniture consisting of a plain table and some folding chairs, principally employed, I was certain, by the headquarters poker gang. But I had not been invited to play five card stud. Sitting at the table, in a chair facing the door, was a short, pudgy civilian in suit and tie, whom I shall call Arnold. He rose, we shook hands, and he introduced himself as an Assistant United States Attorney for the Southern District of New York. This was a poker game of a different sort.

"Marty, I think you know why I am here." He immediately launched into his "bad cop" bluff. "Marty, I have carefully reviewed all the files and we know you got into this unit under what I shall describe as 'unusual circumstances' and for starters I would like to talk about that." Hey, I was now back on my home turf – two civilian lawyers screwing with each other's brains. I said, "Come on, Arnie, let's not bullshit each other. If you really read the files you know I got into this unit because some army dweeb I never met shut down the Graves Registration unit and arbitrarily assigned me to this company. I know who Sal Adamo is, but I have nothing to do with him."

He said, "Yeah, but the FBI interviews say we had lots of guys who wanted to confess to paying Adamo, but they all shut up after you spoke at that meeting." I described the meeting, told the AUSA exactly what I had said to the group, and countered, "Arnie, I did the right thing. If you were there instead of me, you would have done exactly what I did. At least I hope so." He sighed, "Yeah, okay," and then out came the real reason this AUSA from New York City took the trouble to travel down to the boondocks of Virginia to talk to a witness who had seen and heard nothing other than what 200 other witnesses had seen and heard. "OK, Marty, you're right, and I am sorry I got off on the wrong foot. I apologize. But listen, this is a big matter for us. The army is embarrassed. Can you help us out? We are not after these kids. We are after Adamo. The guys in your unit apparently look up to you. Could you just tell them to cooperate with us?"

I said, "Arnie, you know I can't do that. If they paid money, they are exposed to criminal charges. Each of those guys needs a lawyer, and that's not me. The only thing I can promise you is while I won't advise anybody to cooperate, neither will I advise anybody to refuse to cooperate, and if anybody does seek my advice, I will tell him my advice is get a lawyer and to tell his lawyer to call you. Then you can take it from there. Howzat?"

He said, "Well, frankly, that's not exactly a home run for me, but I get your point and it's better than nothing. Thanks for seeing me." I laughed. "Arnie, you are such a civilian. I would have met with you if asked, but nobody asked. You don't have to thank me for seeing you. I was ordered to come here. I'm in the army."

I went back to the 411th orderly room, and later on, Sal Adamo went to federal prison for taking bribes to enroll people in the unit. That solved the mystery of the Dead Souls. His bribe fee not only bought a slot in the unit, but the right to skip weekly meetings. Adamo controlled the roster reports to headquarters and he would mark his clients as "present."

My exit interview with Mr. Big at the law firm had been the last straw, and I used my active duty interlude as a transition opportunity. From my orderly room typewriter, I peppered friends and classmates for job leads. One of my friends was Gerry Stern, a Paul, Weiss associate who had been a law school classmate.

The Paul, Weiss litigation department in 1962 was hardly the powerful colossus it is today. The entire firm had just under fifty lawyers, divided among the Tax, Corporate, Trusts and Estates, Entertainment, Real Estate, and Litigation departments. The latter group had only a handful of associates. When Arthur Frommer, the entrepreneur author of the series of books starting with his ground-breaking *Europe on Five Dollars a Day*, found that his writing and publishing activities were now making time demands that were inconsistent with his obligations as a mid-level Paul, Weiss litigation associate, he told the partners he intended to leave. The word spread, and Gerry contacted me, asking if I were interested. I responded "Gerry, are you kidding? Yes, full speed ahead, please!," and he sent a memo that served as my resume to Sam Silverman, the head of the litigation department. Within days, I had scheduled for my forthcoming Christmas furlough, interviews with partners Sam Silverman, John Wharton, Martin Kleinbard, and Bud Taylor. A week after those interviews, Sam reached me in the orderly room and offered me a job. I was ecstatic.

The 411th had disgraced itself so severely, the United States Army couldn't get rid of us fast enough. Ours was one of the first units in the country to be demobilized. Less than two months after accepting the job offer, I was back in New York, working as a Paul, Weiss litigation associate at an annual salary of $12,500.

I had won the lottery.

Part VII:
RETIREMENT

Gone Fishin'

After 47 years in harness, I retired at the age of 71. My partners who are approaching retirement age constantly ask me, "Oh my God, what am I going to do with myself?" I tell them all the same thing: "Retirement is the best job I ever had."

Some of my retired colleagues keep busy doing good works, some are writing, and some are suffering from inactivity. But I am busy. I spend winters in St. Barths and summers in Montauk, and I started to write emails to friends and colleagues to stay in touch. As my list of emailees grew, I feared I was becoming a spammer, and switched to writing a blog; my pals could tune in if they wanted, or not. I wrote about anything and everything, including descriptions of life in the French Caribbean (a happy but sometimes frustrating blend of French and tropical cultures), current political and legal banter, (mostly U.S.-centric, but some stuff unique to St. Barths or Montauk), reports on my frustrations with my favorite newspaper, *The New York Times*, which consistently refused to print my pithy letters, (though they did take an Op Ed last year,) and my favorite Montauk activity, fishing, fishing, fishing.

I conclude this memoir with a blog I posted on the latter subject. It's all true, and one of my favorite essays:

MARTY'S BLOG

http://londonsbh.blogspot.com

January 10, 2015

Wanna catch a big fish? Look at this:

It's easy. I'm gonna tell you how.

First, you need a rod and reel. Go to the store. Whatever you buy will probably be fine. Truth is, the fish don't see that stuff until it's too late for them anyway.

Second, you need tackle. This is fisherman-speak for a hook and a lead weight to keep the hook lower in the water column where the fish are hanging out that day. Their precise location is revealed by the Garmin electronics people. Their device shows you what is happening under your boat. Of course, the picture usually shows there are no fish down there while guys on boats all around are struggling with bent rods. Hmmm. Probably Russian hackers screwing with your sonar. Then again, sometimes the machine does show fish – but that is only when they are not hungry, i.e., when "the bite is off." Why does "the bite" turn on and off, and when does it do that? Sorry, I am not allowed to tell you that.

Let's go back to tackle. The most important element is a fish hook. The manufacturers of hooks, in an effort to justify charging a dollar apiece for something that costs them three cents to manufacture, make hook selection as complicated as possible. They assign numbers to the hooks, and, of course, the smaller the number, the larger the hook. You knew that, right? Then they put zeros adjacent to the numbers to confuse the size issue further, so that 6/0 is different from 6. Aside from size, you would think a hook is a hook, right? Hah, there are a plethora of different shape hooks, and every guy at the docks is certain that the shape he uses is better than the one you use. Long shaft, short shaft, offset, straight, circle, octopus, it goes on and on.

All fish hooks do have two important things in common: i) a sharp point, and ii) a barb just below the point. The function of the sharp point is to facilitate the easy entry of the hook into the fish's lip or the fisherman's thumb, and the function of the barb is to keep it there. I have made use of both characteristics. Two stories:

First time this happened, I was fishing with my 10-year-old son Robert. We put a very unhappy bluefish in the box. The fish had taken one of the hooks on the treble hook I was using. In case you haven't already figured this out, a treble hook is basically three hooks stuck together so they have a single shaft, but the bends in the hooks face different directions. The fish was banging around in the box, and I reached in to get him. Dumb, dumb, dumb. Not only did the fish defeat me by staying on his hook, he managed firmly to impale my thumb on hook number two. There I was, harpooned, and worse, the pissed off fish was still jumping around and I was like a marionette, dancing and howling to the tune of this green chopper. Robert ran and hid under a boat cover. Fortunately, two guys fishing nearby were watching the show, came alongside, and one of them hopped aboard our boat and managed to snip hook one and separate me from the fish, leaving me still sporting hook two. And this was before body piercing became fashionable.

Okay, with just the hook in my thumb I could manage the boat, but obviously would need medical attention when I got ashore. Steve Jobs had not yet invented mobile phones, but I did have a VHF radio. The joy and pain of VHF is that everybody listens in. It's one big party line. I called the Coast Guard, told the Coastie radioman of my problem, and asked him to telephone my wife and ask her to meet me at the dock and drive me to a doctor. I don't need to tell you how many guys came on the radio when I was finished with that conversation. I received all sorts of advice. Some of the proposed strategies might even have worked if I weren't such a coward. Anyway, the Coast Guard radioman passed my request on to the duty officer, who passed it on to someone else, who passed it on to a clerk who called my wife. I have no idea exactly how garbled the message was by the time it got to Pinks, but what she gathered was that there was a United States Coast Guard emergency call involving her husband and son at sea! She was in a great lather a half-hour later when she met us at the dock, and when she discovered the "emergency" was a hook in my finger, she was furious. "For this you called the United States Coast Guard, who called me and told me of an emergency involving my husband and my son? I was already contemplating widowhood. A fish hook in your finger? That's it?"

This happened 25 years ago, and the memory of this incident is now so dim that she brings it up only once a week.

We did go to a local clinic, where the laid-back doc removed the hook and dropped it into a tray of similarly removed hooks. Why he kept them, I dunno. Pinks was still pissed, but he laughed. "This was easy. You oughta see what goes on here when the mother learns the father took their daughter fishing and hooked her anywhere but in the earlobe."

Hook incident number two occurred several years later. My friend Sandy Herzfeld and I were drifting for striped bass in the Shinnecock Inlet. I was no longer using treble hooks, but did use a rig that had two striper hooks about a foot apart. I hooked what I thought was a big fish that was surprisingly docile. Maybe that's because my "fish" was a three-foot chunk of water-logged telephone pole. When I got it up to the boat and leaned over the gunnel to disengage from the log, I demonstrated once again how little I had learned about self-preservation. Instead of snipping the line and letting the !@#! thing settle back to the bottom, I tried to save my rig by pulling the bottom hook out of the log.

That effort failed, but I did succeed in driving the top hook deep into the meat at the base of my thumb. Now I had a non-wiggling log pulling on the bottom end of a leader that at the top end was attached to a bass hook firmly seated in the fleshy part of my hand. Barbs on fish hooks really do their job. I was about to succumb and jump overboard to relieve the pressure when Sandy responded to my howls and snipped the leader.

This time I was really hurting and did not see how I could navigate my way home through the tricky Shinnecock Bay shoals. What to do? Of course, call the Shinnecock Coast Guard Station, which was but a couple of miles away. They came roaring out in their big red RIB boat, siren howling, blue lights flashing. They came alongside, a crewman hopped aboard, and they escorted me to their dock, where an ambulance was waiting to take me to Riverhead Hospital. A little excessive, ya think? Hey, it's all "by the book."

I get into the ambulance and the EMT tells me to lie down on the stretcher so he can strap me in. I say, "Wait a minute, can't I just sit here with you? I am not critical; I just have a hook in my hand." Nope, once again "the book" prevails, and I lie down, get strapped in, they take my blood pressure and the guy said it was the highest blood pressure reading he had ever seen in his life. Off we go to Riverhead Central, more lights and sirens.

This was the July 4th weekend, which had two consequences. First, the ER was jammed, and the triage nurse put me in Triage Group Three, which is reserved for those of us who are so minimally injured, we get to ripen in the waiting area indefinitely. Second, the recent med school grads begin their internship on July 1st. As a result, the guy in the white jacket I finally got to see was a pleasant child prodigy who was trying to grow a mustache but couldn't quite succeed.

When he looked at the hook in my hand, I saw panic. He was a born and bred city kid who had never seen a real fishhook in his life, and they hadn't covered this at Harvard Medical School. Bottom line, he had no clue how to get that hook out of my hand, and because he was so new at this job, was reluctant to get off on the wrong foot by bothering his boss, a real doctor who was busy treating patients in Triage Group One. I had more experience at this than my caregiver, and told him how to do this: Step one, local anesthetic. Step two, push the hook all the way through so that the point and the barb come out in the open. Step three, snip off the hook just below the barb. Step four, back the now-barbless shaft out the way it went in. Step five, a shot of antibiotics. Step six, apply a Band Aid and send the patient home. He was grateful for my instruction, executed steps one and two with adequate skill, but when he tried to snip off the hook below the barb with what looked like a pair of cuticle scissors, he could not dent, no less cut through the heavy bass hook. Neither of us was happy. He surrendered, and departed our cubicle to consult. Minutes later he returned with good news. A maintenance department guy was coming with a more suitable tool. Sure enough, five minutes later, the distinctive tool-belt jangle from the corridor signaled the approach of the cavalry. The maintenance supervisor, who had never before so directly assisted in a treatment protocol, swaggered into the treatment area, selected a small bolt cutter from the holster on his belt, and proudly plunked it down on the instrument tray. The doctor and a nurse audibly gasped. There was no way they could use that unsanitary device. What's more, he had just contaminated their entire instrument tray. All offending instruments were immediately removed, and an hour later, when the bolt cutter had been degreased, scrubbed, and sterilized, I got my third Novocain shot, the hook and barb were snipped, the hook shaft was backed out, I got my band aid and antibiotic shot, and was set free.

Pinks, who had received an accurate telephoned report from Sandy, had arrived at the hospital soon after I did. This was her revenge. "You rode in an *ambulance* because of a hook in your finger? Ha, ha, ha." "Strapped down on a *stretcher*? Ho, ho, ho." *Flashing lights and sirens*? Hilarious." I still love her dearly, but have not forgiven her, and will not.

Okay, back to catching a fish.

Now, to get the fish to eat the hook, ya gotta give 'em some sort of incentive. There are lots of methods. Some fishermen tie feathers to the hook and jig it back and forth. (Feathers? For fish? You kidding me? Fish mistake the hook for a chicken? Fish like chicken?) Then there are things called bucktails – a hook with deer hair attached. I am not kidding. When have fish encountered deer? Why would fish eat hair from their tails? There's more. Some guys put a two-inch-long strip of pork rind on the hook. Pork! Yup, a guy named Uncle Josh has created a whole industry of different colored pork strips to put on bass hooks! Hey, everybody loves bacon, right? But fish? All I know is it works. And then there are the guys who hide the hook in a piece of rubber tubing. Surgical tubing. Different colors yet. Why do fish wanna eat surgical tubing? Are fish really that stupid? Yeah, they are, and that's why it's our job to kill 'em and eat 'em.

My preference is none of the above. I bait my hooks with eels – without a doubt the single most disgusting creature in the sea.

Okay, you buy a mess of eels, put 'em in a bucket with small drain holes in the bottom, then ice them down to freeze their tiny brains a bit, lest they commit eelcide by tying themselves into knots. Literally.

Eels have several other attractive characteristics. When they are distressed, they emit a white slime along the length of their bodies that makes them totally unmanageable. Ugh. So when the time comes to grab an eel, you use a washcloth you have stolen from home (the ones with the purple flowers from the guest bathroom seem to work best, and when your wife remarks upon their gradual disappearance from the linen closet, you can blame the guests), and then try to hold the small snake steady enough to put the hook in under its chin and out the top of his head – through the eye is best. This is really a fun part of the day on the water, especially when the eel has recovered from the temporary brain freeze, wraps its tail around your wrist, and puts out enough slime so that the washcloth has the coefficient of friction of a wet Kleenex. Sometimes the eel escapes your grasp, and you get to chase it. Picking up a slimed wriggling eel from the deck of a small pitching boat is a hoot. I am surprised Parker Brothers or somebody hasn't made a parlor game of it. I guess nobody really wants eels in their parlor, but it is a barrel of laughs, right up there with a hook in your lip. I once heard a charter boat captain on the VHF radio say that he fishes with eels once every year so he can always be reminded how disgusting they are.

That's how easy this is – you attach a hooked eel to one end of the leader, a lead weight to the other end (more secrets – what shape lead, what weight, what kind of attachment, there is no end of choices, and the fish really cares), clip that rig onto the end of your fishing line, and drop the thing overboard. While you are drifting with the tide, you put your pole in the rod holder on the gunnel, wipe your hands on your shirt to get rid of some of the eel slime, take out your lunch sandwich (hey, it's 9 a.m. already!), and as soon as you take that first bite, the rod bends and wiggles, line peels off your now-singing reel, you jump out of your chair, your sandwich falls into the eel bucket, and the game is on. If you fish like this for 10 or 20 years, you might get to catch a striped bass just like the one in the picture.

It's all so easy it makes you wonder why everybody doesn't do this all the time.

Acknowledgments:

How do I begin to mention and thank all the people who have contributed to my story? They fall into so many groups. So here goes.

Group One: My RFL, Pinks, my beloved, beautiful wife of 33 years, who was my first-draft reader, editor, critic, and major cheerleader. My children, Jesse, Liz, Stephanie, Robert, who ate all those meals without me while I was off slaying dragons, this mention is hardly adequate recompense for my absences.

At Paul, Weiss, a salute to my partners and associates, paralegals, clerks, mail room personnel, and the vast team of professionals and others who examined witnesses, researched and wrote briefs, scoured documents for helpful bits and pieces of evidence, typed the papers, watched the calendar, answered the phones, delivered the mail, carried the stuff to court, and brought some semblance of organization to the stressful and distracting life of a trial lawyer. In particular, my respect for my departed partner-colleagues at Paul, Weiss who helped clear the path for me: Simon Rifkind, Martin Kleinbard, Eddie Costikyan, Morris Abram,

Ted Sorensen, and Cameron Clark. I started out this section with a plan to name all the people who worked on all my cases but soon realized that is impossible to do without leaving out too many important people, so I have switched to a "You-know-who-you-are" mode. Thank you. And while we are discussing the firm, I need to make specific mention of the team that always kept me pointed in the right direction, my once upon a time "secretaries," now "administrative assistants," but most important, dear friends and helpmeets, the departed Edith Kaplan, and her successors Isabel Maddaloni, Ellin Ossandon, and Laura Biancavilla.

Three more groups need mention here:

My enduring gratitude to the clients who were brave enough to entrust their honor, their coin, and in some cases their freedom, to my efforts on their behalf. Without them, no career, except maybe as a plumber. Mind you, I admire plumbers, but I don't think they have as much fun as I did.

Then the group that was so helpful in structuring and editing this memoir, some of whom read the entire manuscript, some read parts of it, all made valuable suggestions and corrections. My whole-hearted thanks to Maureen Barberio, Bruce Birenboim, Lew Clayton, Lewis Kaplan, Ruth Feycych, Marty Flumenbaum, Jordana Haviv, Ricki Herzfeld, Jeh Johnson, Maria Keane, Bob Kravitz, Scott Lucas, Colleen McMahon, Toby Myerson, Andy Peck, Lynda Sheldon, Jane Singer, Maria Vullo, Liz London Wright, and, of course, my "Reason for Living," Pinks. And in the cheerleading section, special thanks to Sarah Hochman at Penguin for her advice and encouragement when the project seemed overwhelming, and Brad Karp, who urged me on from the beginning. And I never could have overcome the complexity of the physical production issues without the brilliant interior and cover design work of Deborah Perdue, of Illumination Graphics.

Finally, my thanks to my "retirement teams." In St. Barths, Dawn and Dofy Gumbs are the invaluable interpreters, managers, and best of all, dear friends, who make life so comfortable in a foreign land. In Montauk, Vicki and Skip Rudolph are our local anchors. It's Captain Skip who taught me how to "turn on the bite" at the Point, and helped me enjoy the sea and at the same time, keep the freezer full. And none of that would have happened without the help and friendship of Tom and Maureen Sennefelder, Bobby, T.J, and the rest of the team at the *Gone Fishing Marina*.

Like I said, I'm a lucky guy.

Index